The Wilderness,
The Wild Man &
The Wound

A Sacred Quest for God
and the Masculine Soul

Brian Christian Meagher

DEDICATION

This book is dedicated to the Holy One in whose image I am created in and to Jesus Christ who redeemed me by his death and resurrection.

This book is also dedicated to Mary, the Mother of my Lord, who became my spiritual mother in 2003 and then took me through the fire.

And finally, this book is dedicated to all who have and will journey through their own inner wilderness so as to make the kingdom of God their own.

To any woman who might
be reading this work:

I welcome you! Although I have written this book to the masculine soul, the stories, the truths and the primal energies of God that I write of are universal. I wrote, not to be exclusive, but to honor my journey. I believe that in the deep work of transformation men need to gather with men and women need to gather with women. For this reason, I wrote this book as a quest for God and my masculine soul.

Be it known, I believe the quest for our authentic self is universal, that both men and women are all called to a passionate relationship with God, awaken these primal energies, and become our wild and true self in Christ. May you find insight, wisdom and strength in this story.

Blessings!
   -Brian

CONTENTS

ACKNOWLEDGMENTS

It is humbling to be trusted by God to walk such a road. Thank you Lord for calling me in March of 1983. I could have never imagined.

Thank you to my wife, Kathryn. I could have never made this journey without you. The love and commitment we share is sacred. The woundings are sacred as well.

Thank you to the circle of men that I have journeyed with for nearly six years. Brothers, what can I say that hasn't already been expressed in the circle.

A special thanks to the men who have cleared a path to my masculine soul through their books or programs: Richard Rohr for the program M.A.L.E.s (Men as Learner's and Elders), Dr. Robert More and Douglas Gillette for writing King, Warrior, Magician, Lover, John Eldridge for his book, Wild at Heart, and especially to the Mankind Project.

Thank you to my parents. Your love and support during this long and winding road has meant much to me.

Thank you to my Mother-in-law, Janice Schuler, who has been an incredible support in my life.

Cover photos-courtesy of the National Park Service, Grand Canyon

1 IT IS TIME

There is a time when a man must journey into his heart and strip away the layers that separate him from God...

There is a time when a man must stand like a warrior, draw his sword and pierce the shadows that hold him hostage...

There is a time when a man must reach within and embrace the wounds of the boy...

This is a powerful time in a man's life. It is the beginning of the masculine journey, the claiming of his passionate love for God, the awakening of the primal masculine, and the profound descent into his own humanity. It is also a frightening time because the heart is a frightening place. It is a wilderness, the most foreboding wilderness I have travelled. There are dragons in this wilderness. Real dragons, ones that can devour a man's heart, steal his soul or crush his spirit. There are also caves, deep and dark; it is the place of our wounds, the masculine shame we dare not trigger, the fear of rejection that binds us or the anger that holds us hostage. So we place a stone over the entrance of this cave and mark it off limits, daring not to go in, choosing to walk the safe road and hold the false belief that all is well. Until one day our world crumbles, leaving us in the ruins of our pursuit to greatness. It is then, stripped bare and seemingly alone in the great wilderness of our heart, that a voice, ancient, primordial and more powerful than our fears, beckons us to roll away the stone to the dark cave within us. It is the great moment in a man's life. Hell trembles. Yes, hell trembles because it knows in the depths of this cave, beneath our wounds and bound by our fears resides the primal masculine of the wild man, that primordial energy of God that empowers a man to break addictions, face pain, bring shadow to light and darkness to dawn. For a brief moment heaven and hell sit in the balance. A great battle is taking place. Light and dark struggle. Faith and fear wrestle. Then in the midst of the great storm and in a moment of surrender that powerful voice that beckoned you and I to roll away the stone becomes a tender voice of compassion, mercy and love, saying, "It is time my son, it is time.".

2 INTO THE WILD

As the road weaved through the mountains of Northern California, I surveyed the landscape with a sense of anticipation, waiting for the inner movement of the Spirit of God to reveal the place I was to spend a year in the wilderness. Yet, with each passing mile my heart seemed to shrink in doubt. Anticipation became anxiety. As we crested a pass, I looked over at my sister and said, "This isn't the place." There was a moment of awkward silence. .

"What are you going to do?"

My mind scrambled. "I hear the Olympic Peninsula is nice," I said.

"I don't have the time to take you there. Perhaps as far as Bend, Oregon." Keri replied.

"That will work."

Olympic Peninsula

The bus meandered through the dark, wet forests of the Olympic Peninsula. It was a strange and beautiful world, the kind of place you read about in fairy tales in which foreboding creatures rise out of dark places. Perhaps it was the perfect place for my year long rite of initiation, although it wasn't what I had planned for nor expected. The bus rounded a bend then began a small descent toward a river. I checked my map then peered into the forest at the moss covered trees that lined the road. I took a breath then pulled the stop cord.

My vision was to spend one year alone, learn the way of the wilderness and the ancient ways of survival then integrate them into my relationship with Jesus. My hope was to return to the Yupik Eskimo Culture to create a program that integrated wilderness and God for young adults. But there was more to this quest than just returning to Alaska with new skills and a deeper love and understanding of God. Upon leaving Steamboat Springs, Colorado, I had liquidated my few belongings except what I was to a carry in the wilderness. This emptying of my possessions was an outward manifestation of my desire to break my ties with this world and embrace the path of a pilgrim, a man devoted to God, simplicity and the sharing of God's love poured out through Jesus in whatever context I found myself.

The bus slowed to a stop. I grabbed my pack and worked my way to the exit. "Is this the place you wanted?" asked the driver.

"This is it," I nodded in feigned confidence.

The bus disappeared and soon a strange and surreal quiet fell upon me. It was a lonely moment, void of any type of ceremony, ritual or even a sense of peace from God. Quickly, I stepped into the forest to conceal my presence. I then turned back toward the road that represented my last ties to the world, possible marriage, and financial responsibilities that had come to burden my soul for the last couple years. I then slowly turned into the deep woods. I now belonged to God, the freedom of the wilderness and the quiet whisper of the Holy Spirit. I wanted nothing else.

My pack was loaded with the basics, one tarp, knife, sleeping bag, cooking utensils, matches, a couple changes of clothes and of course a rather large bag of trail mix and other food. Even after years of wilderness travel and some survival training, I knew there would be a learning curve. I couldn't afford hunger and the weakness that follows.

I worked my way up river, foraging on wood sorrel then set up camp in a small mossy clearing among giant Douglas Fir trees. A soft rain was now falling. Soon, I had a fire crackling. I then crawled under my tarp, wrapped myself with my sleeping bag and began to pray, quieting my mind and opening my heart with the simple phrase, "Come Lord Jesus." There was peace in my soul.

As dusk gave way to night time I laid upon the soft moss-covered earth. My body relaxed as the scent of rich fertile soil filled my nostrils. Mother earth held me in her loving embrace. I was home. The presence of God fell upon me. Sometime later sleep came.

Survival

I woke with hunger. I grabbed my throwing stick that I had prepared the day before then started out into the forest. I had learned the throwing stick at a survival school months ago and had practiced the technique ever since. I stalked through the coniferous forest, following the sound of squirrels working the forest floor. Knowing movement would frighten them, I moved slowly until I settled in some ferns near the tree they frequented. I then crouched with throwing stick in loaded position. The thrill of the hunt was running through my blood. Five, ten, maybe fifteen minutes passed. An unsuspecting squirrel scampered along the forest floor, then turned toward the tree. This was it. Excitement and anticipation raced through my body. I released. The throw was accurate but in a split second the squirrel jumped the stick then ran up the tree and gave me a verbal lashing.

It was an odd moment. As I walked over to grab my throwing stick an intuitive knowing came over me. Something intangible was missing. I couldn't name it but it was there, nagging at my gut, telling me something I perhaps didn't want to hear. I shrugged it off then started out for a new squirrel. After several more failed attempts I returned to camp for a breakfast of trail mix.

Questions ran through my mind. Perhaps I had dreamed up this one year alone in the wilderness. I mentally traced back to my forty days in Canyon Lands, to the moment the idea was conceived. It was a God moment. I was certain of that, but still, something was missing.

In the days that followed I let go of survival and spent most of my time wandering though the dark forests, seeking God's counsel, which was eluding me. As each day passed, a sense of unrest settled upon my soul. About a week later and with supplies nearly exhausted I broke camp then placed my thumb out for the coast, knowing survival would be significantly easier on the shores of the Pacific Ocean, which it was.

I spent weeks on the coast, gathering the endless supply of sea lettuce, kelp, mussels and other creatures at low tide. Life was simple, somewhat sustainable, although I did replenish my food supply once during those weeks. My spirit had slowed down and now ebbed and flowed more with the rhythm of creation as my intuitive sense heightened. I grew more aware of the plant life and took notice of species that turned out to be edible. More than once I would be walking along the beach and feel a sense of alarm, only to see a bald eagle just ahead on a low branch, eyeing my presence with an intensity that was daunting. It was good. I came for this reason, to know the wilderness. I also came to immerse myself in the silent language of God that speaks in the stillness of my soul. I came to fall in love again and to express that love the only way I knew how, to be alone with God in the wilderness. Yes, a sweetness of soul was taking hold. But still, my gut told me something wasn't right. Finally, and after days of discernment, I set out for drier climates on the east side of the Cascades, hoping a change of landscapes would bring the peace I sought.

Changes

Through Seattle and over the Cascades I found my way to the wilderness again, thinking to myself, *"This is it!"* My plan was to find some lonely mountain meadow and build a small structure that I would call home for the next several months. I paralleled a mountain stream as I worked my way farther into the wilderness, gathering mushrooms and cattails to supplement dinner. By night fall and amid giant trees, I made camp alongside a stream that was roaring with spring run off.

That night, while quiet in prayer, a word of God came into my heart, "I have a change for you." There was joy, which comes when the word of God is spoken into my heart. There was also excitement. The next morning, I broke camp with a sense of urgency, that God needed me to be somewhere, although I had no idea where 'somewhere' was. I just knew I needed to hike, and so I did, from dawn to dusk, over one mountain pass until I collapsed in a deserted roadside campground alongside a river. That night, while praying, the quiet whisper of God came again, "I am going to bring a woman into your life."

I might have let out a laugh at the paradox of it all as my heart then fluttered with unexpected joy. Even though I had chosen the life of a pilgrim I could not deny a growing desire to share my life with a woman. *A woman,* I thought to myself. *Crazy, only God would do a thing like that.* I had to laugh. On the eve of this adventure and knowing I was about to cut all ties to a worldly life, I had expressed my desire to take a vow of celibacy. God's voice came back, "No," which surprised me. *A woman in my life,'* I thought to myself again. *I like that idea.*

I woke with the same sense of urgency. By mid afternoon I found my way to Chelan, Washington. My plan was to catch the inland ferry to Stehekein, a small village at the end of Lake Chelan, that borders the Glacier Peak Wilderness, get some work, camp in a nearby wilderness campground and let God go to work. But, as I walked the streets of Chelan the fire of God began to fade in my heart. I took this as a sign this was not the place. *Perhaps Leavenworth?* I thought. I then walked to the edge of town to thumb a ride to Leavenworth. Within ten minutes a dark van began to approach. A knowing told me this was my ride. Just as the van was about thirty yards away, this wild looking man seemingly jumped out of a patch of briars and stuck out his thumb. The van swerved over to pick him up and left me standing. "Okay Lord, Chelan is it."

The next morning I bought a ticket for the *Lady of the Lake* Ferry and took my place near the bow of the boat, enjoying the Cascades and the blue water below. As I settled into my cushion seat an older woman, perhaps in her late seventies, sat next to me and started reading a book about wild edibles. Surprised, I glanced over and asked some benign question like, "I have not read that book; do you like it?"

She then launched into a spirited discourse about the author coming to Holden Village in the coming weeks. She then looked me then asked, "Are you coming to Holden?"

"No Ma'am," I said.

Without hesitation she responded, "I think you ought too!"

"Is that so?"

"Yes, and as a matter of fact the staff coordinators are on this boat. I think you should go back there and speak with them right now. Tell them Gertrude sent you."

Holden Village, once a mining operation, is a remote Lutheran retreat center located high in the North Cascades just on the border of the Glacier Peak Wilderness. There is one road in and out, maintained by Holden Village, accessed only by the *Lady of the Lake Ferry*. The village, in peak times, can support nearly 500 people.

A peace rested upon my soul as the Holden bus rolled to a stop in this quaint retreat center amid towering mountains. After lunch I walked through the large pine and cedar trees along railroad Creek. The air was summer sweet. I rested on a large boulder and began to pray. A sacred presence fell upon me that told me I was welcomed.

I quickly settled into village life, working six hours a day, attending evening worship, and making new friends. Life was rich. I chose to sleep on the earth just outside the village. The earth comforted my soul. Railroad Creek soothed me to sleep. Dreams were deep.

I began to share God in the wilderness sessions for guests and other volunteers. During my off hours I was often asked to go for walks with those in discernment. It was good. I had wilderness, community, ministry, work and incredible worship. More than once I prayed, 'This is enough, God!' I am complete." And yet my radar was scanning the horizon for this woman that God had spoken of.

About two weeks later I walked into the dining room, subtly aware of a young woman sitting at a table doing the final paper work that is required of all volunteers. As I glanced at her my spirit leapt within me. It was profound and unmistakable. There was no doubt in my soul this was the woman that God had spoken of. I went over to introduce myself. She was beautiful. My stomach was giddy with delight. As I began to leave the dining room and as she stood up to finish her paperwork I caught sight of a ring on her left hand. I looked harder. It was a wedding band.

Kathryn and I were assigned the same work area and shared many shifts together. I let a friendship form as we spoke of spirituality and shared music during non-work times. Under any other circumstances I would have run out of there in a minute. But it was God who brought me to this place. It was God who told me that a woman would be brought into my life. I could not run. I didn't want to run. I would have to trust that God had a wisdom that I could not see.

A couple weeks later I was approached by a woman on teaching staff to help facilitate a ritual during an evening worship. I, of course, offered my services. A couple days later I walked into the small worship space for the 10:00 P.M. service. To my surprise, there was Kathryn speaking with the woman leading the service. The facilitator welcomed me and said, "I forgot to mention that you would work with a second person. I have asked Kathryn to help during the hand washing ceremony just after Eucharist. I assume you two know each other? Is that okay?"

For a moment I was taken back, as was Kathryn. To share such an intimate act with Kathryn was frightening, mostly because I feared owning my feelings for her. There was also another part of me that was saying to myself, "This is crazy, you are way off base, how could this be of God? Get your butt back to the wilderness where you belong."

After the Eucharist, Kathryn and I began the beautiful ritual of washing the hands of those gathered, pouring the water and drying their hands. It was a beautiful expression of the servant Jesus who washed his disciples' feet. As we poured water over peoples' hands and gently dried them, a part of me shut down so as keep my growing feelings for her in check. As we completed the task and with relief I began to place the water basin on the rock center piece. But Kathryn, with pitcher of water held out and the drying cloth

9

wrapped over her forearm, gestured me forward. For an instant, I stood bewildered. Then the realization that we were to wash each other's hands dawned upon me.

Eternity can pass though us in a moment's glance. The kingdom of God can be built or torn down with a simple choice of "yes" or "no" to the work of the Holy Spirit. It was that kind of moment. I nearly cried, but by some measure of grace I held myself together. In humility, I offered my hands to Kathryn. She gently began to pour water over them. In that moment, with eyes embraced, the Spirit of God rushed through me. It was then, as the water dripped through my hands, I consciously surrendered myself to the Holy Spirit and to the will of God, wherever that may lead. As she finished I gently grabbed Kathryn's hands and began pouring water over them. Her eyes, wet with tears, spoke of love, fright, and unknowing.

After the service, I grabbed my blanket from my room and walked into the velvet black of the North Cascades' forest. There, with tears of anguish and love, I knelt upon Mother Earth, buried my face in my hands and wept, knowing our souls had touched. And Kathryn, married only a year, had returned to her room with her husband and silently wept through the night. During the few hours of restless sleep the Spirit of God came upon her and awakened her soul further.

David

I ask you not to judge it. Even though you have every right to do so. But before you jump to conclusions I invite you to let the story unfold. I also refer you to the story of David. Each time I had read the account of David and Bathsheba, that is, prior to meeting Kathryn, I had scorned David, holding him in judgment and contempt. Jesus said, "Judge not, lest you be judged." That scripture had now come full circle. But the story of David does not end with his sin with Bathsheba nor the killing of Uriah. The story of David and Bathsheba is about a God who is willing to take our humanity and bring about the Kingdom of God. Yes, there is suffering as a result of his choice, that much is clear. But of all the women David married, God choose his union with Bathsheba to begin the lineage that would lead to the birth of Jesus Christ, the Lamb of God who took upon himself the sin of the world. Certainly, God could have wiped out that relationship and chosen to bring the Son of God through a different lineage but God didn't. So out of brokenness, out of sin, out of David's humanity came the power of God. It is a wisdom that is too high for me to grasp.

I don't use the account of David to justify my story nor manipulate God. I simply put it out there, knowing that sometimes God is outside the box, a box that God seemingly set fixed parameters too.

Three weeks after Kathryn's arrival a group of us rode in the back of the luggage truck, bound for the loading dock, sharing our last few moments together. Torn into a thousand pieces and uncertain what the future held, Kathryn and I rode in silence, wishing this moment would never come, wishing circumstances were different or wishing time would stand still. But it didn't. Our time together was now measured in minutes.

The *Lady of the Lake Ferry,* that had brought me to Holden docked and was now waiting to take Kathryn back to Chelan and onto New Jersey. Tears blurred my vision. My heart ached. The captain gave a last call. It was crazy. It was unbearable. Kathryn and I embraced farewell. The pain and paradox of it all tore at my innocent understanding of God. I had come to the wilderness to divorce this world and become God's own. Yet, here I was, torn into a thousand pieces and so profoundly connected to a younger married woman. The captain gave the final call. As we pulled back from our embrace, our eyes, streaked with tears, locked. There were no words. As I dropped my hands from her shoulders to let her go my soul ripped within me. Yes, I could feel the tear deep within, ripping through the sacred chambers that had been carefully laid the last eight years of my journey with God. She started up the ramp. Everything inside of me was screaming, 'This is wrong! It wasn't supposed to happen like this!" Kathryn stood on the back deck of the boat as the captain maneuvered the ferry boat away from the dock. The engines revved louder. White water began to churn behind the large ferry boat. Kathryn remained standing on the deck, looking, looking. I stood there also, watching and watching. Soon, she was unrecognizable among the people. I remained until the *Lady of the Lake* disappeared.

The Dark Night of the Soul

A dream came. In this dream, Jesus and I were walking along a mountain path. There was peace. The next moment the trail stopped and before us was a cave. As we approached the entrance I was struck with the absence of light in this cave. It was dark, utterly dark. In the dream I did not understand the cave nor even fear it. I just knew it was dark, that was all. Then Jesus motioned with his hand, gesturing to me that it was my time to enter this cave.

I awoke with a knowing, the hour of shadows was upon me. My dark night of the soul had come. There was no running, there was no place to hide, even the wilderness would offer no solace. It was time.

Kathryn and I wrote often, speaking of our lives and sharing of our pain. There was no remedy for the pain. She was married and that was reality. But our feelings grew and as they did Kathryn began to struggle in her infant marriage. This was too much to bear for me, to be in the middle of this painful situation that seemingly had nothing to do with the God that I had known so deeply for eight years. Finally, the burden, the guilt and the confusion became so great, that by Kathryn's initiation, we chose to cut communication between us.

It was the right thing to do and yet it shook my world to pieces. By the week's end, I loaded my pack and took off for the wilderness. I followed Railroad Creek ten miles or so to Domkey Lake, which rests in a small basin just above Lake Chelan. For two days I poured out my grief to God. There was no relief. Sunday morning, amid broken skies and a slight rainfall, I worked my way toward Lake Chelan to catch the bus back to Holden Village. As I rounded a knoll that overlooked the lake, my eyes caught sight of one of the most brilliant double rainbows I had ever seen.

Upon my return to Holden and immersed in pain, I did the unthinkable while living in winter community at Holden, I took a vow of silence and began a ten day fast, excluding work duties and one meal per day. I told the community I was struggling with a deep personal issue and needed to draw my boundaries and go inward for guidance. It was my deepest prayer that at the end of this prayer and fasting 'novena,' my deep feelings would be washed from my heart and soul.

I said my prayers with conviction and lost some extra pounds but there was no lightening bolt from heaven nor washing of these feelings, and despite my commitment to break free, my feelings for Kathryn only intensified, leaving me with a desire for her like I had never known. By day ten, I had given up my false hope of purging my feelings for Kathryn and owned the truth. I loved her and desired her like no other woman I had ever known.

On the other side of the country in the concrete world of New Jersey, while Kathryn was completing her second year of seminary, she was experiencing the same wave of emotions for me. It was then, Kathryn began to face the reasons why she married her husband and pondered if she could emotionally survive in the marriage. As the divorce word began to come up in conversation something inside of me snapped. I couldn't take it any more. I then broke my commitment with the Holden winter community and returned to the wilderness.

Arizona

My dark night followed me to the land of coyotes, cactus and desert sun. I knew it would, but at least I had the expanse of the day to pray and the quiet of the wilderness to comfort me. But the wilderness closed her heart to me, as if she were saying, you are not welcomed at this time. It was frightening. I was lost and I knew it. God was silent, the wilderness didn't want me, and I was in love with a married woman in New Jersey.

I stumbled around the desert dumbfounded, putting in my time, while vainly hoping some guidance would fall upon my soul.

Somewhere in my agony the thought of the Grand Canyon flashed into my mind. By now, the south rim, which sits at 7000 feet above sea level, would be thawing out. I broke camp and started toward Flagstaff, Arizona.

With my pack loaded and a seven day back-country permit in hand I stood before one of the most powerful landscapes I had ever trekked. The Canyon, with its endless expanse of smaller canyons, red rock spires and desert shrubs seemed to welcome me. There was hope, that perhaps in such an austere and powerful landscape, I might find God and the direction I so deeply needed.

From the Ponderosa Pine forest of the south rim, moving lower into another climatic zone of the Pinion Pine and Juniper forests I weaved lower into the earth. Several times, I remained motionless as I gazed upon the rugged beauty of this land. In reverence to God for such an awe inspiring landscape I took a three day vow of silence, which is not hard to do when a person is alone but still, it was my act of reverence to God for such a place, believing I was walking on holy ground.

All around me jagged canyon walls had torn through Mother earth, leaving a gaping wound that seemingly led to the underworld. It seemed no accident that I was descending into her depths. It was my dark night of the soul, my journey to the underworld. What better place to ritualize this profound journey than the Grand Canyon.

The pines and junipers gave way to desert shrub. A lizard darted here or there but for the most part and to this untrained eye, the Canyon seemed void of life. I laid my sleeping bag under the stars on the Tonto Plateau. Prayers were said in the silence of my mind and the quiet chambers of my heart.

For days I hiked, slept under stars, cried out to God and uttered silent words of despair. But the darkness only intensified, leaving me with an agony of spirit like I had never known before. By the seventh day and with my back country permit expired I hiked up to the rim, renewed my permit and returned to the austere and beautiful world of the Grand Canyon.

The Canyon Desert blossomed, really blossomed. It was an explosion of yellows and pinks and other assorted colors. I was grateful for the opportunity to witness it. I traversed along the plateau for several days. Daytime temperatures stretched into the eighties. Sweat rolled off my forehead as I walked five, ten and sometimes fifteen miles a day. The physical exertion brought relief to my agony of spirit. For two nights I camped along the cool of the Colorado River, resting my body and being quiet in spirit. There was no word from God nor solace that I could grab hold of, and so, as my permit expired, I returned to the rim, renewed my permit and descended into the Canyon a third time, toward the confluence of the Colorado River and the Little Colorado.

I remained there three days, fasting and praying. The spiritual oppression was so intense I could barely function at times. By the end of the third day I knew my answers were not in the Grand Canyon. It was a frightening reality. If I couldn't find my answers here after nearly four weeks in the Canyon where were they? That is, if there were answers. And so, I began a slow and deliberate hike back to the rim. With each step closer to the world that I had hoped to divorce and to Kathryn and her husband my heart sank further into grief. As I crested the rim of the Canyon, I was almost numb with disbelief. My inner compass that had been so faithful and true for the last eight years had failed. I was lost, really lost, and now I was to return to civilization, broken, in love with a married woman and with no vision for my life. This was hardly the rite of initiation that I had set out to live almost a year ago. It was almost unbearable.

The Navajo Man

Dusk settled upon the Arizona desert as the state trooper pulled off the highway. He stepped out of his car and walked deliberately toward me. I braced myself for a battle.

"What are you doing son?" he asked.

"I am hitch hiking back to Colorado," I replied.

"I can see that," he said with a hint of sarcasm.

For a moment our eyes embraced. His face then softened as a look of concern came over him.

"Do you know that you are on the edge of the Navajo Reservation?"

"I know that," I said.

"I can't stop you but I don't recommend it, especially at night. Go north through Salt Lake."

"I want to go home," I replied. "This is the shortest route."

"Go north!" he spoke again.

"I am going this way," I replied.

He shook his head in frustration then looked me in the eyes. "Be careful son!"

I should have heeded his warning but it was not a rational time. I was in pain. I had just spent two months in the Southwest, praying, fasting and searching for a word from God. Strangely enough, the time spent in prayer had only intensified the pain. A part of me was angry. Yes, angry at God that Kathryn was married, angry that the agony of this dark night was so intense, and angry about the fruitless labor of unanswered prayer.

I watched the officer's car disappear into the vastness of desert, wondering if I should reflect upon his words. I then stuck my thumb out at passing cars bound for the heart of the Navajo Reservation. Just as night swept over the landscape and the hope of catching a ride dwindled a Ford truck swerved to the side of the road. A jolt of fear gripped my heart. The truck door opened and a man much larger than myself with long black hair stepped out and yelled, "Get in!"

He said it which such conviction, as if he knew me or had been expecting me that I looked over my shoulder to see who he was speaking to.

"I am speaking to you! Get in!" came his command.

His boldness flustered me and without thought or prayer and wishing I had the strength to stand up against him, I started toward his truck while thinking to myself, *this guy is either sent by God or is going to kill me.* At the moment, I hardly cared either way. I threw my backpack in the back of the truck then climbed into the passenger seat. He then put the truck in gear and drove off into the Arizona blackness.

By the lights of the dash I surveyed this man, his distinct Navajo facial features, and simple dress of jeans and a denim shirt. Time passed, the night deepened. I sat with arms crossed, watching the desert stars come to life, wondering if I had made a fatal mistake. My answer came as his voice broke our silent truce.

"I am going to tell you a story. And you are going to listen." I didn't respond. "I am going to tell you about my life. How I lost everything to drugs and alcohol. How I lost my children, my wife, and even myself. I am going to tell you what it means to walk through pain."

A tear began to swell in both eyes.

"There was a time when I didn't even know myself. There was a time when I lay paralyzed with pain, refusing to get up, refusing to change. I wanted only to drink until the pain no longer existed. That is darkness, when there is no hope and no will to live. You ever been there?" I didn't answer. "But I want to tell you something about being in darkness. You either live or you die. Do you hear me?" I didn't answer. He continued, "I don't know how much time passed for me like that, but I do remember the day a Road Man or priest as you might call him visited me, saying, "This is not the path the Creator wants you to walk. I am going to teach you the sacred way. But I can't do it for you. Do you hear me? I can pray. I can lead you through sacred ceremonies. But I cannot do it for you. Only you can walk this road. You are the one who must call upon the Creator's Power. You are the one who must believe you have the strength to face your pain. You are the one who must break your destructive cycle with drugs and alcohol."

As he spoke silent tears streamed down my cheeks. I knew for this moment I had fled to the Southwest and had labored in the wilderness for two months. I started to pray, giving thanks for this Navajo Man. Just then his voice broke cadence.

"Do you know what faith is?"

"I haven't a clue," I said.

"Faith is when you get on your knees and pray. And whether you feel God's power or not you get up. And you do the right thing. Do you understand me? You get up! That is faith."

I remember thinking to myself, *'my God, who is this guy and how did he know?"*

Sometime later his truck slowed to a stop. "The turn off to my ranch is just ahead. This is as far as I can take you. Will you be all right?"

"Yeah, I've got plenty of gear," I said as I climbed out of the cab, grabbed my backpack then slowly returned to the cab to say thank you. As I opened the door, he looked hard at me and pointed his finger saying, "You got to have Faith! You hear me! You got to have Faith!"

I wanted to burst out crying but held on, nodding my head in acknowledgment of his words. I closed the door then walked fifty feet into the blackness of the desert. As I dropped onto my knees, I wept tears of surrender and tears of faith, knowing my rite of initiation had just begun.

3 JESUS IN THE WILDERNESS

The phrase 'rite of initiation' conjures up images of indigenous elders beating drums around a fire as they prepare young men to face themselves in the wilderness. The air is crackling with suspense, unknowing, and the certainty of being tested. There is also fear. It is a time of testing, endurance, and pain, all of which strips away the psychological dross of life so that one might discover the gold within. There will be suffering in this wilderness and psychological death. The way of the ego-centered boy, his magical thinking and his idealistic world must give way so the mature masculine can take root. Death and resurrection are painful stuff. The young men know this. We all know this. After the drums fall silent the young men scatter into high ridges, lonely meadows and small outcroppings where they will fast, call upon the Creator, face their shadow and perhaps find a new name and their life's mission.

If we are honest with ourselves there is a part of our masculine psyche that aches for such an experience, to venture into some wilderness, to test our skills and call upon that raw and primordial masculine so that we might emerge an awakened and powerful man, a man with a new name that only God and we know and a man with a mission that will give purpose, direction and meaning to our life. And you know, that is exactly what needs to happen. Because it is only when a man is stripped raw and seemingly in an uncharted wilderness that his true self is awakened and realized within himself. This is the wisdom of God revealed to us through the life of Jesus, a wisdom that even Jesus could not circumvent. So I take you to Matthew 3:16 into the powerful drama of Jesus' rite of initiation.

"And when Jesus had been baptized, just as he came up from the water, suddenly the heavens were opened to him and he saw the Spirit of God descending like a dove and alighting on him. And a voice from the heaven said, 'This is my son, the Beloved with whom I am well pleased.' Then Jesus was led by the Spirit into the wilderness to be tempted by the devil. He fasted forty days and forty nights, and afterwards he was famished. The tempter came and said to him, 'If you are the Son of God, command these stones to become loaves of bread.'

But he answered, It is written, 'one does not live by bread alone but by every word that comes from the mouth of God.'

Then the devil took him to the holy city and placed him on the pinnacle of the temple, saying to him, 'If you are the Son of God, throw yourself down; for it is written, "He will command his angels concerning you, and on their hands they will bear you up so that you will not dash your foot against a stone.'

Jesus said to him, "Again it is written, Do not put the Lord your God to the test.'

Again, the devil took him to a very high mountain and showed him all the kingdoms of the world and their splendor and he said the him, 'All these I will give you, if you will fall down and worship me.'

Jesus, said to him, 'Away with you Satan! for it is written,' Worship the Lord your God, and serve him only."

Then the devil left him, and suddenly angels came and waited on him.""

The Baptism

In this account of Jesus overcoming the temptations, he claims his power as the son of God and goes forth to do God's work. But to understand the fullness of the story and in the context of a rite of initiation, we have to go back to the baptism, to the Spirit of God descending upon him and receiving the words, "This is my son, the Beloved, with whom I am well pleased." This is it, the foundation, the core and the very guts of the masculine journey we need to live. God cannot and will not take us into our own wilderness until we come to a place of intimacy with God and an outpouring of the Holy Spirit upon us. This is where our work will begin, moving into that place where you and I hear those incredible words given to Jesus, leaving no doubt to whom we belong to and whose image we bear.

The Wilderness

This baptism by John and the outpouring of the Spirit of God upon Jesus is powerful and seemingly more than enough for Jesus to go forth and do God's work. But it isn't. It is only half the equation. So God leads Jesus into the wilderness. Why? Jesus has to realize the fullness of his baptism and this power within himself, and that demands going into the desert and overcoming the temptations of self preservation, power, and prestige. There is no other path. True power is not freely given, not even to Jesus. It must be earned and called forth.

It is the same for you and I. It is not enough that we are born again, baptized, church-going or saved. Nor is it enough that Jesus died on the cross for you and I. Yes, he took upon himself the sin of the world and through him we have salvation. But still, it is not enough. St Catherine of Sienna in her work, *the Dialogue,* which is a written account of the inner dialogue between her and God, pens these words as spoken to her by God, "It is not enough that I built a bridge between heaven and earth with the work of my Son. Now you must walk across it." And so, there is a wilderness awaiting you and I, a rite of initiation that God has designed for each of us. Why? The answer of course is our Father's love, a love that yearns to share the incredible joy and power of the kingdom with each of us. So God leads us when we are ready into our own wilderness so that we might be tested, experience psychological death, and emerge a new and awakened man, a man with a new name, a man with a mission.

Called

Jesus was led into the desert. We need to get this. He did not go of his own choosing. This is crucial. This joyful, exhilarating and difficult path of God's initiation for each of us is the work of the Holy Spirit. There is no going into this desert by our own initiative. It is the movement of God. It is intense. We must be called.

This calling will be unique to each of us. Sometimes call and crisis go hand in hand. Perhaps circumstances have spiraled out of control, or your marriage is in difficult waters or an addiction that you have kept well contained is beginning to work its way out and wreak havoc upon your life, and so you find yourself at the edge of some abyss, knowing your life could crumble at any moment. Perhaps you find yourself comfortable, too comfortable, yet knowing there is a deeper purpose yet to be discovered, that somewhere in your heart, laying dormant beneath your complacency, your fears and your insecurities, is your passion, your dreams, your divine purpose just waiting to be called forth. One thing is for certain, it does not matter the circumstances, it is the knowing that matters, that powerful moment when we hear God's voice whisper, 'It is time," in the quiet of our souls. So for whatever reason you are here, I welcome you. It is a sacred place, perhaps a painful place, but it is real and I want to share with you, that you stand on the threshold of your fullest potential in Jesus Christ.

The Wounding

The song, *I can only imagine*, by Bart Milard of Mercy Me is the title of one of my favorite songs and seems fitting to use as we speak about the forty days in the desert. I can only imagine the physical, psychological and spiritual wounding endured by Jesus. I can only imagine that the baptism he had received had faded and there he was, seemingly alone, hungry, thirsty and taunted by dark forces, holding onto to the words given to him by his Father that had become like a dream or a distant memory. I can only imagine Jesus being pushed to his limits, far beyond what any of us can understand or will know. This wounding might seem cruel, yet at the very heart of this wounding is love, a Father's love that longs to share the hidden treasures of the kingdom with His Son.

This dark corridor or wounding is a universal truth, given to us by God, passed down through prophets, sages and all those who have chosen to venture into this wilderness to make the kingdom of God their own. This is the wilderness time of our lives, when all seems lost, when faith is but a glimmer of hope and our wounds are laid bare. It is the cutting open of the psychological scar tissue that has calloused around the wounded areas of our heart and the breaking of the false self that has robbed us from our masculine power. Painful, you bet it is. God's Word cuts deep, like a two edged sword, slicing soul and spirit, bone and marrow. But here is the good part. Beneath our wounds and shadows, held captive by our shame and insecurities, bound by our fear and self-serving pursuits dwells the God-given masculine energies. These primal forces, the lover, the warrior, the seer and the king, are awakened and honed as we allow God to strip away the protective layers of our psyche and lead us into and through our darkest caves and deepest fears. This my brother, takes a wild man.

Jesus was tempted....

After forty days of intense hunger and prolonged psychological and spiritual battles, the very essence of Jesus was put to the test. Of course this test came when he was stripped bare, void of followers and without great deeds or mountain top experiences. It will be the same for you and I. We will be pushed to our limits and stripped bare just as Jesus was. Then when all seems lost, we will be tested, tempted, and tried. It will be agonizing. It is then we will be required to use these newly awakened masculine energies to pierce the shadows, to stand firm against the arrows of the evil one and to break the family dysfunction. It is here, as we align the wild man energy with the Spirit of God, that the power of addiction begins to dissolve within us and we begin to reclaim that which was lost to darkness and chaos. Here is the place we are given the courage to see our wounding as a gift from God. This is the place where forgiveness flows, our humanity is embraced and our masculine power in Christ Jesus is realized. It is worth fighting for. It is worth the pain suffered.

The Invitation

Let's pause at this time, breathe, reflect. Take inventory of your heart and the desires that dwell within, take measure of your life and the legacy you want to leave behind. There are roads before each of us, choices that have a profound affect upon our lives and our loved ones. The kingdom of God is at stake. There is, of course, the safe road. The well traveled path that slowly drains a man of his power. We have all left footprints upon this path, giving God 99.9 percent of our heart, following what society asks of us, living in denial, blaming others, choosing passive silence, putting in heartless time as a father or doing just enough to get by. I won't belabor this path simply because it is not the path God chooses for any of us. The road I speak of begins where the conventional road ends, where there is no path, only an unchartered wilderness through the foreboding landscapes of the inner man. At such thresholds we tremble with fear, because we know there is real pain in this wilderness, and we wonder if we have what it takes to survive. There is also an intangible sense of excitement, adventure, quest and the unknown. At our core we ache for adventure, a vision or a quest and yet, there it is, within each of us, an unchartered wilderness that will lead us to our masculine soul in Christ. We need only to accept the invitation given to us by God through Jesus.

The Lord of the Rings

In the mythic saga, J. R. Tolkein gives story to the spiritual battle between good and evil and the ancient rite of initiation. In the first of the three trilogies we meet Strider, an heir to the throne of Gondor who is on the run, living as ranger from the north, seeking to distance himself from his lineage. Why? It was his ancestor who should have destroyed the ring of power in the fires of Mordor thousands of years ago, therefore ending the struggle between good and evil. But his ancestor's humanity got the best of him and he took the ring for himself. Strider,'which is really his false-self name, fears the same weakness in himself and instead of confronting his weakness and owning his true lineage, he compromises his true self by running, doing good but not living his true self.

Let's be honest, there is a Strider within each of us, a part that is on the run and doubts whether we have what it takes to overcome our weakness, our false self or go into the wilderness of our heart and face the enemy. For good reasons, the stories of those who sought to follow God suffered. This isn't cowardly stuff here nor a road lined with roses. It is real. God is real. There will be pain. We can be certain of this. The Strider in us knows this and so he is on the run, hiding behind the veil of doing good, putting in our time at church, giving to charities or volunteering in the community. There's no doubt Strider is a good guy and on the right side. But the fact is, he is on the run and unwilling to own his true lineage and face his weakness. We have all been there.

As the story evolves Strider engages in the quest to destroy the ring, and as he does, he takes on his real name, Arigorn. It will be the same for you and me. As we accept the invitation to become our authentic self in Christ and engage in the struggle against the forces within and without that seek to destroy us, our soul name begins to emerge.

As Arigorn's story unfolds and just before the battle at Gondor, when doom for the world of men seems inevitable, the king of the Elfish people, Elrond, rides into camp, carrying with him the sword of Elindia, once broken now re-made, which represents the king energy and the lineage of Arigorn's ancestors. Elrond confronts Arigorn with the reality that his army is out numbered, that he is riding to war but not to victory, that he needs more men. Arigorn responds by telling him that there are no more men. Lord Elrond explains that there are the accursed dead living in the mountain. Lord Elrod then pulls out the sword of Elendia and says to Arigorn that they will answer to the true king of Gondor. He then invites Arigron to let go of the ranger and become who he was born to be, that he must take the road into the mountain, the dimalt road to gather the accursed dead.

Arigorn, now faced with the reality of defeat and the possible destruction of the world of men and knowing he alone has the power to change the course of events, finally grabs the sword and owns his true lineage as the King of Gondor. And where does Arigorn go from there? To summon the courage of his commarades and to the battle? No! He, with his two companions, take the Dimalt Road under the mountain, symbolically the road to the underworld to gather the army of the living dead.

This mythic saga is another expression that true power is awakened in the dark times. Each time we enter the cave or pass through the dark lands and face the trials that demand we go deeper into God and deeper into our masculine power we emerge with a new masculine power in Christ. It is then we know who we are and the power we wield in Christ, answering that deep question of validation that haunts every man. "Do I have what it takes? Am I worthy?" The answer is obviously yes. But until that yes is owned and realized within us, it isn't real. Please get hold of this, until that *YES* is owned and realized within us, it isn't real. That is the great poverty, men who have what it takes but aren't willing to go into the dark mountain and make it their own. So they are left wondering, living with half a heart and seeking the validation that only God can give them through a rite of initiation.

The question we now need to ask ourselves is; are you and I willing to put aside the Strider within us and own our true lineage in Christ? Are we willing to surrender our all and let God guide us through the wilderness of our heart and into the dark cave of our wounds so that God might awaken the primal masculine within? As you ponder this call and possibly question whether you have what it takes, I take you back to the old Testament story, 1 Samuel 16:13 "Then Samuel took the horn of oil and anointed him in the presence of his brothers; and the Spirit of the Lord came mightily upon David from that day forward."

This journey I speak of is the work of God. None of us has what it takes by ourselves. None of us by our own might can journey into the wilderness of our heart and face the false self, overcome addictions, pierce the enemy and come out an awakened man. It is impossible. But the moment we surrender our all, the moment we reach into our guts and say "yes" to God and God's mission for our life the Spirit of the Lord will rush upon us and give us the power to do what we could never do by ourselves.

If you have never experienced the power of God this will be a great leap of faith. I encourage you to trust though and take that leap through the veil of the unknown, to begin your journey just as David did, from tending sheep to the throne of Israel. I assure you, you have what it takes, every man does, it only needs to be awakened, called forth and set in motion. Will it be easy? Of course not. Do you have what it takes? Yes! You were born for this hour, to fight, to bring honor to your soul and to your God.

So, as you ponder these words I invite you to take pause. Perhaps you have the chance to walk in the wilderness, to sit by a stream or climb a mountain. Maybe you have only the quiet of your apartment. No matter where you are, draw a circle around you, claim your sacred space before the Lord. You are God's son, a true heir to the kingdom and a chosen instrument. As you claim your space before the Lord I also invite you to quiet your mind and empty yourself as Elijah did at the mouth of the cave at Mount Horeb. Certainly, the Lord will speak to your heart when you are ready.

I can only imagine what the Lord of Host might say to you.

Before we go any further, I need to put it on the line. This rite of initiation I speak of is a joyful, passionate, difficult and dangerous road. If we accept this profound invitation, we will know the peace that passes all understanding, the unspeakable joy of God's Spirit within us and experience the power of God working through us. We will also know the agony of battle. There will be wounds suffered and pain endured. There will be critical moments, when everything within us wants to quit. I can assure you the adversary is not going to let you or I grasp our masculine heart without a fight. Most likely, we will find ourselves on the front lines of the cosmic struggle between good and evil. If we remain true to God, even though we stumble, the new dawn will come. But there will be dark nights, a piercing sword and times when we all seems lost.

For those who hear the call, who long to get out of the boat and live a more passionate life, who are willing to let God probe deep into the psyche and bring pain to healing, I believe God can and will change the world through you. I dare say the kingdom of God rests upon the shoulders of those, both men and women, who are willing to enter this dark cave and awaken their powerful selves in Jesus. So I conclude this chapter with the words spoken through the prophet Isaiah, chapter 43: verse 14. "'But now thus says the Lord,'" He who formed you, 'Do not fear, for I have redeemed you. I have called you by name, you are mine. When you pass through the waters, I will be with you; and through the rivers, they shall not overwhelm you; when you walk through the fire you shall not be burned, and the flame shall not consume you.'"

4 YOU ARE MY SON

It's time to get to work, to create an inner sanctuary in which we will experience the indescribable joy, peace, love and power of God and hear those incredible words spoken by God to Jesus in the core of our being. Again, this is the very core of the masculine journey I speak of and from which all other truths are built. If this foundation is not firmly in place, if intimacy with God is not our deepest desire, if there is no outpouring of the Holy Spirit upon us, there will be no going into the wilderness, no awakening the primal masculine, nor facing the shadows or claiming our power as a son of God. Simply put, intimacy with God must be the foundation of our journey. To begin this work I need to share with you a teaching story that I came across years ago that speaks to the very heart of this issue.

There once was a young novice who eagerly sought God but to no avail. Upon hearing of an Abbott who possessed the rare gift of bringing people to God he set out to find him at a far away monastery. After months of travel, he knocked upon the door of the Abbot's cell. The Abbot opened the door and then asked what he could do for him. The young man replied, "I have been searching for God for years but cannot find God. I have been told you have a gift for helping people find God."

The Abbot looked with compassion upon the young man and said, "Follow me." The Abbot took off at a fast walk and nearly broke into a run. The young man, panting, followed. Much to the young man's surprise the Abbot ran right into a river. Again, the young man followed. Waist deep in water the Abbot turned with a jerk and grabbed the young man around the neck and dunked him in the water. The young novice panicked and began to lash out. But the strength of the Abbot prevailed. Just as the novice was about to drown the Abbot jerked him out of the water. After the young man regained his composure, the Abbot grabbed him with a sense of intensity and said, "When you want God as bad as you wanted that first breath out of the water you will find God!"

Author, unknown

describes? or ?

I love this story because it explicitly (tells) the spiritual truth that when we desire God above all else we will find God. This truth became clear in my own life nearly 28 years ago, the moment the grain of wheat first fell to the earth and died. Just after I had graduated from college my world crumbled. It was a series of falls. As I was about to journey to Alaska to commercial fish I met a young woman. We dated for nearly a month. An intimate relationship was formed. I went to Alaska with half a heart. I came back with less. Our relationship grew. Months passed. More than once she began to speak of a lifetime together. I teetered on the fence of indecision for a while. Then something in me shifted, really shifted. I wanted to marry her. About the time I was about to ask her to marry me was about the time her heart went elsewhere. To keep hope alive I had foolishly turned down my dream job in Montana to take a nightmare of a job in the heart of industrial Denver. Two weeks after I betrayed my inner self and shook hands with the CEO to accept the job, she ended the relationship. It was the final blow to my young heart.

In the wake of that pain my sister invited me down to Lubbock, Texas. Sunday morning we attended a large non-denominational church. Through eyes seared with pain I took inventory of the young men neatly dressed, carrying a Bible and sharing pleasant conversation while thinking to myself, *that's not me.'* 'This is not me.'

Drawn inward and protecting the pain that was unbearable, I endured the worship service. Just as the pastor gave the final benediction a large man with a booming southern voice took the microphone and said, "I know someone is out there struggling and needs Jesus in their life."

I didn't hear a word of that church service but when those words were spoken I jerked my head up, knowing an unseen sword had just pierced through my protective pain. He continued, "If that person would like to make a commitment to Jesus I invite them to stand up and walk down the aisle to where these elders are standing. My lower lip began to tremble as the pain started to leak out. I watched several stand up. His offer came again. I could barely hold back the tears. More stood up. Then his offer came a third time.

I grew up Catholic and have always loved church but didn't really know God's voice. But in that moment the voice of God spoke clearly to my heart saying, "If you stand up, your life will be more different than you can ever imagine." For a brief second eternity passed through me. Two roads lay before me. I saw them plainly in my spirit. I could hold onto this pain and live a fractured life or I could risk giving away my pain and my shattered dreams to live in Montana and stand up and give my life to God, knowing my life would be different, a different that was veiled from my spirit. The pain grew. My gut wrenched. I had a choice. About that time my sister leaned over and asked, "Do you want to stand up? I will go with you, Brian." I opened my heart then took the great leap as I nodded yes.

As I walked down that aisle grief and pain came out of every cell in my body as the old self shed from my psyche like snake skin, leaving a huge void for the risen Jesus to take up residence. My journey began that moment.

I share this story so we can explicitly come to an understanding about surrender. It is the surrendering of who we are to God that creates the space for the Spirit of God to dwell within, giving birth to an intimate relationship with God. This intimacy is the platform from which we will hear those powerful and healing words given to Jesus at the threshold of his wilderness experience. This is a universal spiritual truth, unchanging, set down since the foundation of the earth. Jesus said, "Very truly, I tell you, unless a grain of wheat falls into the earth and dies it remains just a single grain; but if it does die, it bears much fruit." John 12:24 Metaphorically speaking, the grain of wheat that must die is the self.

So here our work begins, in the very depths of our soul, taking ownership of our choices before God. So I need to ask you. Have you come to that place in your life where you desire God more *than* anything else? This a tough question, a deep question! It is easy to fool ourselves. It is not about being good, going to church, being spiritual, following the rules or saying our prayers. We could do all those things and still not surrender our deepest self. It's about the *Surrender of the* heart, all of the heart. I have never experienced an outpouring of grace when I have given God 99.9 percent. The power of God moves when I get into my guts and die to self. *Completely, ego?*

We must desire God above everything. Certainly, a PHD title is no different than the belt I just earned in martial arts. Hold this belt above my desire for God and the grace dries up and power seeps from my soul. Ten dollars is no different than a million dollars. Cling to it for security and we have placed a wedge between us and God.

The list is endless and unique to each of us. Causes *our beliefs* can be a stumbling block *to us* as well. Not that we shouldn't fight for what we believe in but we need to be careful. Whether it be abortion, religion, evangelization, peace, social justice or ecology, the ego can quickly grab hold of such causes for meaning and power as well as create the illusions that we have surrendered all to God.

Okay, enough words about surrender. It is time to get to work, to pull out the sword and cut deep. The question is: Have you crossed that threshold in which you have given your entire self to God through Jesus? Does the fire of God burn within your heart? Is Jesus your Lord and Saviour? Are you there now? We don't need a Lubbock, Texas to get there. Jesus stands at the doors of our heart, waiting for you and I to gather the courage to open the door wide and give all that we are and all that we posses to him. This my friend, takes a wild man. *and that*

For those who long to live this truth, feel they have surrendered all but have not experienced the fire of God, I invite you not to give up in your journey of surrender. When you are ready, the Spirit of God will sweep you up to new levels of your human experience. Be patient, trust, and persevere. God spoke to St. Catherine of Sienna in these words. "It is I who choose your day of consolation, not you." There have been countless times I have gone to the wilderness, put in the hard work of days and sometimes weeks of prayer and surrender only to hear the words, "You are not ready. There is still more work to be done." The soul is a vast wilderness and God is an endless expanse of Love and Mystery. There are many conversions along this path, although I must confess, Lubbock, Texas is a *remains* treasured moment. *as the beginning of my journey.*

5 A NEW WORLD

Back in from the deserts of the Southwest, I boarded a plane for West Michigan, in love, spiritually fractured but holding onto the faith the Navajo Man spoke of, that sometimes we don't feel God's presence or power working in our lives but we stand up, we believe, and we move forward.

By this time Kathryn had forged through the agonizing process of dissolving her first marriage. In general, I don't believe in divorce, it is most often the boy's path, but I don't judge it either. How could I? There I was, in love with Kathryn whom had just been married and was now divorced. We all like God to be predictable. But this time, God was outside the envelope, stretching my comfort zone, inviting me to embrace my own humanity and the humanity of the world.

To embrace my own humanity and the humanity of this world did not come easily. For most of my life I had run from my own brokenness as well as the dysfunction of others. I had run into the heart of God where I thought I would be safe. There is no triggering the wound or facing the shame when I am alone. The inner world is safe, God is all that I want God to be. At one time I deemed this the holy path, being celibate, surrendered and with few possessions, and perhaps it is for a season or for the boy within who needs his world to be safe and feel special. But this is about a rite of initiation, the journey from boy psychology to man psychology, a journey that

34

demands the crossing of a great chasm, a chasm in which the only way across is down and back up.

My plane touched down. We had not seen each other for almost a year. Upon our first embrace there was no doubt our love was real and God given. I settled in an apartment close to Kathryn and on the shores of Lake Michigan. They were great times, swimming in the waves of Lake Michigan, long talks deep into the night, sharing quiet prayer and evening walks on the beach. I was enchanted with Kathryn. She was the one, my soul mate, the person God had chosen for me, and so, like many of my pursuits in life and like many young lovers, I jumped into our relationship with no sense of caution or prudence, forsaking the words of a friend who said, "Go slow, so you may go deeper."

New romantic love doesn't know anything about caution nor does the boy within seeking to fill the mother wound. Knowing she was the one God had chosen for me, I did the most foolish thing possible. I consciously let down the walls that had protected the wounded boy within and let Kathryn in, certain her love would heal the wounds I carried. Now if this doesn't make you cringe, please stay with this story. My guess is that you might have some 'work' to do in the area of what power woman has in your life. Like I said, I was enchanted with Kathryn. Not only had I entrusted my wound to her but in a moment of thanks to God for being chosen to journey with such a woman the word *goddess* shot through my mind before I had time to hold it back, which scared the hell out of me. I didn't know where it came from but it was there and I knew it was not a good thing.

Our summer was magical. We were deep in love, sharing spirituality and enjoying Lake Michigan. But in the midst of such joy and promise there was also a tremor of fear running through my soul. After so many excursions deep into the wilderness: Alaska, Canyon Lands, Rocky Mountains, Grand Canyon, and the Northwest I was painfully aware there was no undoing the way of the wilderness within me. During the countless days, weeks and months walking through red rock desert, praying under the vastness of the heavens, climbing mountains or sitting for hours beside a stream in prayer something had shifted in my psyche. A part of me had become wild.

The wilderness coursed through my blood and called out to me in the quiet moment between dark and dawn. I would hear her voice in my dreams, asking me to come back. The truth was, I was in love with the wilderness, not like being in love with Kathryn, but still, in love with her. She had embraced me as her son, taught me her wisdom and welcomed me as I was. Mostly though, she had guided me into intimacy with God through Jesus and for this I loved her.

It was a paradox, to be so in love with Kathryn and yet torn. There were times, while driving through industrial Michigan that the fatigue of the land nearly suffocated my spirit, and often, as I struggled to find my domain in Kathryn's family system and was absolutely lost concerning a career, I knew the wilderness within me was unreconcilable with my new life. Many nights, with tears streaming down my cheeks, I relived my encounter with the Navajo Man and replayed his words in my mind, "You got to have faith." I did have faith, a faith that I was called to journey with Kathryn. But my faith would cost me. I was certain of this. Some part of me was going to die.

Colorado

At summer's end Kathryn and I ventured to Colorado Springs to meet my family. One afternoon we were driving up a dirt road that weaves through tunnels and into the mountains. As we entered into the darkness of a tunnel the dream of Jesus inviting me into a dark cave came to mind. We then burst into the light. A tear of relief came, perhaps my time in the dark cave was coming to a close.

We parked where the road was gated off and continued our journey by foot, hand in hand and sharing the quiet of the wilderness. Within a mile we veered onto a trail that parallels a stream. As we entered the forest and under the canopy of the Douglas Fir trees, the presence of God began to wash over me, healing the pain from the last year and releasing my soul from the grip of the adversary.

Through the gift of tears, I saw Kathryn, holding the presence of God within and simply letting the moment unfold. As the pain and oppression left, and with new strength and clarity, I grabbed Kathryn's hand and we began farther up the trail. But only for a moment. The Spirit of God was still working within me, and then I knew. I stopped and embraced Kathryn.

"What is going on?" she asked.

"Would you marry me?"

When the flame of God subsided the realization of what I had just done overwhelmed me. *Marriage,* I thought to myself. *Are you sure God? Oh God I am scared.*

In the years preceding Kathryn, I had become a pilgrim with little desire for material things and the road most men travel. My life was God's. My desire was for simplicity, wilderness and a ministry at some time. Until now there was no room for marriage, house payments, insurance and all the trimmings that seem to go with the road of marriage. Then the thought of children came into my mind. Now this really scared me. *Oh the responsibility, the time commitment, how am I ever going to find time to pray?* In a moment of mental survival I began to push the thought away. Just then my eyes traveled across the ravine, walking silently through the forest was a doe with two fawns. I knew.

The Inner Wilderness

If in my early thirties and after so many wilderness excursions someone would have told me there was a gaping wound working beneath the surface that was robbing me of my masculinity, I would have of course denied it then gone off on some self righteous discourse about my masculinity, which is exactly what happened.

"He is a soft male," came the words from a friend of Kathryn's family. I, of course, reacted strongly, which is a sure sign there is *work* underneath the reaction as I launched into my litany of accomplishments that assured me I was fully a man. Denial is a powerful built-in defense mechanism. We all use it in one way or another. Most often, the coded message beneath denial is, I can't go there. This is too painful to face, and it is, until we have to! This is where the wounding comes in. If God never allowed us to be wounded, we would never face the core issues that rob us of our masculinity. The truth was, I was a soft male and reflected more of the feminine qualities of masculinity. I had consciously and unconsciously rejected the world of men and the archetype of the warrior. The world of men was too frightening, confrontative and had seemingly little to do with spirituality and my expression of God. The feminine language of bride of Christ, lover of God, intuitive, gentle, fit my ideology well and kept the wounded boy safely guarded from the way of the warrior.

Years later, while Kathryn was sharing a cup a tea with a woman friend, I walked in. Kathryn politely said, "Brian can we finish this discussion in private?"

Just as I nodded sure and was about to leave her friend said, "Oh that is okay, Brian is just like one of us." That about says it all. Now how would you like that on your masculine resume? Pathetic! The worst of it was, it was true.

Without the warrior online we run from conflict, which is something I had done as far back as I could remember. I don't know about you but emotional conflict rips me into pieces. I have seen this in almost every person I have journeyed with, the fear of conflict and the defense mechanisms of fight or flight that kick into gear when things get hot. Fight or flight are both the same, a learned or adopted response to conflict which best protects our wound, that is, the masculine shame or sense of rejection that emerges out of our family system. Fight is verbal aggression, manipulation, control or twisting the facts to avoid ownership of the mistake which therefore protects the wound and the buried shame. When we are *right* there is no need for self reflection and without self reflection we can avoid triggering the buried wound. The other side is flight, retreating into some hidden cave, denial, silence, burying the emotions or passively acquiescing to the other person's point of view. Flight is no different from fight, both are protecting the wound.

Kathryn and I had two different styles of responding to conflict. I was more about retreating into some hidden cave, silence, burying my emotions or passively acquiescing to her. She was more shoot from the hip style, aggressive, clear on the facts, pressing the issue. I kid you not, when Kathryn and I were in conflict, I couldn't have had a straight thought if I wanted to. The tension would go up, voices would be raised and then there was this confusion that was void of any type of masculine strength. Even my body language, which slumped with shame, spoke of the wounded boy.

The body never lies. Our words can hide our true feelings, bury our shame or speak the untruth that all is well, but our bodies tell the real story. Our eyes, our posture or even our physical health all speak of who we are and whether we are living in the wounded boy or a mature masculine psyche. I have worked with men who have tread a similar path as I. As they tell the story of their marriage and the conflict with their spouse their body language takes on the posture of a seven year old boy being scolded by a strong mother figure. As they continue to tell their story I have challenged them to listen to their language that speaks of a boy. Most of them respond in a defensive mode, assuring me and themselves of their masculinity and the pain they have endured. I hear their pain. It is real. But still, the body never lies. They are operating from the wounded boy and the archetype of the victim. Divorce is almost sure to follow.

Shortly into our relationship and after several minor conflicts I had this dream in which Kathryn and I were about five years old. In the dream we were beneath large pictured windows of the house that I grew up in. As the dream progressed the little Kathryn began picking up small stones and throwing them at the pictured windows. With each stone she tossed, a sense of horror overwhelmed the little Brian and I begged her to stop. She then picked up a rather large stone, about the size of a grapefruit, and hurled it with all her might at the picture window, which then shattered and fell to the ground at my feet.

You don't have to be a Joseph or the prophet Daniel to get the deeper meaning of this dream. The symbolism is clear. That even at the age of 32 there was this little boy within who was terrified by emotional conflict and feared having my fragile family system disrupted. I had protected this wounded boy by charisma, avoiding

39

confrontation, lack of boundaries, aloneness, and spirituality. And now, by the wisdom of God, my inner boy's fragile world was being rocked if not shattered by the very woman I had entrusted him to.

The Boy Within

My life is about integrating my whole self into a passionate relationship with God and awakening the primal masculine forces within. But in order for me to make this leap it was necessary for me to embrace and understand the boy within. This is not a "let's make love to our wounds" session, neither is it an "oh, poor me" session, nor is it a blaming of others. That is not what men's work is about. God is not glorified nor is our true self served when we dwell in our wounds. Embracing the boy within is a powerful ingredient to becoming our full masculine self. It is about integration, wholeness and self discovery. And mostly, it is about allowing the Spirit of God to embrace and restore the fractured parts of our self. This truth is made evident to us in the simple but profound story of Jesus healing the woman crippled for eighteen years.

"Now he was teaching in one of the synagogues on the Sabbath. And just then there appeared a woman with a spirit that had crippled her for eighteen years. She was bent over and was quite unable to stand up straight. When Jesus saw her, he called her over and said, "Woman you are set free from your ailment." When he laid his hands on her, immediately she stood up straight and began praising God." Luke 13:10

To understand how it relates to the wounded boy we need to grasp the deeper implications of this story. Women were not welcomed in the sanctuary. They were separated, perhaps by a latticed fence. Now as Jesus was speaking the woman who is bent over appears. Remember, Jesus is fully awakened, mind, body and spirit and is well aware of this woman's affliction and the shame she had most likely internalized from the cultural understanding that illness represented being out of favor with God. But Jesus is about breaking down such walls, restoring the broken fragments of our life and making straight that which is bent over.

Jesus calls her forward into the sanctuary with him, as she is, a woman who is crippled, a woman who is not welcomed in the sanctuary with men and a woman who is silently shunned by her community. It is the moment of great risk for this woman. She must risk further shunning of the community, risk breaking religious tradition and risk giving away her belief she is not worthy, which is probably the most difficult of all. Internalized messages of shame, unworthiness, rejection, or not being good enough are hard to let go of. They are core messages that have been coded into our psyche since our earliest years. These messages, such as, I am nothing when I fail, or I am not worthy are the lenses in which we see ourselves and this world, even if we can't admit it.

These messages go underground in the world of the unconscious where they work their magic upon our lives. So often, with every failure the messages gets triggered, sending a shock wave of shame or rejection through the psyche, which is why these messages must be pierced or faced, which is exactly what Jesus is doing with this woman. He is challenging her to walk through them instead of skirt them. This is what healing the wound is about, going into it, not around it.

As Jesus calls this woman forward a critical moment is upon her. Time probably stood still as she looked into the eyes of Jesus. She was probably trembling with fear, hope and the knowing that she was about to touch the Sacred. She courageously sheds the false belief that she was not welcomed and answers the call.

Jesus could have easily worked within the confines of the Jewish law and stepped outside the sanctuary to heal her but he chose to present to her the opportunity to move through her shame, release her faith and claim her dignity as a daughter of God by inviting this woman as she was, bent over and shunned, into the sanctuary with him. Her weaker self probably would have preferred to have Jesus work in some deserted alley away from the crowds. But this story isn't just about healing of the body. It is about risk, integration, deep healing, being worthy and the knowing that we are welcomed in the sanctuary as we are.

Jesus is the same yesterday, today and forever. He is still radical. We can be certain at some point in our journey, perhaps at a retreat or a men's group, he will call forth our wounded, neglected or perhaps abused boy who is so often cast aside, silently shunned, seen as a weakness, bound by shame and protected by layers of the false self into the sanctuary with Him. Be assured it will be a moment of great risk. Because to risk bringing the wounded boy into the sanctuary with Jesus is to open ourselves up to the boy's pain, pain we have been running from all our life. I have worked with men and have been there myself when that pain is cracked open. It is a frightening moment. But that is the risk you and I must take if God is to heal the fragments of our life and awaken the primal masculine.

Our First Rite of Initiation

So let's go back to the beginning of the boy's life and God's design for each of us. The womb, warm, soft, moist and safe; the infant and the mother are one! Union in the deepest sense. But this sense of security is a passing moment. As the infant grows his secure world becomes cramped, and if his journey is to continue a radical change must take place.

I wasn't going to veer off to this teaching about birth but I feel I must because the natural world reflects the Divine and holds within it profound spiritual truths. As the contractions begin the water breaks and the only world the infant has ever known is crumbling and must crumble. The contractions increase in intensity, the infant is now being pushed through the dark tunnel of the birth canal. The Mother is screaming. The infant is being squeezed. There is trauma. For a short while, the infant is between worlds. The old has crumbled and the new has not come. Metaphorically, this is the time of growth, inner transformation, facing our issues, uncovering grief and owning our fractured self.

The birthing process has all the ingredients of a rite of initiation. The loss of our security followed by the crumbling of our world, the journey through the dark tunnel and the push to new life. Isn't it ironic that our human pilgrimage begins with a crisis? For if the infant is to grow and become all that God has intended the infant to be, its safe secure world of the womb must crumble. It is the same for you and I. God leads us to green pastures, allows us to drink of the healing waters, experience peace and a union with God, and then, with seemingly no warning our secure world begins to crumble. Soon, God's voice grows faint and our steps fall on shifting sand. We cry out to God who answers in the agony of silence. We grip tighter as circumstances seem to spiral out of control, and soon we find ourselves asking what we have done to deserve this or even question the wisdom of God. And even worse we begin to fight God through blame or anger at those around us or even at God, unwilling to give up our world of security and journey through the dark tunnel of the unknown, unwilling to look within and see how we participated in the crisis, unwilling to learn lessons that God has placed before us.

We must heed the lessons of our first rite of initiation, that even in the womb, crisis precedes a leap in consciousness! We must embrace this reality. Jesus lived this truth! Forty days in the desert-followed by the realization of his full power as the son of God! Gethsemene and the cross-hence the resurrection and the path of salvation opened to all. We are not immune from the way of transformation. We are called to drink the same cup that Jesus drank. If God is going to move us from one state of consciousness to a higher one, that is, to a place of deeper union there will be the crumbling of our world and the knowing we must leave that which has become familiar and journey to a land which we know not! There might be emotional and spiritual trauma, there might be financial stress or marital struggle and the sense of being out of control. This is the Christian story though, given to us by Jesus through his death and resurrection and now, it must become our story.

The Mother's Love

So let's take a look at this new life for the infant. Out of the womb, nursing the breast, skin to skin. Doesn't sound so bad does it! In fact,

43

it sounds like the marriage bed and sexuality, but we will leave that for later. The infant is drawing the very life force from his mother. Deep emotional and physiological needs are being met. Hormones are being released. The infant learns he or she is loved and safe. Please key into those words loved and safe! They are going to show up again and again!

Throughout the child's growing years, the Mother provides nurture, comfort, care, intimacy, with of course, boundaries and strength. The mother is the boy's first love. This mother/son bond will be the one of the most intimate human relationship he will have, certainly the most formative. It will set the stage for his journey into manhood and give him the emotional grounding necessary so that he will reach out into his world of adventure and masculinity.

What is crucial here and what I am hoping to drive home is that it is God's design, that the Mother's love, that is, the feminine energy is meant to soak into every cell of the infant and young boy, giving him that deep assurance that he is loved and safe for who he is!

Exercise: In your quiet moments with God, with pen and paper in hand and when your mind is turned off and your heart is open and your are ready to listen to your core ask God to reveal to you the images of mother within you! And simply write, without judgement! Perhaps stories, images or just feelings and associations! We are just scratching the surface here. All that is asked of you is authenticity.

The Father's Blessing

The infant and the Father, snuggled together, close, intimate, a different type of love, one with strength, compassion, and playfulness. As the boy grows the Father's love, blessing and validation becomes expressed through play, adventure, wrestling, and working together. Masculinity begins to take hold. He finds his strength through his father's approval and the taking of risks. Throughout the years, as they grow together, the boy's deepest desire is to have the father look into his eyes and hear the words given to Jesus by his own Father. "You are my son, in whom I am well pleased." These heart-centered words answers the deep need for validation that is at the core of a young boys being. It is this validation that empowers him into the world of adventure and masculinity. And just a note here, it doesn't have to be those words. But, what is important here is the essence of that authentic approval or blessing that is given in the daily tasks that the father and son share!

Exercise: I ask you to repeat exercise 1 except with the father image. Just write, it seems best, in the morning, when you are alone and your mind is clear of the day's toil.

The Wound

When there is a breach in either of the mother or father's love a void is created within the human psyche. None of us gets the whole package. Some get more than others. But when these needs are not met a void is created. Once the void or wound is set in motion it evolves into a relentless hunger for love, affirmation or validation that is played out in every aspect of our lives and in every relationship we find ourselves in. No matter how religious or spiritual we become, how perfect we strive to be or how much love or sex is poured into us, the hunger never ceases.

We all serve our wound. This is universal, whether it be the mother-wound that manifests itself in our relationship with women, our spouse, pornography or emotional distance or our father-wound expressed through seeking validation, reckless adventure or obsessive need for success. Becoming a Christian does not erase the wound! This is important. It is our relationship with God that gives us the strength and courage to go into the wound. Yes, our sins have been forgiven, but the wound remains. Healing the wound is the sacred pathway to our masculine self.

The wounding is as varied as each of us. The circumstances as unique as our own life-an emotionally distant parent or overworked corporate father who simply doesn't have the emotional reserves to play catch with his two year son for more than a minute or two, or the career-parents who shuttle their children off to daycare. This wounding may be deep and painful, a divorce, a death or the inner knowing you were not wanted by your parents. And of course, there is verbal, physical or sexual abuse which betrays trust and scars the fragile psyche of the growing child. The possibilities are endless. The results are always the same.

Through forestry I have learned that when a tree is injured it responds in two ways. First, the tree compartmentalizes the area around the wound to prevent a systemic infection, and second, the tree calluses the tissue that has been wounded, which essentially kills that part of the tree. Both responses are a survival mechanism that protects the tree from systemic infection.

There is a profound lesson here. Watch a child when they are shamed or belittled. Their eyes dim as they internalize the shame and their heart closes with the pain of rejection. The young child is responding just like a tree does when it is wounded. They are compartmentalizing and callousing the wounded area of their heart and psyche. Why? It is a survival mechanism, graciously given by God, which protects the young child from the intense feelings of shame and rejection, feelings that most adults struggle with.

This compartmentalizing and callousing is not only for the growing child. Each time we shut down after an argument and say to ourselves 'I will never be vulnerable again like that,' we add another layer of callused tissue to the already existing wound. The more layers of psychological scar tissue, the deeper the sword must pierce! Because underneath the psychological scar tissue are raw and painful emotions that go underground, into the unconscious where they work without us even knowing it.

Recently, in our men's group a man who had just been diagnosed with diabetes began to share the trauma of having to poke himself with a needle every day. He also mentioned the grief of the life change and compromised health. He then said, "I cannot change the trauma I feel about the needle but I can change my attitude about the illness and the life change."

After he finished speaking I challenged him with the words that his fear of needles was not a personality trait but most likely hitting on a deeper issue. He gave me a perplexed look then boldly said, "I have no idea how to get there so I will trust you on this one."

In men's work the goal is to give a man his power not do his work for him nor take away his power, which means asking questions as opposed to stating his reality. So I simply asked him, "When did you first experience a fear of needles?"

"What?"

"I asked you, when did the little boy in you first experience the fear of needles?"

He thought for a few minutes. As he did, I saw his hand begin to tremble. I knew he was onto some of those raw and traumatic emotions. He then began to retell the story of the family doctor coming to his house to give shots and the fear he experienced as a boy. He spoke about running to his aunt and parents for comfort but was playfully mocked. As he finished his story I asked him, "Do you want to do some work around this issue?"

"Yes," he replied.

We set up a drama to go into the emotions of the boy. It was powerful, touching the grief and fear of the boy, but still missing the mark.

"It is my judgement there is something missing," I said.

"What?"

"You worked on your fear and emotional pain but what about the anger piece. "

"There is no anger," he said.

"Really!"

"You just told me at the age of five you ran to you parents and aunt for protection but were mocked. And now you are telling me you don't have any anger about this."

"I have forgiven them."

"What about the boy? How does he feel about it all?"

"I'm okay about it, Brian."

"Okay, where is the wild man in all this?" He looked up rather hard at me. "Can I cut a little deeper?" He nodded yes.

We then went through one more process to touch the anger and awaken the primal masculine. As our eyes locked in a hard stare and with us both holding the staff we use in men's work, something inside of him gave him the permission to touch the primal rage of the young boy. Immediately his eyes flashed anger as his body coiled then struck out. In an instant this gentle, soft spoken man became a tornado of rage, ritually striking out against those who had injured him so deeply fifty years ago. For a brief moment I became the object of his rage as he pushed me against the wall with staff at my neck level. With our eyes still locked he slowly began to press the staff into my neck. Immediately, the man to my right yelled, "Safety, Safety!" Slowly his eyes softened as the rage subsided.

"I need to stop," he said. "I never knew this stuff was so deep." He then took several breaths. "I will revisit it when I am ready," he wisely said.

We all carry these raw and traumatic emotions. It is part of the human story. No one is immune. They work underground, poisoning our relationships and tainting our lenses through which we experience life and God. They also give birth to depression, and illness and rob us of our masculine power.

Blame

When these raw and underground emotions get triggered we blame those who have triggered the deep pain as if they are completely responsible for our emotional discomfort. Remember the dream of the little Kathryn and the little Brian. Her conflict style was the piecing sword that began to penetrate the calloused tissue of my heart, therefore exposing the raw and traumatic emotions that were compartmentalized in my growing years.

Each time my wounds got triggered through conflict with Kathryn, I believed it to be Kathryn's issue not mine. This is called blame. It is about not owning my own stuff and operating from the wounded boy. In short, I was saying, "change so I will feel loved and safe!" In my mind she was the source of my pain and if she would have tempered her style of conflict the wounds of the boy would have never surfaced and all would have been well. But if that were the case, I would be still be running around this earth as a charismatic preacher with a gaping wound within me, seeking to fill the void, connecting with women and unwilling to own my humanity, all in the name of God and ministry. And yes, by the grace of God people would have been touched, but I, would have never awakened the primal masculine. That is why the wounding is so crucial.

The False Self

There is one last issue that needs to be addressed, the false self, that part of our personality that arises out the wound and a dysfunctional family system, which includes every family I know. An example of the false self would be a boy who gets harshly disciplined for expressing negative emotions at his parents. Next time negative emotions come up he has a choice, share his feelings and experience the pain of what the child perceives as rejection and possibly emotional trauma or stuff his true feelings and create a false self to receive and maintain his parent's love and approval.

Most often, out of emotional survival, the child will choose his parent's love rather than his authentic self, which he should. He is a child. It is not God's design that a young child has to hide who he is to receive his parent's love. So the false self, that protective layer or mask that hides his true self, is created and given a domain within the child's psyche.

I have worked with many men who struggle to release negative emotions because the family message is so powerfully coded in their psyche they dare not risk triggering the fear or trauma they have buried beneath the false self, even after the family member is deceased. So in the midst of their anguish and pain they hit a wall, a wall that offers them two choices; stuff their emotions again, which feeds the false self, or gather their courage, break through the wall of fear, face their pain and allow God to unravel a layer of the false self. The latter is men's work.

The false self can also be created when the father or mother projects his vision onto their child. They want their son or daughter to be a doctor. Each time the child strives to break forth and live his true expression he is gently guided toward becoming a doctor or possibly shamed by his father or mother for seeking his authentic passion, which is not their passion. A parents' scorn cuts deep, ripping a young heart in two. Soon, the boy chooses his parents' approval over his true self and buries his God-given passion beneath his need for his father or mother's love.

It is a survivor's choice and one that we all make as a young boy. Until one day, crisis comes and the young man or even older man can no longer carry the pain and grief of not living his authentic self and so he gathers his courage and begins to dismantle the layers of the false self and heal the wound.

The macho man is classic expression of the false self. I was on a retreat with a man who seemingly had it all. He was a body builder, blond and seemingly comfortable with himself. Until, that is, we began the deep work of dismantling the false self. Within minutes of the process the macho man crumbled in tears, and there in the ruins of his false self, was a young boy that was riddled with shame aching to undo the message of "I am worthless" by becoming what he thought was a powerful man. Of course, it didn't work. It is impossible to build a man's world on the foundation of a wounded boy.

We all have a false self and we all have protective layers or wear masks that keep us safe or meets our needs. It is not to be judged, disdained or looked down upon. At the time it was necessary, an internal survival mechanism that keeps the child safe. Without it, most of us would have never made it into our adult years. So please, don't disdain or see the false self as weakness, but rather, as we spoke about in the story of Luke 13:10, embrace the false self with compassion, invite that part of you into the sacred spaces with Jesus, knowing it was necessary. And realize also, there is a time, when we as men must begin the joyful and difficult work of bringing the false self into the light and facing the emotions buried beneath the protective layers.

This is a process, a necessary process as we cannot fully serve God and our masculine self if we are unconsciously seeking to fill the void, protect the wound and feed the false self. So we have some work to do. We have to go back so we can understand the void, own the wound, see how it has shaped our lives and bring it into the light. This is crucial! If the kingdom of God is to come through us, if the authentic Jesus is to be revealed within us and in this world, it is necessary we do this work. The evil one would like for us to keep these issues in the dark, in the unconscious where it can grow and gain power. Because each time we suppress our wounds, deny our anger, bury our shame, cloak our fear or hide our inner self, no matter how fractured it may be, we create shadow.

Evil lives and operates through shadow, through our buried anger that can fester into hatred. The Spirit of the Lord is squelched by fear that settles into our psyche through traumatic experiences. Consciously or unconsciously we live into and through our fear, anger or shame, creating walls between us and God and giving the evil one power in our lives. Jesus said on the cross, "Father, forgive them for they know not what they do." We all crucify Christ in some way or another. Jesus rebuked Peter with the words. "Get behind me Satan." Be it known, we all carry shadow and we are all capable of doing the same.

Most of us are not even aware of these underground emotions, the false self, the void nor our attempts to fill the void until God shakes up the boy's world and breaks open the false self. Painful, you bet it is, because the false self has emerged out of the wound and the raw and frightening emotions of anger, fear trauma and grief that now must be faced. So the wounding comes, the loss of a job, a relationship dissolves, addictions take hold, childhood memories surface, our naive or rigid understanding of God and religion crumbles or a combination of any of these events. From the boy's perspective this wounding seems violent. Be it known, it is God's mercy that ordains it and blesses it. For without the wounding we will never make the ascent into manhood. We would never be initiated men in Christ. And so my wounding came, through the life change of leaving the wilderness and through marriage, the last place I wanted it to.

6 SHADOW

In the months preceding marriage and as our relationship intensified, I experienced an intensity of emotions; of course love, and joy but there was also anger. I didn't like this! Anger didn't fit with my idea of what a spiritual person should feel and second, I didn't know what the hell to do with it. In my family system, I had learned to passively skirt this issue. I have a distinct memory of my mother barging into the guys' room and unloading at my older brother and myself for not cleaning our room. Much to my brother's credit, he stood his ground and went face to face with my mother about the demands of his life and that he was intending to clean the room. But I, frightened of any type of emotional conflict, simply said, "Sure Mom, I'll clean it later," with no intent of doing so in the immediate future. After she left the room, I cornered my brother and said, "Why do you need to argue with Mom so much. Just tell her what she wants to hear and forget it."

He looked at me and said, "Because I felt I was right."

Somewhere in my hardwiring I didn't get that or did not want it. My family nickname was Gentle Ben, given to me by my Mother. Be it known, our personalities and our wounds are woven together into a complex fabric that only God can understand. I came into this world sensitive and easily wounded. I own that. It has been my gift as well as my burden and has played out over and over in my life, creating a cycle that feeds the false self and gives power to the wound. My brother, on the other hand, who came in with more warrior energy, created a completely different drama for himself. I dare say we carry the same wound, although our responses have been different. That is why there are no roads through the murky waters of our unconscious. My wilderness will be different from yours. There are spiritual truths that anchor our life and wisdom given to us by those who have tread a similar path. In the end, we must each forge a new path through this foreboding wilderness.

Back to anger though. I really struggled with it. To share it with Kathryn was to risk facing her defense mechanism of an interrogative approach to conflict, which only traumatized the boy within me further. The other option was to bury it and pretend it wasn't there or wish it might dissolve into the universe through silent prayer. Two roads were before me, but there was no real discernment process. Without the primal masculine online I wasn't foolish enough to charge into a battle without a weapon nor a shield, and so I did what I always did, because it was familiar and because it had worked for 32 years of my life, I internalized the anger, prayed it away, forgave and trusted all would be well.

I call this eating pain, which has nothing to do with the primal masculine and the Gospel but has everything to do with serving the wound. To state the obvious, this isn't a sustainable way of being in a relationship. The human psyche has only so much capacity to hold the emotions of anger, bitterness and resentment before it begins to work its way out in passive aggressive ways or as commonly referred to in our men's group as coming out sideways.

In every reactive moment we can almost be certain there is a backlog of emotion behind it. That backlog is referred to as shadow, that which we hide, deny and suppress or that which we are not even aware of. It is potent stuff. Get enough of it and rage, addiction or a breakdown is soon to follow. In men's work, it isn't really the reaction that matters but the wound beneath the reaction, that root of rejection or wounding that needs to be brought to the light. This is called regressing the wound. When I worked with the man who feared needles I helped him regress the wound. When the wound is regressed true healing can take place.

Marriage and the Boy

'The boy never gets married,' are the words spoken by my good friend Steven. Words that came at a price. He had travelled the painful road of divorce. During his first marriage he said his back pack was always packed and ready to go, next to the front door. I asked him, "Metaphorically?"

"No!"

We don't have to have our back pack strategically placed by the front door to leave our marriage. As conflict arises and as we refuse to deal with the pain, the heart hardens. With a hardened and bruised heart we find excuses to stay at work a little longer, enjoy casual friendships with other women, bury ourselves in sports, give ourselves completely to our children or turn to alcohol or other addictions. Yes, the boy never gets married. I also add, that the boy, with all his dreams and idealistic hopes does get married, but when things get tough, he runs and when conflict arises, he blames. When he doesn't feel safe, he sends the message, 'change so I can feel safe.'

Marriage

As our marriage date neared and as conflict came and went, the boy in me began to tremble with fear. He wanted to run because he knew he didn't belong in this world. I used rational thinking, mentally relived our engagement day and assured myself this was God's will, which it was, but the boy within me wouldn't be convinced.

Jesus said, "The two shall become one flesh." Kathryn and I were married five months after our engagement. The wedding was anointed and intimate, only family and a few friends. We spoke our vows, cried tears of love and began our journey. We lived a simple existence at a retreat center in Michigan, close to the earth and sharing community. I pounded nails for work. Kathryn remained at the retreat center. Coming home each day was a great blessing. We embraced, shared a meal, prayed, played music and slept together. The world of sexuality opened. I liked it.

It didn't take long to figure out, that is, once we began sleeping together, sharing meals, a bank account, house cleaning and of course the bathroom, I married my opposite. Most of us do, the reflective marries the outgoing, the dreamer is coupled with the realist, the emotionally strong marries the passive and so forth. This is the wisdom of God who has cleverly placed the keys to our own transformation in the heart and wound of our mate.

This weaving of opposites could not have been more evident in our own journey. Kathryn and I, fire and water, earth and spirit. Even our wounds reflected this polarity. During Kathryn's upbringing there was a separation of her parents at one time, the moving to a new school in the middle school years, the illness of her mother and then the tragic loss of her father in a plane crash. The result, a core issue of stability and a deep need for security. So who does God send her, a pilgrim with 185 dollars to his name and an unquenchable desire for adventure and the wilderness, not to mention a person with little desire for earthly wealth or a career.

Then there's me, an emotional, sensitive person with a hunger for the gentle feminine, and fear of any type of conflict. So who does God send me? "Snake Woman." It's a family joke-the woman who speaks her truth, interrogates during conflict and a realist who presses the facts. Mix it all together and you get a passionate marriage in which their wounds are easily triggered by the one they love. A match made in heaven? For the wild man, yes! For the boy, hell no!

My Mother Wound

Without the mature masculine to navigate conflict I ate pain in my marriage. Within two years and while living in Seattle, a mountain of pain was growing within me. The wound was festering and the unmet need of the boy began to assert itself in my dream life. I started having dreams of befriending women. They weren't intimate dreams but dreams of casual friendships. As they kept coming I knew some need within was crying out to be heard and validated. It was a red flag, a sign of emotional distress, that much I knew. Like my anger though, I just didn't know what to do with it and in typical guy mentality, I thought God and I could handle it.

It was about that time that Kathryn sensed my growing anger and began to distance herself physically, which was a natural response. Until then, sexuality was nice, always welcomed but not an issue. But upon her withdrawal sexuality became an issue, not so much sexuality as of itself, but the trigger for a deeper issue called feminine rejection.

My own mother wound, the hunger for the feminine, has been with me for as long as I can remember. Yes, I had good male buddies growing up, but always there was this current to connect with girls and to be their friend. During my high school years I didn't have enough guts to be their boy friend. That took too much masculinity and self confidence, both of which I lacked. I could be their friend though, the nice guy. That was safe and filled my need to connect with the feminine.

This pattern really began to play out in my mid twenties, set in motion by the painful break up that preceded my conversion in Lubbock. I was young, just out of college and naive. It was her rejection that inflamed the feminine hunger, setting in motion an unconscious mission to connect with women, really connect with them, not sexually but emotionally, that is, married women, single women, it did not matter. The funny thing about it all, as God began to put my life together through such events as a two month solo-cycling trip through Europe, contemplative prayer, wilderness travel and teaching skiing at Steamboat Ski Area, I re-discovered myself, and as I did, women were attracted to me. This was a revelation for me, a new experience. I liked it. The worst of it was, the more spiritual I became the more women were drawn to me.

I am not alone in this drama! There is a boy within all of us, who is either aching to be filled by the feminine, giving away his power to his spouse, rejecting feminine intimacy for fear of triggering the mother wound or unleashing unconscious anger upon women. Any of these dramas is serving or protecting the wound, specifically the mother wound. What needs to be made clear is that in my own drama with Kathryn, the mother wound was in motion long before I met her, although being unschooled in the way of the masculine soul and still not willing to take ownership of my own stuff, I could not accept or own it. My first eight years with God had been story book with adventures and intimacy. My world shifted when I embarked upon the path of marriage. The obvious conclusion was this incredible pain, triggering of the mother wound and the fear of conflict was Kathryn's issue, not mine. Again, this is called blame.

Checking in

So I invite you to take a moment and check in with yourself and see how the mother wound might be playing out in your life. A couple questions here. Have you given your power away to a woman? Or have you taken away her power to feel powerful and in control? Are you asking her to validate you? Do you run from intimacy? Do you fear your wife's scorn? Or are you angry at women for no apparent reason? All of these questions lead back to the boy within. Perhaps it is time to embrace his story.

So let's probe a little deeper. The picture I painted of the mother nursing the infant boy sounds a whole lot like sexual intimacy...skin to skin, kissing the breast, feeling loved and being validated by a woman. Kathryn recently read an article that stated the same hormones are released during nursing as in sexual intimacy. Now if that isn't a curve ball. The bottom line is, sexuality is fire. It's a man's world, not a boy's. When we bring the boy's needs to sexuality we weaken our relationship with God, cut ourselves off from the masculine power, create more pain and eventually find ourselves in addiction.

So the question is, what do we as men bring to sexuality? Our masculine strength or our mother wound? Perhaps a mixture of the two. How do you react when it isn't there? Men, there is a huge amount of work in this issue. Only you and God can know. Or, if you are feeling rather courageous, ask your wife. She probably has a good handle on what energy you are bringing to the marriage bed.

Then there is pornography. I have never been drawn to pornography. For this I am grateful. My understanding is, though, it is a powerful addiction. No judgment here. Only owning who we are: facing it head on. What is the root? What drew you into a woman's body so deeply: adventure, mother hunger, only you can know! I believe when we are ready, God will reveal the core issue.

This is the way of the mother wound, the unmet needs of the boy or the buried anger and rejection that has gone underground and is now working through us, consciously or unconsciously. Whether it be consciously or unconsciously it does not matter. The issue is, it is there. Shadow never magically dissolves. It is either dealt with or pushed deeper through denial. One leads to our masculine soul, the other feeds the wound further.

So here we are, at the cave of our heart. The still small voice beckons us. Do we roll away the stone and dare go in or do we push on with business as usual? Remember, beneath our wounds and shadows, held captive by our shame and insecurities, bound by our fear and self serving pursuits dwell the God-given masculine energies. These primal energies of God are awakened and honed as we allow God to strip away the protective layers we have constructed and lead us into and through our darkest caves and deepest fears. This my brother, takes a wild man.

7 DESCENT

"For our struggle is not against enemies of blood and flesh, but against the rulers, against the authorities, against the cosmic powers of this present darkness, against the spiritual forces of evil in heavenly places." *Ephesians 6:12.*

Since the dream of Jesus inviting me into the dark cave, there had been a growing presence of evil around as well as within. The evil came at many levels, in my thoughts, dreams and even while I was reading scripture, seeking to drive a wedge between God and myself. If I wasn't consciously praying most of the time I was vulnerable to them. Dark thoughts came with an energy also. It was subtle but very real, as if a wave of confusion and darkness washed over me in an instant. With each dark thought, a part of the kingdom of God suffered within me.

Nights became a place of battles and attacks. Many times, while sleeping, I would wake with the knowing an evil presence was camping in the room. My soul would go on alert and I would begin to pray, "Jesus Christ is Lord of my life." In my first eight years with God that simple confession would have sent the evil presence fleeing. But not so now. An outer wall of the sacred sanctuary of my soul had been breached, giving access to demonic power.

At the time I was concerned but not desperate. Jesus was Lord of my life. All would be well; I was certain a break through was just around the corner. But the warfare intensified. Several times I woke in terror as the evil penetrated farther into my psyche. One night, the sensation of being trampled upon by a black horse came over me. I tried to call upon Jesus but the evil had seized my ability to cry out and then the sensation of being pushed into the underworld came over me. With a seemingly paralyzed voice and body I ached to call out to Jesus but was bound by the power of evil. As the sensation of being pushed farther into hell intensified I finally jerked up in bed and audibly screamed.

Kathryn grabbed me, "What's wrong?"

"Oh God!" I whispered.

"Bad dream?"

"Yeah, really bad dream."

Remember the words Jesus spoke to Peter, "Satan has demanded to sift you out like wheat. But I have prayed that your own faith may not fail. Once you have turned back, strengthen your brothers." Luke 22:31 Have no doubt as you and I seek to live fully into God and take hold of our masculine heart, the evil one will seek to sift you and I out like wheat. It will not come with one blow, but over time, little by little, with sharp arrows directed at the buried wound or the unmet need. We want to succeed, get things done and realize our goal. The closer we get, the more we become fixated on achieving our dreams. Everything in our ego says succeed! You deserve this and so we compromise our true quest, which is union with God for the things of God. It is just a little compromise though, nothing to worry about. And then, there is our marriage, perhaps in rough waters, like all marriages are at one time or another. Temptation comes when the woman who works in the same department starts up a benign conversation. We linger a little longer than normal, enjoy it beyond a simple conversation. Remember, Satan will not take you or I out with a single blow, but over time, relentless, tempting us in our deepest need and our most painful wound, hoping to drive a wedge between us and God.

We need to pause and get clear on this issue of wounding versus spiritual attacks through our wounds. God wounds us so that we will bring these issues to the Jesus, heal the broken fragments of our life and enjoy the love and power of a deeper intimacy with God. During our wounding time it is crucial that we remain in the presence of God, trust God and do the work that God intends for us to do. Satan attacks us to destroy that which God has built up. Shadow is one of his great weapons. If we choose to bury our pain, dwell in our wounds, hold onto bitterness or pursue our unmet needs we give power to the enemy.

The Debate

After Kathryn's three year program ended in Seattle the discernment process of where to settle had finally come to a head. The West or Michigan? That was the question. It was one of the great struggles of our marriage. It was a charged issue that neither of us could approach with emptiness. The wilderness is my link to God, the place where energy, vision and power flows into my soul. To think that I would live away from the West, the mountains, the expanse of blue skies and towering peaks was inconceivable. For Kathryn, the West represented another fracturing of her already fractured family from her father's tragic death and mother's illness. Like I said, it was a charged issue.

Mid summer we visited Colorado to facilitate several workshops. There was the hope of settling in Colorado but it was in vain. The conflict was too great. The chasm too wide to bridge. As we left Colorado I raised the white flag and said, "Michigan."

We returned to Michigan to begin the search for a home. While driving from the Michigan Lake shore, I crested a hill then swerved to miss a painted turtle. I quickly pulled over, stopped the car and said, "I need to get that turtle out of the road." Kathryn jumped out also. We ran. Just as we were about five feet from the turtle a large black sedan came speeding over the hill, probably around 65 miles an hour. I grabbed Kathryn. The turtle exploded from the crushing weight of the tires. It was an awful sound. In that instant I could hear the Satan laughing in my spirit. I knew. Kathryn looked at me and said, "Perhaps we should venture back to Colorado."

"I am done running Kathryn. Michigan is it."

Six weeks later we closed on a log cabin on three acres in Michigan.

Now that we were settled I began sharing at new levels. By the grace of God a ministry of renewal and healing was given to me. I led evening programs, speaking from the Gospel stories of Jesus, inviting people to a deeper conversion and praying for those who so desired. Despite my humanity and despite that I was still in the valley of darkness, the Spirit of God moved.

It was good, but, we can't build a man's world on the foundation of a wounded boy. Even if other areas of our life are going well, the wounded boy and all his needs must be addressed. It is a temptation though, when one area of our life is working well to ignore the wounded areas. This is called denial and leads to more shadow and this is exactly what I did.

A wise woman once asked me, "What did you do with your little boy?"

"I pissed on him," I replied, half jokingly yet knowing there was a truth to my words. We both laughed.

"Do you think that is a problem?"

"Perhaps?"

I metaphorically pissed on him because he represented everything I had run from; weakness, vulnerability, shame and neediness. I ran through great deeds. The higher I climbed the better I felt about myself, which seemed a worthy antidote. So with the ministry going well and the joy of preaching burning in my soul I lacked the understanding and the strength to heed the wounded boy who was crying out for the mature masculine to make sense of his psychological mess. I knew there was pain, pain that was triggered by Kathryn's distance and pain that was taking hold at deep levels. It wasn't so much denial but perhaps a lack of tools or lack of emotional intelligence, not that I mean that in a self-condemning way, but the fact was, I believed if I prayed and was faithful to my God that all would be well. But it wasn't and each night as we rolled to opposite sides of the bed, the pain inflamed further, not by much, but like interest on a loan, the burden grew.

Kathryn, who could be a therapist, tuned into my growing anger and discontentment with our marriage. Several times, as we sat up in bed working things out, she would say, "Just go ahead and get angry. Get it out on the table. At least I can deal with that." Remember Gentle Ben, the guy who skirted anger since childhood. I couldn't do it. I couldn't break the wall down for fear of the backlash. It wasn't just Kathryn's backlash that I feared, it was the generations of the maternal and paternal wound working within me, that getting angry means rejection and more trauma. It was a wall of blackness that I simply couldn't penetrate and so I cowardly said something like, "Perhaps I am a little angry," with a smile of course, even though every part of me wanted to scream out "I am so angry at you! I feel criticized! Emotionally unsafe and rejected!"

"So then, putting away falsehood, let us speak the truth to our neighbor, for we are members of one another. Be angry but do not sin; do not let the sun go down on your anger, and do not make room for the devil." Ephesians 4:25-27 Well, I missed that scripture. Most of us have. Authenticity is the mark of a man.

Time passed, months then years. It was business as usual, ministry, growing shadow, spiritual warfare and a hell of a lot of pain. The psyche can only hold so much. I still remember the morning I woke with the knowing something had fractured in my psyche. The pain of all those years had finally taken its toll upon my inner self and now it had finally broken under the weight of eight years of spiritual and emotional stress, creating a further breach of my inner sanctuary. I knew it wasn't good. I remember thinking that morning, *okay God, someday and somehow we are going to have to repair this tear.*

The Grand Canyon

"It is time for you to return to the Grand Canyon. You have unfinished business down there," came the whisper of God while walking the woods. There was a tremor of trepidation, a knowing the Canyon would be an intense time. There was also the thrill of adventure, conquest and the wilderness. I couldn't wait to go, certain this dark night was about to come to head. I was ready to take back all that was lost to darkness, kick Satan's butt out of my sanctuary forever.

Just before leaving I caught a chest cold. It wasn't bad, just enough to weaken my body. I wasn't concerned though. I had soul work to do in the Canyon that demanded being sedentary and prayerful. Several days later and after a red-eye flight that weakened my body further, I signed for my back country permit and walked toward the trailhead that would lead me into the Canyon.

The air was January crisp. Snow crunched beneath the weight of my footsteps as I walked through the Ponderosa Pines of the South rim. The wilderness was welcoming, a sweet reunion as I felt her embrace deep in my soul. I arrived at my trailhead. For several minutes I remained at the rim, searching the expanse of the Canyon, savoring the untamed landscape while trying to grasp the meaning of standing on the cusp of two worlds. They had not reconciled within me. Behind me hummed an occasional passing vehicle. I was eager to distance myself from that world and the business it represented so that I might finish the work that God had prepared for me. I looked out over the Canyon; my soul took flight like an eagle catching thermals from the inner canyon. I then fastened simple cleats to the soles of my boots and began my descent.

The trail switch backed amid stunted pines and junipers then traversed along the Canyon wall until more switch backs. As I worked my way lower into the Canyon and deeper into desert ecology the snow packed trail became earth. My pace remained slow and deliberate. Hours later I crossed the Tonto Plateau then began my final descent into the inner canyon where I would cross the Colorado River and make camp at a back country site on the North side of the canyon. It was a simple trip, just down, remain at a campsite for nearly six days then back up. With my cold sinking deeper into my chest, it was as much as I wanted. By evening, I had crossed the Colorado, passed Phantom Ranch, then skirted up an adjacent canyon to a deserted campground.

The morning came, crisp, cold and clear. My devotions were said in the comfort of my down bag. Sunlight kissed the canyon rims then slowly descended toward the inner canyon. With my body weakening further from the cold I remained there for quite a while, enjoying the sensation of laying upon mother earth while immersed in my prayers.

By mid-morning I crawled from my down cocoon, wrapped myself in my sleeping bag then savored my breakfast of dried fruits, nuts and seeds. Shortly afterwards, I worked my way over gentle terrain toward the warming sun then nestled into an outcropping of rocks. The view of the South rim was splendid. The sun was warm. Below me the song of water falling over rocks as it made its way to the Colorado River gave texture to the desert quiet.

I have always loved the red rock country. There is a sacred quiet among the red rocks that takes me inward, to a place where the silence of God speaks to my soul about inner simplicity and the presence of God in all creation. So often, as I walk and pray in such landscapes, my soul seems to travel beyond the confines of my conscious mind. I am aware of the timelessness of God, that countless generations have walked the land before me and many will come after me. I am aware that in some way beyond what I can understand we are all connected through the Spirit of God, the past, the present and the future. In humility, I know I am but a drop of water in a seemingly infinite ocean, and yet, I am loved as a son, cared for, that even the hairs of my head are numbered. Who can grasp such wisdom and expanse? Certainly, not I. I can only drink, choose gratitude and live surrender. I pray it is enough.

As I remained snuggled in my rock outcropping, absorbing the winter sun and close to the earth, I imagined a song of praise coming from the earth, the rocks and the heavens above, crying out, 'Holy is the Lord of Hosts,' and so I joined in with them, my feeble little voice in the vastness of a universe that is beyond what I can ever understand. I was at peace.

The days moved slowly. The toil of prayer took hold. Time is a crucible in the wilderness, a grinding of the psyche that brings psychological dross to the surface. That is why I come, though, to strip myself of the of daily tasks that occupy the mind to devote myself to God and the multi-layered issues of surrender, healing and trust. Four days passed. There were healing moments with God but no breakthrough or unfinished business.

On the morning of the fifth day, while laying in my sleeping bag, the word of God came into my heart like an arrow, "In order for you to go any further in me, you must give up everything you have gained in me!" Yes, the Word of God came, not with comfort nor words of 'well done' but as a sword, piercing the very core of my existence. I had come expecting a breakthrough not to be sent farther into hell. I remained psychologically paralyzed as this *Word* kept stabbing the very essence of self. I contemplated the words, 'Give up everything.' I foolishly tried to imagine my future. There was only blackness. What will become of me? Where will I go? What will I do? Flip burgers! My walk with God had been my life for the last fifteen or sixteen years. I had no other resume nor skill to fall back upon. There was only God and the hope of sharing God to support Kathryn and myself.

I breathed deeply, trying to hold onto my sanity. My growing anger at God, like a dragon within me, wanted to unleash itself and lash out at God in fury. Time passed slowly. The word 'everything' kept churning in my mind. A sense of utter blackness enveloped me. The abyss was opening. Satan was pulling. I was slipping. "Stop thinking!" I told myself. "Pray!"

"Lord Jesus Christ have mercy on me!" I muttered, not once, but over and over. I can't remember how long I remained in this frozen-like existence, perhaps an hour maybe two. But as time wore on, the immediate crisis began passing. Strength was coming back to my soul. I peered into the darkness of what my life might look like and thought to myself, *I will be a nothing. My life will be misery. I don't know the way. I am lost. I don't know the way. But if that is what God is asking of me, then I must go.*

In that moment, like a shaft of light that pierced the darkness, John 14:6 shot through my spirit. Jesus said, "I am the Way, the Truth, and the Life." I began to pray it out loud while imaging Jesus and myself walking into the darkness of my future. "I am not lost," I said to myself, "I am not lost. I know where I am going. I know where I am going. Jesus is the Way, the Truth and the Life. That is the way I am going."

It was the critical moment in my quest. The unfinished business God has spoken of. By the grace of God I was given what I needed and now it was mine. An incredible peace filled my heart as I lived into that scripture. I could feel Satan's grip loosening upon my soul.

On the morning of the sixth day, under winter blue skies, I started my hike out of the Canyon, uncertain whether I possessed the strength to make the 5000 vertical foot ascent. My lungs, now gripped with viral infection, seemed to be succumbing to pneumonia. I stopped at the Phantom Ranch and bargained for a bulb of raw garlic. Garlic is an incredible antibiotic as well an energy booster. Egyptian warriors ate raw garlic before battle. I ate a couple pungent cloves then started my ascent. There was a peace in my soul though. Prayers came easily. I crossed the bridge that spans the Colorado River then edged along the side of the inner canyon, ascending slowing. About an hour into my ascent and while looking over the bottom of the canyon I heard Satan's voice inside my head, "I will be waiting for you back home."

By nightfall I stumbled into the halfway camp, eating more garlic and barely functioning. Fearing night chills I cinched my down sleeping bag then draped my broken tent over my sleeping bag. The stars came to life. Sometime later, moon rise came. Frost fell hard.

The next morning I laid in my bag for a long time, foolishly hoping the sun would find its way into my little crevice of the Canyon. It was all in vain, unless I wanted to stay snuggled in my bag until midday. Anticipating a warm dinner at the lodge I unzipped my bag. The warmth vanished, replaced by the biting cold of a January morning.

I started the second half of the climb. Slow and methodical, saying my Jesus prayer. I never stopped. Several hikers on their way down inquired of my well being. I nodded all was well and continued on my way. I fooled them but not myself. Pneumonia, fever and dizziness was setting in. "Just get to the rim," I told myself. By mid afternoon I collapsed in the front seat of my rental car and nearly passed out.

Battles of the Spirit

When Jesus was tempted by Satan in the desert his defense was clean, crisp and rooted in scripture. There wasn't a dramatic discourse about the love of God or his recent baptism. He was grounded in God that gave focus and power against the arrows of the evil one.

This is the great challenge, to stay centered in Christ so I can deflect the arrows of the evil one with the power of God. The minute I overreact, strike out with too much aggression, engage in the mind games of spiritual warfare, give room for fear and anxiety or bury toxic emotions, my balance in God becomes weakened. Perhaps not much, but enough. Remember, Satan will not take us out with a single blow, but over time with each little compromise or poor choice that weakens our position in God.

In the wake of my Grand Canyon experience, I committed myself to staying grounded in God, rooted in scripture as well as praying in the woods of Michigan. But over time, the way of the world, the fear of feeling estranged from God and the stress of daily living and marital pain eroded my sense of being connected to God and the wild.

This battle seemed to play out in my mind, which is one of the great battle fields of spiritual warfare. Thoughts have energy. In a split second they can bestow a blessing or wield a curse, either of which leaves a residue upon our soul, a residue of good or evil. In Phillipians 4:4 to 4-8 Paul exhorts the church to rejoice in the Lord and in verse 8 he writes the popular words, "Finally, beloved, whatever is true, whatever is honorable, whatever is just, whatever is pure, whatever is pleasing, whatever is commendable, if there is any excellence and if there is anything worthy of praise, think about these things."

Paul was asking the faithful to guard their minds. This is warrior energy, to discipline the mind, especially in the critical moment of an argument or some other crisis. In most relational conflicts there is a fraction of a second in which we choose God or descend farther into the wound. It is a fleeting moment, barely noticeable, but carries profound ramifications in the spiritual and emotional realm. The inner warrior is awakened to this moment. He has trained himself to choose God in the critical moment rather than shrink into his wounds and the false self.

There is an old proverb out of the Asian culture that goes like this, "It is better to light a candle than curse the darkness," which is another expression of Paul's truth. I tried to live this wisdom but as I moved from one unbalanced state to another and as the peace and strength I had realized in the Canyon slipped from my soul, I found myself in hand-to-hand combat with Satan, seeking to make secure the many breaches in my psyche where streams of darkness were penetrating. Even prayers became a place of warfare. I found myself interjecting the words 'I reject you Satan,' in the middle of my prayers to block his power moving through my psyche.

In the months that followed I experienced my body tensing while drawing closer to God. It was subtle but real. I knew the meaning of it, the adversary had gained a little more ground within me, and now, some part of me was in need of spiritual healing. It was another grief and another blow to my already breached inner sanctuary. Depression crept in. I began to lose faith that I could sustain my passionate relationship with God in this world and in marriage. Anger and blame took hold. Yes, my anger at God grew. I was angry that God had seemingly placed me into a lifestyle that offered no way to Him. No matter how much I cried out or said my Jesus prayer I kept losing ground spiritually and emotionally. I began to blame my marriage with Kathryn and question the wisdom of God in this matter. Some call it rebellion.

Sand Lakes Quiet Area

Finally, seven months after my Grand Canyon trip, I approached Kathryn in desperation, "I am spiritually and emotionally drowning. I need to go into the wilderness for an extended period."

"How long are you thinking?" she replied.

"One month."

"One month! Are you kidding?"

"No! For me to do the spiritual and emotional work I need a chunk of time. Otherwise I cannot go forward in my life with God."

"Where are you thinking?"

"Close to home in the Sand Lakes Wilderness Area. I can camp at a nearby lake. You can live with me, sleep with me and stay with me when you are not working. I need to go though!"

The Sand Lakes Wilderness Area is only ten minutes from our home. The walk into the lake was another ten minutes. Kathryn could come and go as she pleased, but I would remain, sleeping close to the earth, immersed in prayer and seeking God the only way I knew how. It took all of two days to move and set up the furnishings to support myself, Kathryn and our five month old golden retriever for the month. By the end of the second day my month long-quest had begun, praying the Jesus prayer as I walked around the seven mile loop once or twice a day. It was medicine for my soul.

A week into my wilderness retreat Kathryn came in with tears streaming down her cheeks.

"What's wrong?" I said.

"I am pregnant!"

"That is great news!" We both cried with joy.

"I need you at home," she said.

"What?"

"I need you at home!" she said again.

"I can't leave now," I said.

"I need you," she pleaded.

We dialogued for nearly an hour. I stayed in the wilderness.

Getting Clean with God

With three weeks left of my retreat my work in the wilderness intensified. I said, "Okay God let's have a direct and clear every issue that stands between us. I am ready." I started this work with my marriage, owning the fact that I fell in love with a married woman, praying "Lord, it was you who brought us together; but still, I am responsible for my thoughts and actions." I knew what the scripture says: this is adultery. I owned this before the Lord. For the longest time I just held up this issue before God, asking God that we might clear any debris between us. It was then God brought me back to a dream I had three years before meeting Kathryn. At the time I was in Bethel, Alaska as a volunteer in the Yupik Eskimo Culture. I dreamed of a young man who was incredibly angry at me, yelling and screaming and full of rage. In the dream I remember thinking, *what have I ever done to make someone so angry at me?* As the dream was about to end, he looked at me hard and said his name with the words, 'remember me.' Yes, his name was Ted, Kathryn's first husband. The next morning I wrote him a letter, sharing my grief, taking responsibility and asking for his forgiveness.

For three weeks, I went through my soul as if with a fine toothed comb, down to the smallest of details. There was living in Michigan, leaving the wilderness, rebellion about marriage as well as anger at God. As I brought each issue into the light there was a cleansing of my soul.

Several days later, deep in the night when sleep and the conscious mind become indistinguishable, the spiritual realm came upon me in a surge of demonic anger and hatred that sought to unleash itself at God. The battle raged as cosmic forces seem to collide within me. I tried to call upon the name of Jesus but was somehow spiritually restrained. Another surge of evil came over me as it pulled upon me to lash out and even curse God. By a knife's edge I resisted. The battle continued. A sense of real fear of falling into darkness came over me. In my spirit I screamed, "NO!" then cried out, "Jesus." The darkness broke. There was peace. A day later I left the Sand Lakes Quiet Area a renewed man, walking home to a beautiful woman who was now one month pregnant with our first daughter.

In the months and even years that followed the Sand Lakes Quiet Area I experienced a deeper peace and renewed power in my prayer life. I had faced my demons and brought my issues to the light of God and now there was peace. Yes, I had been to the dark cave that Jesus had invited me into eight years ago. I had given away all that I had gained in God. Even the ministry had taken on new life. Months later I met with a publisher who was interested in a project entitled,

71

The Joyful Monk-practicing the presence of God in a busy world.
The Spirit of God was moving.

As I began to pen the words that came with difficulty and as my retreat schedule dwindled I began to hear the faintest of whispers, "Your most difficult hour is before you." It was so faint and so unbelievable that I shook it off as the work of the enemy, believing he was seeking to instill fear into my fragile soul. But in the months that followed, the words to *'The Joyful Monk'* never came. No matter how much I sat before the computer and wrote, the words were lifeless, leaving no doubt, the book was my idea, not God's.

Time passed slowly as I waited upon the Spirit of God to move. There was no movement. A tremor of fear entered my soul as the words that I received in the Grand Canyon recycled within me. "In order for you to go any further in me you must give away everything you have gained in me." I thought I had lived those words, gone through the dark night and was now ascending. But they came back, with a haunting strength, giving more voice to that faintest of whispers that now echoed louder in the empty halls of my soul, "Your most difficult hour is before you." My retreats dwindled and then died, leaving my life blank, void of vision and purpose, triggering that deep message of the father wound, "You are nothing without accomplishments." I never knew how powerful that message was until I had nothing, until all my passionate pursuits of sharing God through music, words and ministry were laying in a heap of ashes. The father wound had been unleashed.

It was then a vivid dream of my dad, older brother, and I came. In the dream my older brother and I were sitting across from my father at a small table. We were taking a test. Upon completion, we handed it to our father who graded it then gave it back. With great exuberance and remarks of praise he returned the test to my older brother who has followed my father in a successful career in science. He then grievously looked at me and apologized with the words, "I'm sorry but I had to give you an F# minus."

The dream reflected my devastated life and the unconscious reality that churned in the dark recesses of my psyche. I was a nothing. I had failed myself and in doing so I had forfeited the father's blessing that was rightfully mine.

This decimation of my pursuits was the wounding, the scraping away of the psychological scar tissue that encased my masculine shame. As I look back the father-wound had been working under the surface long before my crisis. I carried my need for validation into my relationship with God and the wilderness treks. Not that I wasn't called into the wilderness, but mixed in with my authentic call was the motivation that I was going to prove to the world and myself that I was indeed special because deep down there was this shame, the underlying message that I was not worthy and so I was hell-bent on gaining God's blessing, seeking others approval and destroying that message of shame within me.

Years ago, that was one of the driving forces of my journey into the Alaskan Wilderness. In late August, just as my commitment ended as a volunteer, I made preparations to venture into the Alaskan Wilderness. The Denali Park Bus dropped me off after a ninety mile trip to Wonder Lake. It was a frightening moment, standing alone in the vastness of the tundra with a month of wilderness travel before me. A strange numbness came over me as the bus rolled away, wondering if I had just sentenced myself to death. With a slight mist falling I began a course west toward mystic pass, traversing the tundra with a pack that weighed over ninety pounds.

After ten grueling days in the back country that should have cost me my life I set down my pack to make camp for the night. As I collapsed on my pack in exhaustion the gentle whisper of God spoke into my heart, "Whose baptism are you seeking, mine or yours?" The question pierced soul and spirit, revealing my deep need for validation that I had brought into the wilderness. I had set before me an undoable trek, believing that if I had accomplished this feat, I would have gained that inner validation from God, myself and from this world that I so lacked. Yes, I would have deemed myself worthy, worthy of God, worthy in the eyes of my family, worthy in the eyes of this world to be a man of God. I remained there for three days, regaining my strength before retracing my steps back to Wonder Lake.

The Father Wound

The father bestows validation, that inner knowing that the boy and young adult has what it takes. Without that truth anchored within, there is the void, the unconscious aching for validation that will play out in our lives in almost every circumstance. We will go to great lengths to search for that blessing, perhaps in the work place, giving away our power for our supervisors approval. Classic men! We have all done it, seeking that surge of emotional validation of a job well done. When it doesn't come our inner world crumbles, leaving no doubt we are seeking to fill the void as opposed to working for own sense of integrity. Giving away our power to our priest or pastor is another attempt to fill the void. Men, we are not designed to give our power away to anyone. Respect yes, power no, not even to our pastor. If we are giving away our power and he or she is taking our power, we both have soul work to do. Another classic example of the father wound set in motion is the man who pushes his son or daughter to excel in sports or other activities. Usually at the core of this behavior is the man's own lack of inner validation that he projects onto his children, basically he is saying, "Be the best so I can feel special!"

I have seen the father wound wreak havoc on men in many ways, shutting down to emotions, passive silence, cutting themselves off from their dreams, reckless adventure, and the relentless need for success. In more subtle ways, needing to be the center of a conversation, to be the expert or conform others to our way of thinking. Brothers, a man speaks his truth out of integrity to God and himself, not to conform others to his way of thinking. To seek to conform others to our way of thinking comes from a deep insecurity and is seeking to meet our own needs. It is serving the wound, which does not bear fruit in God's kingdom.

To be honest men, I have seen myself in most of those scenarios. Just recently at a family gathering that celebrated my fiftieth, my older brother and I entered into an idealistic tug of war. It wasn't about ideals though, at least for me. It was about validation, a struggle for power and identity in the family system. It began as a harmless dialogue between my brother, myself and my Dad. Nothing like family to bring out our deepest issues. Remember the dream about the test, my brother, myself and my Dad sitting around at table; and of course, receiving a F# minus and the pain of my father's disapproval in the dream? Here we were, sitting around the table, a golden opportunity to unconsciously claim my space in this triangular power struggle. This is a perfect example of the unconscious at work. So often, we are not even aware of what is going is on. At some point in the discussion my older brother threw out a comment that went into my wound, into my need for validation. So instead of holding my ground and staying centered, I pulled out my sword and went to work, seeking to dismantle my brother's wisdom and emerge as learned and wise man. It got ugly, an oh God I have done it again, moment for me. I should have known better. As Paul said, "I do the very things I hate!" Romans 7:15

The next morning, I felt drained of the primal masculine. I had brought my need for validation to my brother. The wounding of God had followed, leaving me powerless and feeling like a fool. Perhaps you have been there. This wounding is a gift, a window into our wounds, revealing the unmet needs of the boy that robs us of our masculine power. We need to listen to God through this wounding. During my walk that morning I owned my stuff and said, "Okay God, I did it again." The core issue is the need for inner validation, a validation that never happened, a validation that only God can now fill.

Wrestling with God

"In order for you to go any further in me, you must give up everything you have gained in me!" Those fearful words had now become reality. My pursuits of ministry had crumbled. My many excursions into the wilderness to reclaim God had now faded into despair. My openings with two publishers had dissolved. I cried out, "I need something God!" but nothing came. I had successfully exhausted every dream and vision, pursued them with a passion until they withered like dust before me.

In desperation I returned to Sand Lakes Quiet Area. In daylight I stripped down, naked before God and the world. I then stepped into ankle deep water and covered myself with clay. I looked into the heavens, held my hands up and said, "Here I am God, your servant whom you called. You have buffeted my road. You have torn me down countless times. I am tired of wrestling with you. I will not fight you any longer and so I say, tear down what must be torn down. Only spare my soul!"

I meant every word of it, if God wanted to tear me down to nothing I was ready. I wanted to get to the core issues, to be done with this insanity and go forward. I returned home, cut my hair short in grief, mourning the loss of everything that I had worked for and said, "Okay God, let's get after it!" Several days later, after my walk in the wilderness, Kathryn silently handed me a note. It read:

"Dear Brian, God gave me a word during prayer this morning. 'I do not take away your visions to decimate your vision. I take them away to purify your love. I want love for me to consume you as my love for you is all-consuming. No longer shall you hold to the vision to give your life meaning and purpose. I am your meaning and your purpose. Being in love with me-receiving and giving this love and fire between us must be your focus. Many things will come to you and through you but they are only a passing shadow of this love we share. Each day.....LOVE.....the focus of your thoughts, your will, and your thoughts. I love you."

The Abyss

This growing sense of doom in my soul became a reality. How can I explain it, except that some invisible door to the abyss opened and I fell in. It was if all of hell seemed to come upon me, taking me farther into the realm of darkness and evil. Dreams became so evil I could barely stand going to sleep. Often in my dream life darkness took the form of snakes, suffocating my soul with dark power. I fought back but it was in vain. In my prayer life evil came speaking blasphemous words into my spirit, words that I would never write. I cried out, tried to stand against it in the name of Jesus but my confession wrought no power against the darkness.

It seemed impossible, almost a betrayal of my spirit, that after surrendering all, I would be taken farther in the realm of darkness. I prayed incessantly but there was no answer. The abyss had opened. Like being caught in a vortex of evil, my soul was being sucked farther into the underworld. Despite my prayers and my choice to forgive myself and Kathryn anger had become hatred, real hatred, the kind that wanted to lash out at God, myself or Kathryn, I was going down and knew it.

Thoughts became twisted. I found myself be coming attracted to evil things. Even my eyes, always gentle and welcoming, had grown hard. Looking into the mirror was like looking into another person's eyes, eyes that now had a streak of evil in them. For those who have seen *Lord of the Rings* I began to look like Frodo as he neared Mordor, screaming in terror, knowing the dark lord was gaining power over him. It was not much different for me. My attraction to other women was growing. I prayed intensely, fasted then prayed some more. My efforts were in vain. The battle was waging. The war was in full swing. Without any defenses though, it wasn't so much of a war. It was more like a slaughter. I kept thinking, *okay God, this is as far down as I want to go. Let's pull out. I've seen enough.*

Then the worst of thoughts came to me, that by a razors edge, I could become a Judas, a betrayer of Jesus Christ or a King Saul, once the anointed of God, who turned bitter with rage, hatred and fear. This scared me! I mean really scared me. I cried out, "NO! I don't want that road. I will not go down that path. I would rather die now!"

Everyday was a struggle, every day I kept believing the power of God would prevail but everyday took me farther down. Then, in the quiet of my home while reading the Bible, I started to cry while saying, "I am so broken God. I am so broken." Then came God's response, "Are you ready to break?"

"Yes, Lord."

The next morning while bent over praying and moaning Kathryn walked up the stairs. Her presence caught me off guard. A bolt of terror went through my being. Until this moment I had kept my spiritual struggle in the secret of my soul just as I had kept my toxic anger and hatred of God, myself, and Kathryn concealed behind the easy-going guy I projected and had always been. I had also kept my growing attraction to other women well cloaked. She looked at me and asked, "Are you okay?"

The words, "Are you ready to break," flashed through my mind. This was it, I knew.

"No, I am not okay," I replied to Kathryn. In tears of remorse, fear, guilt and shame I revealed all to Kathryn.

8 LAZARUS

"LAZARUS COME FORTH!" Proclaimed by Jesus at the entrance of the tomb, when all hope had been destroyed and when death seemed final. This is the Christian story, the hope of the resurrection that you and I must carry, that in God nothing is lost, not our love for God, not our dreams, nor our hope. This was the hope that barely flickered within me, that even in this utter blackness I would see the new dawn.

Martha & Mary

Before we get into healing the wound, breaking addiction, piercing the darkness and reclaiming that which is lost to chaos and darkness let's go into the story of raising Lazarus and lay down the ground-work of awakening the primal energies of God, that is, the warrior and the lover, expressed through Martha and Mary. To get a glimpse into these two seemingly opposing energies let's go back and recount what Jesus said to Martha, the sister of Mary, in the Gospel of Luke 10:42. Remember the scene, Martha is busy with the details of serving the meal and is frustrated that her sister, who appears like a lazy dreamer, is just sitting at the feet of Jesus listening to his words.

In disgust, Martha approaches Jesus and asks him to state the obvious, that Mary is not pulling her weight. In one quick sentence Jesus turns Martha's world upside down with the words, "Mary has chosen the better part which will not be taken away from her."

Now what Jesus is calling forth in Martha, who is about action, mission, speaking her truth and fairness, which is warrior energy, is devotion to God, inner simplicity and receptivity, which is the way of the lover. This is the better part, the one thing in which all other truths stand upon.

We see truth, not once but several times in scripture. "Mary has chosen the better part," and "This is my son the Beloved in whom I am well pleased," and "Seek the kingdom of God first," all speak of intimacy with God. Again, this is the core of the journey I speak of, and yet, as we shall soon see in the raising of Lazarus, the way of the warrior is called forth when the lover stumbles in grief.

The drama of raising Lazarus opens up to us as word comes to Jesus that Lazarus is ill. Of course, Jesus, who is operating on a higher plane of consciousness, replies, "This illness does not lead to death; rather it is for God's glory so that the Son of God may be glorified through it. Accordingly, though Jesus loved Martha and her sister and Lazarus, and after having heard that Jesus was ill, he stayed two days longer in the place where he was."

Please note, Jesus loved Martha, Mary and Lazarus. They are good friends. They have gathered at least once, probably more, and so, when Lazarus falls ill they call upon the Messiah, their good friend, to come and do what he has done for the multitudes. But what does Jesus do? He prolongs his stay so that Lazarus dies.

In my own journey, when my prayers are seemingly unanswered, I most often hear, you are not ready, there is more work be done. This isn't a judgment of self but a knowing that there is a wisdom working that I cannot see; and in the world of inner healing, I have learned that Jesus does not take shortcuts. There are also lessons to be learned, masculine energies to be awakened, pain to be brought to the surface and forgiveness to be realized before I am ready to receive what God has for me. This is a place of trust, a place of perseverance, a place of the warrior as well as a place of taking responsibility for anything in my life that might be hindering the power of God.

As we pick up the story, Lazarus dies. He has been in the tomb for four days. There is grief. Jesus is now approaching. Verse 20 reads: "When Martha heard that Jesus was coming, she went and met him, while Mary stayed at home."

Let's begin with, "While Mary stayed at home!" Can you imagine staying at home while Jesus is approaching? The Jesus she loves. The Jesus who has done incredible miracles. Think about it. Mary is so absorbed in her grief she doesn't even possess the inner strength to rise up and meet her Lord. That is heart pain. I mean deep grief, the kind that takes a person's heart right out. I do not want to sell her short but something is missing within Mary. Call it tenacity, inner strength or warrior energy, it doesn't matter. The truth is, it just isn't there. How many of us can relate? I don't want to minimize grief because it is real and the journey out of grief can be long. But what I do want to call forth is that perhaps some of us, like Mary, who live from our heart are nursing our *ego* wounds a little too much, playing the drama over in our minds and refusing to get out of our grief when Jesus comes knocking on the doors of our heart.

Now Martha, who has experienced the same tragedy as Mary, responds in an entirely different manner. Upon hearing that Jesus is approaching she runs out to meet him. She is a warrior and a snake woman, speaking her truth and even pressing in on Jesus with the words, "But even now, I know that God will give you whatever you ask of him." That is bold. She is pushing him and putting her faith on the line.

Jesus responds, "Your brother will rise again."

Martha replies, "I know that he will rise again in the resurrection on the last day."

Jesus says to her, "I am the resurrection and the life. Those who believe in me, even though they die, will live, and every one who lives and believes in me will never die. Do you believe this?"

To catch the full implications of this last verse we need to tune into the last line. It is a question, not a statement. Jesus has now turned the tables as he calls forth her faith and her power. Now that is really bold! I don't know if Jesus needed it or simply wanted it from Martha. I tend to believe, though, that at that moment he drew strength from Martha's faith. That is a frightening reality and we see it more than once through the Gospel stories. After several healing accounts Jesus says, *"Your faith has made you well."* That demands a serious look at my faith and trust. Am I wallowing in my grief like Mary or am I rising out of my wounds and pressing into Jesus? What if Martha would have crumbled and mumbled some words like, "Gee, Jesus I, I, um, well I sure hope so." Sounds weak doesn't it, lacking of any resemblance of warrior energy. But there is nothing like that in Martha. She is operating from the primal energy of the warrior.

Soul Mission

Now the last piece of this story is when Jesus is led to the tomb, John 11; 38. "Then Jesus, again, greatly disturbed, came to the tomb. It was a cave, and a stone was lying against it." Jesus said, "Take away the stone." Martha, the sister of the dead man said, "Lord, already there is a stench because he has been dead four days."

"Take away the stone," is a powerful image spoken by a powerful person. It is metaphorically another critical moment in the journey of transformation, a moment we dread and yet the moment our deepest self desires. What if Jesus asked each of us to roll away the stone of our hearts? Would we shrink as Martha did, saying, "Lord there is a stench in there, my dreams have been laying dead for years? Let's just let them rest in peace. I am getting along okay." But Jesus is not about letting that which God planted lay in the buried tombs of our hearts. He is the Resurrection and the Life! So he says, "Take away the stone!"

This is about our soul mission, who we are and the work we have been commissioned to do. Upon our birth, infused into the depths of our psyche is our soul's mission. This mission, calling or work is linked to our personality and the unique gifts that God bestows upon each of us. So I ask you, are you living your soul mission? Or, is it laying dead in your heart?

A good friend said to me, just as many men have, "I am on this earth for a purpose. I just don't know what it is!" That is a real grief and a poverty of soul. There is a Lazarus in my friend's psyche, something dead and decaying. It is his soul work, the very mission God infused into his psyche upon the embarking of his human journey. My friend is a good guy, church going, reverent and full of good deeds. Looks good on paper but something is missing.

In the early years of marriage, the aching to journey into the wilderness was overwhelming. I would hear of friends or my sister speak about climbing peaks in Alaska or back country skiing in Colorado and my heart would nearly burst with anguish. Everything within me wanted to go! The wilderness was calling. Most of the time, I turned the other way. Why? Remember Kathryn's wound and fear of abandonment, a fear that I fed with my anger and emotional distance. To go into the wilderness for a week was to unleash her fears. For the boy, it was easier to squelch my true self to keep a false sense of peace in the house.

Denying our true self is a slow, agonizing and painful death of the inner man. We slowly forget who we are in Christ and the joy of living into our masculine heart. Passion then fades from our heart and our eyes dim with depression. Eventually our soul mission will fade from our inner vision. This is just what the enemy wants. He knows a man void of passion, heart and mission is no threat to his domain. He knows his family will suffer, that his kids will inherit the lie that life isn't really worth fighting for and that religion has nothing to do with a God of passion, vision, adventure and quests.

That is not the life God desires for any man to live. We are called into a life of intimacy, passion, and desire. And so, we as men must *remember,* that is the key to rolling away the stone and raising our Lazarus. We must remember whose son we are, that perhaps the core message given to us by our earthly father is not the core message our true Father wants us to claim and live into. We must believe, even if we have spent most of our life living through the false self, that the God who raised Jesus and Lazarus can raise us as well. This is a guts moment. It isn't going to be easy either.

So how do we remember? It is beyond just a thought process, beyond just a visit to church, beyond doing the right thing and even beyond pursuing our passion. It is a soul thing, a deep and embodied knowing that the love and power that created the universe dwells inside of you and me. If you have no experience of God you might think back to your religious upbringing or to acquaintances that seek to conform you to their style of Christianity, both would be doing God an injustice. God is wild, foreboding, powerful as well as mercy, love and compassion. The prophet Isaiah trembled when he was taken in spirit before the Lord. Elijah, a true wild man of God, covered his face at the cave on Mount Horeb as the Lord passed by. Moses took off his sandals. This is our Father that I am describing here, the rock from which you and I were hewn and the imagine in which we were created. This is our inheritance and our birthright as a son or daughter of God!

Let's get serious here, the rock from which you and I were hewn, created in the image of God, the light of the world, a son of God. Those are the core messages God is asking each of us to live into? Think about it. How many of us are fathers? What message would you want your son to live into, that he is not worthy or doesn't have what it takes. I don't think so. Any true father would want his son to kick butt, get it done and be all that he can be. So, I ask you, is a son living into his weakness honoring his father? Of course not. Is God any different? No! We honor God by living into the truth, that you and I are created in God's image, that we have what it takes to become a man of God on this earth. That is what it means to remember.

So how do we begin to call forth a power that perhaps we have never known before? The answer is a radical conversion experience, perhaps like the one Peter experienced the night Jesus asked him to come to him on the water. That's what a conversion experience is, though, like stepping out of the security of our boat and walking toward Jesus on water!

This story grabs my heart. Can you imagine Peter's first step out of the boat? And how about Jesus, choosing this miracle in the dark of night. What better time, both metaphorically and realistically, to invite Peter to a new level of trust and conversion. Put yourself in the story, on a boat in the middle of the night. Years ago, I commercial fished in the gulf of Alaska. More than once twenty foot rollers smacked our boat in the middle of the night while trying to bring in pots. It was frightening and wild. Imagine Jesus coming to us in that context. How many of us would really step out of the boat and trust? That is exactly what a conversion experience is like, getting out of our same old boat and walking on water with Jesus. Exhilarating, isn't it? What can I say, living into Jesus isn't for cowards! And get hold of this, Jesus doesn't make it easy for Peter either, saying something like, okay Peter, just hold my hand I know you are scared. And, if you are okay with that put your toe on the water and see if it works for you. There is nothing soft about Jesus' invitation to Peter. It comes from his soul and with one word,

"COME!"

Integrating Soul and Mission

To accept that invitation is to roll away the stone of our heart and to give ourselves entirely to God. Only then can we begin to 'remember' who we really are. I have worked with men who seek to by-pass this crucial step, hoping to find their soul work without finding the Author of their soul. It just doesn't work and in doing so they forfeit who they really are in Christ. "For those who want to save their life will lose it. And for those who lose their life for my sake and the sake of the Gospel, will save it." Mark 8:35

But, there is more than just surrender needed. We need action, which is the way of the warrior. This integrating of surrender and action is well delineated in the story of feeding the five thousand, Mark 6:37. Jesus and the disciples have been with a large crowd in a deserted place. As the day wears on the disciples ask Jesus to send the people away so they can get something to eat. Jesus responds, "You give them something to eat." This is about action, doing something, even if it seems inconsequential.

Many of us men are paralyzed by inaction. It is sad but true. We have forgotten how to dig deep and pull out a new strength. "You give them something to eat," means do something! It is that simple. I don't care what, just do something. Even if it seems inconsequential. Just do it!

In this Gospel account, Jesus catches the disciples' bewilderment and responds, paraphrased, "Give me what you have." This is another one of those critical moments that so often precedes God's handiwork. The disciples could have easily looked out into the crowd and collapsed in despair, knowing what they had wasn't enough. Sound familiar? Fortunately, the disciples acted upon Jesus' word and did something! As we follow the story the disciples return with five loaves and two fish.

Those five loaves and two fish represent the sum of our talents, given by God which are intended to feed the multitudes. Get hold of this, if our few loaves and fishes have been laying in a tomb like Lazarus, it can be very difficult to give it to Jesus. Giving away broken dreams is painful. We get used to them, they become part of our story and so often they are intimately woven into our depression, grief or anger and even into our identity. And even worse, broken dreams can give us an excuse to quit.

So what is at risk here? To call forth my Lazarus means I need to give away my despair, my depression and my broken heart? Perhaps it means busting through my shame or releasing my bitterness. There is always a risk. Are you willing to take it? Are you willing to bring your few loaves and fishes to Jesus.

I ask you, do not judge your few loaves and fishes. In the kingdom of God there is no differentiating between talents. That is an ego thing, not a God thing. The smallest of acts brings as much honor to God as the greatest of deeds. Years ago I was in the Rockies on a my week-long sabbatical. My health had been compromised and I was tired of working in the woods. One night, while sitting around my fire I asked God, "Can I be done cutting trees?"

The response I heard in my heart was, "You honor me when you cut trees!" It was the last thing I had expected, dreamed or wanted. In my mind I saw my ecology work in the forest as just a job, a way to support my family until the day arrived that God called me to ministry. But that is not the way God sees our comings and our goings. Each act, no matter how small, once given to God, becomes a prayer to God. So no matter where you are in your life, no matter what you are doing at this time, even if you feel your work has nothing to do with your soul-mission, just get it to Jesus, make a prayer of it and live into as your soul-mission. The moment we do, something profound takes place.

Closing

"The glory of God is man fully alive." – St. Irenaeus.

Healing our wound and raising our Lazarus is exhilarating and agonizing work. This work begins with surrender, which is the way of the lover. But it takes more than just surrender. It takes the guts to "Roll away the stone," and face what must be faced, to look into our wounds and choices that have robbed us of life then be willing to own them, forgive ourselves and move forward. Moving forward is about action. This is our part of the equation. So I invite you to dust off your dreams and grab hold of them. They were given to you by God, not to be destroyed and buried in some tomb but to be called forth and resurrected. As we do, the primordial is awakened and strength returns. God is glorified.

9 THE WAY OF THE WARRIOR

I told Kathryn of the depth of my spiritual struggle that had begun nearly thirteen years ago at Holden, some of which she knew. I told Kathryn of my anger that had turned inward and had become rage. I told Kathryn of my anger at God. And finally, I told her that I was drawn to other women..

It was a painful moment. My life, like an exploding star, was now collapsing into a black hole. My spiritual pilgrimage, the passion, the pain, and the many quests were now being sucked into darkness. My very soul was dying as was my marriage.

Kathryn's disbelief became anger. Insanity deepened. It was everything I feared and more. Kathryn's secure world had come to an end as well. She had been betrayed by the person she trusted the most. She took off her ring then screamed, "Get out of the house. Just go! Go talk to someone, a priest, a pastor, a counselor, I don't care who. Just get out."

I left for our church. The priest who had been through his own crisis was in. I told my story. He listened without judgment. I returned home. Pain was in every moment. Shame was coursing through my spirit like electricity. Hatred of self, God and Kathryn smothered me. There was no off switch. No place to run. It was survival, moment by moment, barely hanging on.

The next day, I stepped into the crisp March air, grabbed my walking stick and took off. Nowhere in particular, just following the snowmobile paths through the forest. I walked. I ran. Sometimes I seemed to stumble under the crushing weight of my reality. There was nothing left of me. My heart was empty. My soul broken. Gone were the lessons of the wilderness. Gone was the fire that once burned in my heart. It was unbearable. Twenty years of a passionate relationship with God had been bled from my soul and in its place was a spiritual darkness, evil and insanity.

I returned home. Before entering I walked to the south side of our home. The ground was still frozen beneath inches of snow, except for a small patch of earth that snugged our home. There, amid the barren earth that follows winter's blow, were a couple of daffodil shoots emerging from their winter dormancy. As I took notice of them I heard, "That's your life." I cried because I knew it was the truth. At forty-four years of age my spiritual journey was about to begin a second time.

A couple weeks later, Kathryn, still pondering divorce, left with our daughter for an extended visit to her Mother's home. Evening came. Darkness descended. A fright took hold as I paced around the house. My soul hung in the balance between life and death. There was Jesus on one side, the Jesus I could not get to. And on the other side was Satan who was pulling me into his domain.

As night fell I spoke my Jesus prayer, but they were prayers of desperation. Fear gripped tighter as strange and demonic thoughts raced through my mind. I had no power over them. They came like arrows, one after the other, sending me deeper in shadow. With each thought a wave of hatred, evil and confusion washed over me. In desperation I called a friend and asked for prayers. I then laid down for sleep, which of course did not come. More frightening thoughts came.

"Jesus! Jesus!" I cried out. "Don't let me be a Judas."

I struggled for minutes which became hours, fitfully tossing, turning and wondering how in the world it all came to this. In the confusion, I began to retrace my journey with God, holding onto the pivotal moments. I relived my month solo in Alaska, a two month cycling trip through Europe, the Canyon Lands Quest and several other adventures. I called back the strength and clarity that was given to me during those times. I then retraced my steps that led me to Holden and the meeting with Kathryn. A spark of hope came from retracing my story, a knowing that the hand of God had been with me. I went back to the dream of Jesus and I walking along the mountain side and the invitation into the dark cave. I didn't believe there was a cave this dark, but perhaps this was the cave the dream spoke of. Then there were the words received at the bottom of the Grand Canyon, my medicine land, "In order for you to go any further in me you must give away all that you have gained in me." I breathed in those words as well as all the experiences God and I had tallied to that moment.

I replayed the experiences over and over in my mind. It was all I had, and in doing so, a trickle of hope touched my soul. I drank of this hope and continued to replay the experiences. It was then, as I *remembered,* that some primordial strength stirred within me. I was in hell, the deepest of hells, but there was hope, just enough to grab hold of and make it my own. I had seen God do the impossible. I would see it again. I laid there for quite a while, reliving my journey over and over. Strength and grief came in waves of tears, tears that seemed to unlock some cavern within. Then from the ashes of my life a primordial force began to stir within me. All of a sudden I cried out, "I am a servant of God! I am not going down the road of darkness, damn it! I am not a Judas. I will not betray my Lord! I am not going down that road, damn it! I have faced the wilderness, I have been chased down by a bull moose, fasted in the desert and nearly froze to death in the Alaskan Wilderness. There must be some part of me that can face emotional pain. There must be some part of me that can rise up and fight. There must be a man somewhere inside of me, a warrior who can fight and face pain. I don't know where the hell you've been all my life but I am calling you forth now. I am calling you out of the recesses of my soul. Wherever you are! I need you. I am calling you forth!"

In that moment, a spiritual tremor rocked the foundation of my soul, rolling away the stone to a cave that had been sealed off, releasing the primordial energy of the warrior. Tears poured from my eyes as this masculine energy coursed through my blood, rose in my spirit and surged into my heart. It was pure warrior energy, God's warrior energy, primordial, powerful, and ancient. Tears now flowed freely as this new strength, a strength I had never known before, filled my entire being. I cried out, not as a plea anymore, but as a statement to the universe. "I will not be taken down! I will not be taken down. I am a son of God. I will not be taken down." I then sat up in bed, looked south toward Kathryn's mother's house 130 miles away and proclaimed, "Kathryn, I will fight for our marriage. I will fight!"

Healing the Wound

Healing the wound, breaking addiction or becoming a new man in Christ is like rebuilding the sacred temple of our soul and reconstructing the infrastructure of our psyche. To begin this profound work we must uncover the debris until we are at the very foundation of our innermost selves because if the foundation is not firmly and carefully in place all other work will be in vain. This work begins with our relationship with God through Jesus, the corner stone of our new sanctuary. I invite you back to the chapter about intimacy with God, because it is everything I want to say about building a sacred foundation. There is however, one last angle that needs to come to the light, especially when dealing with addictions, the painful wounds of abuse or rejection, and spiritual oppression. This angle I speak of is found in a couple of the Gospel stories concerning healing. The first comes from Mark 5;25, the woman who has been suffering for twelve years with a hemorrhage and the second story comes from Mark 2:3, the paralytic being lowered down through the roof of Peter's home.

In the first story we find the woman pressing through the crowds, perhaps pushing, shoving, who really knows. This woman has had a flow of blood which has rendered her unclean for twelve years. She is an outcast, which means she has no right to be in public yet alone pushing through the crowds. Yet there she is. Why? She has hit the

91

wall, rock bottom, which is the very place the primordial is awakened. So what does she do? She says the hell with Jewish tradition and the hell with being an outcast and comes out of hiding as she breaks the psychological chains of isolation, fear and shame and goes out searching for Jesus. I can only imagine her thoughts, 'I am going out. I am going to press into Jesus if it is the last thing I do. I want to be healed!'

The second story exemplifies the same truth. Jesus is preaching in Peter's house. The room is packed, the courtyard is packed and perhaps even the streets. Four men carrying the paralytic seemingly arrive late. Are they daunted by the crowd? We don't know. What is given to us though is that these four men will not be denied their opportunity to get their friend to Jesus, and so they push through the crowds, stretcher and all, climb the side of the house, stretcher and all, walk on Peter's roof and then have the audacity to begin tearing apart Peter's roof. Why? Tenacity! A spirit that says I will get to Jesus no matter what!

The common thread that unites these stories is their tenacity to overcome any obstacle that separates them from Jesus! Why? They have come to that place where they know their only hope is Jesus. That is a powerful place to be!

Let's be brutally honest. If we as men are passive about reaching Jesus then I dare say we aren't really serious about healing the wound. We are sitting on the sidelines, magically hoping someone will do it for us or unwilling to take ownership of our stuff. In short, we are faking it. So the question we need to ask ourselves is, "Do we really want to be healed?" It is a basic question but I am serious. Do we really want to heal the wound? To heal the wound means our life must change. We must take responsibility, which means we can no longer blame. It also means we have to give away our excuses. The old line, "That is just the way I am" is a coward's path. I am speaking of the false self here. It would be more authentic to say, "That is the way I choose to be!" So I ask the question again. Do you want to be healed? If the answer is "yes," then we need to get to Jesus. It's that simple. We must do whatever it takes, climb over any obstacle or press through any hurdle. It doesn't matter. Just get to Jesus.

The Real Jesus

In the last two thousand years Jesus has become many things he isn't. We have made him a conservative and aligned his message with the ideals of politicians. We have also adorned him with excessive religious practices and even smothered him through the scriptures. Jesus says in John 5: 39 "You search the scriptures because you think that in them you have eternal life; and it is they that testify on my behalf." Why? We want to control this Jesus of Nazareth, make him predictable and mold him into an image that fits are ideals. It is easier to change the image of Jesus than change ourselves. So out of our wounds, our fear and our need to control we subtly begin to shape Jesus into an image that fits our wounds and placates our false sense of security.

I am not alone. In my early years in the ministry, while trying to be predicable and nice, I decided to get involved with the Catholic Church I was dutifully attending. After going through the basics of learning the ropes of distributing communion the priest took me behind the altar and held up a crystal jar of oil and said with a sense of pride and power, "This is where we keep the Holy Spirt." I about fell over backwards with disbelief. Everything inside of me wanted to scream, Let Her out! Let Her out! No wonder the church is suffering so much.

This is shadow stuff, the work of the false self. I don't have to go far to find the false Jesus. I need only to look within. I carry shadow. I carry wounds and so I shaped my Jesus accordingly. He was more of a lover than a warrior, deflecting conflict and always a peace maker, no doubt, a people pleaser. He was the aloof, hero Jesus who stood alone rather than with community or with a band of brothers; that way my Jesus would avoid rubbing up against other people's dysfunction or my own. He was also the ascended Jesus, the Jesus that despised my weakness and was neither of this world nor in this world. And so I molded my mission around this Jesus.

We are all human. We all carry shadow. There is a real Jesus in us just as there is a false Jesus. Perhaps it is time to look within and begin the painful yet life-giving process of dismantling our false Jesus. For example, if our life has been chaotic, where boundaries weren't clear and family dysfunction ran rampant we might create the rigid Jesus. A rigid Jesus gives our inner world clear boundaries so the wounded boy can feel safe. We quote scripture, take everything literally or cling to our religious practices as if they were Jesus himself. Why? Most likely it is a safety issue. The child never felt safe and so we project that deep need for security onto Jesus, which we should; the only problem is we create a false Jesus instead of letting Jesus heal the original wound.

If insecurity is our issue we might go out and evangelize everybody we meet, unconsciously seeking to make everyone like ourselves so we can feel safe. Insecurity is threatened by diversity. An African American pastor invited me into his inner city church with these words, "Jesus doesn't cut corners, he crosses lines." Crossing lines is frightening because the false self wants to control Jesus, make him predictable and even nice and church going. But Jesus is not about being nice and predicable. This is the guy who singled out a Samaritan woman, a woman who had been married four times and now living out of wedlock with a man, to be his herald. Unpredictable, isn't it?

Jesus stabbed at humanity's need to have a God that is both safe and predictable. He threatened their understanding of power, both individually and through the power structure of the temple. He challenged them to face their shadow and own their humanity. They couldn't do it, so they crucified him.

This is all radical, especially healing the servant of the centurion. We can't understand how radical this is unless we place ourselves in the mind-set of the Israelites. They hated the Romans. The Romans were their enemies. They were expecting a Messiah to come and obliterate them off the face of the earth. Does this language sound familiar? A decent comparison might be if a middle eastern country took over the United States. Imagine how each of us would feel toward a foreign government lording themselves over us, demanding that we pay taxes to them, keeping us dependent. I suspect most of us, myself included, would have some level of animosity toward them, if not hatred. And to fuel the sense of self-righteous anger further we are expecting an old testament God to come down with fire and brimstone and wipe out our enemies.

In this context Jesus comes on stage and does just the opposite, healing one of the servants of a top ranking military official in the Roman army. In one quick moment Jesus delivers a piercing blow to the conscious and unconscious hatred of the people of Israel. This is no accident. This was a premeditated act of God and Jesus. He was going right after their deepest shadow, calling it into light, asking them to look within at their own hatred instead of projecting it onto the enemy.

Unconscious hatred needs an enemy to hate. It is that simple. That is the way it survives, grows and gains power. It is covert stuff, working beneath the surface under the guise of a self-righteous ideology. Several years ago I was working with a Christian. We began to share stories of our journey. The Spirit of God was there. Then somewhere in our conversation the word gay came up, triggering an unconscious hatred in this man. Immediately the Holy Spirit left as the man pulled out his shadow sword and went on a personal crusade of how all homosexuals should be shipped to some barren island to die.

On a grand scale and in the wake of 9/11, the Iraq war was sold by tapping into the wounded and unconscious hatred of Americans. Many Christians bought it. We all need an enemy to hate so we don't have to deal with our own hatred or even self-hatred. This is called projection. We all do it. It is a hell of a lot easier to hate a certain group than to deal with our own hatred. Politics is full of hatred. It is tragic. Many politicians have become masters of control through hatred and fear. Listen to any of them as they express extreme political views on either side. Ask yourself what emotions are they triggering in you!

What I am getting at here is that our unconscious shadow creates a Jesus that molds to our wounds and buried toxic emotions. It is easier to create a Jesus that hates gays and lesbians than search for the real Jesus who crosses lines and pierces the unconscious hatred in you or me. This is frightening stuff here. Not for the faint of heart. It takes a warrior to look within and ask God what part of our false self is controlling Jesus and shaping him into something he isn't. It can rock the very foundation of our understanding of our God and ourselves.

For myself, the old expression of Jesus, was now laid in a tomb. There was grief, horror and unknowing and perhaps even a sense of betrayal. Yes, my world had been rocked. My old Jesus had died. The resurrection would be slow and painful, that much I was sure of. There was much work to do to prepare for this resurrection and much to let go of. I had used Jesus to run from my shame and ascend out of my humanity. I wanted ascent, great deeds and wilderness treks. Fortunately, that Jesus died. Sadly it took an earth-shaking crisis to finally let him go.

Retracing the Wound

"It is time," Kathryn said.

"I know," I said as I started to cry. "I am afraid." Yes, I was afraid to enter this dark cave of my humanity and face the wounds I had been running from all my life. I was afraid because I knew there was real pain in that cave, pain that could rip my heart in two. But it was time. I was scared. I guess that is when we know it is real.

A couple weeks later I was doing a quiet meditation, recalling scenes of early childhood with the help of a therapist. My thoughts traced back to memories of being with my maternal grandmother the first year of my life surfaced. Just for the record she was no pussy cat. Once, she disciplined my youngest sister. According to my mother, my sister was in an emotional coma for three days. Like I said, she was no pussy cat. Even though I was in my first year of life, with no conscious memories of being with her, the traumatic memories were there, calloused and compartmentalized in the unconscious. And now that I had given them permission to come forth, my body trembled as the memories shook loose from the deep recesses of my mind, body and soul.

In the weeks that passed as I began to scrape away the layers of the calloused tissues of my psyche the wisdom of God unfolded before me. Yahweh, the Warrior, was building the psychological infrastructure with the primal energy of the warrior so my psyche could process the excruciating pain without fracturing further. This is an important piece. The wounded boy needs the mature masculine of the warrior to feel safe and begin the healing process. To undo the layers of the wound without awakening the warrior is often unproductive, if not psychologically dangerous.

Jesus as Warrior

Jesus lived into and through the warrior energy. We need to be clear about this. We do him a disservice by making him sweet, nice, church-going, and always carrying a Bible around. Jesus was radical, passionate, committed and focused. We need only to journey with him into the wilderness to understand this. It was no Sunday picnic. He was weakened, famished and psychologically and spiritually worn down. Every moment, I assume, was an invitation to compromise, give into weakness or lose focus. But Jesus did not compromise himself, his integrity nor his commitment to God. He was living through the warrior energy, that is, with firm resolve to the journey of union with God and his mission.

A warrior is fully committed to God and his task and will see it through to its completion. That is a place of power. I had lacked this energy in my marriage with Kathryn. The pain had overtaken me, causing me to stumble, doubt and even rebel. I knew this in my gut, that I was not willing to get into the raw masculine, face the issues and commit completely to solving the differences. Countless times I tried to force myself to awaken this masculine energy even though I couldn't name it as such and live into my marriage as a man but the boy wouldn't go there. There was a wall of fear that paralyzed him. I pushed, but it never happened. Marriage is a man's world.

The second attribute of the warrior I see in Jesus is that a warrior is fueled by pain. I don't mean this in some sick ascetic or macho man way. Life has more than enough pain without heaping it upon ourselves. But pain will come. It is part of the human experience. What I need to call forth here is that the warrior harnesses this pain to fuel his God-given mission. This is one of the signature marks of the warrior. He is not consumed with pain or the frustration of the many obstacles that arise in his path. He uses the pain to hone his commitment, gather his strength and move forward with tenacity.

It is easy to write these words but hard to live them. A month or so after my crisis erupted and after I had awoken the warrior energy, Kathryn and I had a really tough processing session. It caught me at a low moment and tore my newly awakened warrior heart into a thousand pieces. I crumbled inside and said, "I have had it God. I am done with this. I want to come home." For a long time I just sat on the floor as the life force drained out of me. I was falling, but this time, I didn't care. After a while I looked up at Kathryn and our beautiful daughter. God simply posed this question to me, "Are you sure you want to leave this?"

Let's be honest. You and I are not Jesus. We are going to stumble, really stumble. It is part of the human journey, even necessary as we grow into the primal masculine. What I am saying here is that the warrior never gives up! We will fall, we may even lose our heart but the warrior within us will not stay down. He will gather his strength, harness the vital energy of God through surrender and prayer and then channel it into his actions. That is warrior medicine.

Jesus in the Temple

Jesus comes into the outer courts of the temple where they are selling animals for a sacrifice. He knows these merchants care nothing of the sacred. They are thieves, interested in lining their pockets with cash. A justifiable anger, if not rage, is ignited within him. Jesus then grabs a whip, overturns the tables and drives out the merchants.

This moment is about anger, a righteous anger that comes when the sacred has been violated. When there is anger we can be certain boundaries have been crossed, whether that be in the present or past, most likely both as discussed earlier. To deny this anger is a further wounding to the sacred and a missed opportunity to heal the wound.

We cannot fear anger, but rather journey into the anger to heal the wound and set boundaries. Boundaries are about protecting our dignity as a son of God, which means, defining what we will tolerate as acceptable actions toward us. The warrior sets his boundaries, and in doing so, protects the sacred.

In the reclaiming of our true self, the wounded boy needs the mature masculine to set boundaries so he will feel safe and begin to heal. If we have allowed ourselves to be walked upon in our relationships or allowed ourselves to be manipulated by those close to us, it is the warrior that must rise up and set boundaries. If we do not set our boundaries, the violation cuts deeper and the primal masculine is weakened. Rage is soon to follow.

Just after the crisis broke, Kathryn approached me with a vivid dream about how I was untrue in the marriage. It was a dream, a projection of her fears. I understood this but still, the details were not true. As she belabored the dream, anger rose up within me. The warrior was screaming, "This is a violation. Do something!" The critical moment was upon me. It wasn't just about the moment though. There were forty-four years into that moment, a boy who had never learned to defend himself emotionally and a boy who shrank in fear each time he was disciplined. There was also generational baggage into that moment. Both my grandfathers, my paternal grandfather I knew only through stories, had married strong women and in my judgement would be considered emotionally passive. All of that baggage, dysfunction and old wounds were playing into the moment. The boy was crying out for help. The violation was cutting deeper. I took a breath, called upon the strength that I had newly discovered and said, "Kathryn, I can't listen to this dream. If you want to share your feelings or pain I would gladly listen but I can't listen to something that is not true and weakens my soul." It was a pivotal moment, seemingly insignificant, but powerful for both of us.

Defending boundaries is not restricted to our relationships. As said earlier, once the wound gains a stronghold in the psyche, it creates its own energy or life force. It becomes a part of our personality, seeking to be validated by playing the drama of the wounding over and over in our minds. I call this making love to our wounds. I would feel injured through a tough interchange but the wounding wouldn't stop there. For some reason, seemingly beyond my control, I played the drama over and over in my mind, validating the wound and playing into the victim. Making love to our wounds is a sure sign the warrior is lying dormant.

Our Sacred Temple

Let's look deeper into the story of Jesus cleansing the temple. There is more here than just boundaries and anger. Metaphorically, we are the temple that has been violated by thieves. These thieves that rob us of our passion for God and our masculinity in Christ are the self-destroying messages we carry within us. Messages like, "If you don't succeed, you are nothing. Who are you to be powerful?' 'I am not worthy,' and so on."

We need to ask ourselves, is there anything holy about these messages of unworthiness or a false sense of humility that comes from dysfunction? The answer is obviously no. Then where is our whip, our passion and our zeal for the sacred, God's sacred. This about shame, the masculine shame that binds us, robs us of our power and destroys who we are. Shame is a core belief that we are not worthy. Through this core belief we are driven to perfection, mask our authentic self or create a persona that gives us a false sense of power.

Remember, healing the wound, breaking addiction or becoming a new person in Christ is like rebuilding the sacred temple of our soul and reconstructing the infrastructure of our psyche. We must uncover the debris until we are at the very foundation of our inner-most self. We can't outrun shame or gloss it over with scripture or walk around saying we are created in the image of God and expect shame to simply disappear. Remember the body builder who crumbled in shame during a process at a retreat. We cannot build a sacred temple on a foundation of shame. The shame must be pierced so the wound can bleed. Only then can a new foundation of ourselves in Christ be laid down.

Addiction

Before we leave this story of Jesus cleansing the temple we need to cut a little deeper. Addiction comes in many forms-work, video games, sports, neurotic thinking, compulsive eating, violent behavior, and of course the forms of addiction that our society frowns upon, pornography, alcohol, gambling or sex. But certainly the list is not limited to those charged issues. So often addiction takes hold when a wound festers in shadow, creating an opening in the psyche in which dark forces gain a strong hold.

If addiction has taken hold we can be certain the walls of our sanctuary have been breached. The enemy has gained a strong-hold and a long and difficult battle is before us, a battle that must be fought on many fronts. Each of these fronts, the emotional, spiritual, mental and physiological, represents a battle field in which we must reclaim ourselves in God. I consider these fronts or battlefields, energy centers that correspond to the greatest commandment spoken by Jesus. "You shall love the Lord your God with all of your heart, with all of your soul, with all of your mind and with all of your strength." I use the word energy centers because it is through the heart, mind, soul and with all our strength, meaning actions, that we give and receive energy with God. To reclaim our self in Christ, to break the power of addiction and to become all that God has intended us to be we must realign our body, mind, soul and actions with God.

The warrior charges into these four energy centers to uncover the emotional wound, the spiritual sin, the wrong thought process and his harmful actions to self and others that precipitated addiction. In doing so, he is fighting the battle on each of these fronts, bringing them into the light and fortifying the inner walls of his sanctuary, which weakens the enemy's stronghold and diminishes his access to his psyche.

This was my work, facing the pain and undoing the choices that had brought me here. Several times I asked myself, "Why am I here?" The answer was obvious. For thirteen years I had denied my deepest self by hiding my pain, not trusting God and not speaking my truth. These choices were so subtle and seemingly insignificant at the time. Yet, every denial of my true self had accrued a growing debt upon my soul, sending me farther into shadow. I was also here because I had run from shame and marital conflict until they had became a raging tornado within me. There was no running now. Shame, anger and hatred rushed through my spirit like a dark river. Each time Kathryn and I processed the crisis and I was faced with the reality of what I had become it was like being dragged behind a truck going sixty miles an hour. The boy within me cried out, "Stop, stop, I can't take another moment of this shit!" The warrior within stepped up, but even then, by the days end, I couldn't take another moment of life. It was hell, barely surviving, hoping that someday I would know a sense of peace. I was also here because I had made a goddess out of Kathryn, certain her love would heal my wound. I now had to bring the wound to God, not once but every day, facing my deep longing to be loved and valued in a feminine and nurturing way.

Yes, I was here for obvious reasons. But there was another answer that came during those few and fleeting quiet moments. It was an answer that defied all understanding of God. But it came, more than once over the next several years. That answer was, "Because I love you!"

I understood the full implications of the answer. Since meeting Jesus in Lubbock and experiencing him in a profound way during a cycling trip through Europe, I had focused my prayers, energy and intent into one pursuit, union with God through Jesus. "As far as I can go God. Leave no stone unturned," was my cry, not once but over and over. And now, that pursuit had lead me into the dark fire. Why? So that someday I might know the union my soul desires.

Accessing Spiritual Power

Reclaiming God's power in my life was a full time job. There was a hell of a lot of hard work to do, charging into heart, soul, mind and body and undoing what I had done, facing spiritual pain, fighting spiritual oppression and working on my marriage that was hanging by a thread. It was warrior time. It was survival time. The core of my struggle was in the my soul. I knew my greatest weapon in breaking addiction was realigning my soul power with God through Jesus Christ. Without a doubt, soul power is found in the deepest of surrenders. If I hold back just one grain of self from God my soul power is weakened. The enemy knows when I am faking it, speaking like I have given my life over to God but haven't really committed myself.

In the book of Acts chapter 19:13 there is a story of men faking like they know Jesus as if by using his name it would bring power to their lives. It reads, "Then some itinerant Jewish exorcists tried to use the name of the Lord Jesus over those who had evil spirits saying, "I adjure you by the Jesus whom Paul proclaims." Seven sons of the Jewish high priest named Sceva were doing this, but the evil spirit said to them in reply, "Jesus I know and Paul I know; but who are you?" Then the man with the evil spirit leaped on them, mastered them all, and so over powered them that they fled out of the house naked and wounded." In the spiritual realm there is no faking it.

Power and confidence comes through commitment. This is the way of the warrior. There is no middle ground nor the word 'try' in the mindset of the warrior. He either does or he does not. Either he belongs to God or he does not. This is a place of power. Be it known, Satan does everything to keep men and women from living into their warrior energy because he knows he cannot stand against someone who is completely God's and willing to do what ever God asks of them.

The Warrior and his Body

A couple of months after my crisis broke I found work as a park ranger. Often, I rode my mountain bike to work then found myself running a chain saw. It was good to work in the woods again. The rich smell of churned-up earth, the sweat pouring from my brow and the sweet but pungent scent of pine pitch grounded me to my roots as a forester and logger and further anchored me to my masculinity. Yes, it was good to be in my body, to know the joy of a hard days work and to feel alive through the aching of my muscles as I laid down to sleep that night.

Our masculine soul is linked to our bodies. This is the design of God. In the breaking of a sweat, anger and other toxic emotions are released. Simply put, physical exertion is therapy and through it the warrior is honed and called forth. It seems once the mid life rolls start forming around our belly something in the male psyche gives up. It is subtle but real, robbing us of that mental edge that comes from conditioning our bodies through a physical discipline.

I have a friend who is in his mid eighties. He is slight of build and mentally sharp. Recently, we met for lunch. Sometime in the conversation he remarked, "You know Brian, I feel really good."

"What's the difference?"

"I began doing simple strength exercises."

What I am saying here is that it doesn't take much to get on a positive curve with our bodies. A simple work out three times a week, just enough to get some blood pumped into the muscles and the heart rate up seems to be enough. My friend Steven, who told me the boy never gets married, likes to run. It is an expression of who he is, an outlet for stress as well an opportunity to hone the warrior. Every now and then, he pushes himself, not for ascetic reason, but to call forth the warrior energy, that is, to run the last block when his body would rather quit. It is a mental discipline, expressed through the body to keep the warrior energy honed, on line and ready for action when necessary.

Our bodies are linked to our psyche and our psyche is linked to our body. We cannot deny this truth. There is a synergistic energy between body and soul as we train, not just for ourselves but to hone the warrior within us so that we might fight our real fight. It is not just about being in shape. It is about giving 'voice' to the warrior within you and I. The warrior within needs a physical expression, to work out, stretch and feel the sense of exhilaration his body. Martial arts has been that venue for me.

If you find yourself in a fight for your heart, marriage or dreams, or perhaps struggling with addiction, facing traumatic wounds, in depression or simply just existing without direction, I invite you to wake up early, slip on those running shoes and simply go. Or pump air into that deflated basketball and go to the gym to shoot some hoops or lift some weights. It doesn't matter the expression, just do it. Something intangible will awaken within you.

The Word and the Warrior

Say what you mean and mean what you say. If you tell someone you will meet them at 10:00, be there or call in. If you tell your wife you will get a task done, do it. This is about integrity and accountability. It is about the words of our mouth and our actions being in alignment. In our stressed-out world when we as men are seemingly pulled in about a thousand directions it is easy to let the words, "Sure honey, I will get to that later," roll off our tongue without really tightening up what "later" means. I have been that guy in my marriage more than once. It does nothing for me as a man nor does it bring life to my marriage.

The warrior is focused. He doesn't let casual words roll off his tongue without focused intent supporting them. If we make a commitment to get up early and spend quality time with God then do it! If we make an inner commitment to get in shape and lose some extra pounds then do it. Each time we compromise our integrity the inner man is weakened. Our psyche knows this and so does the enemy. Again, "Say what you mean and mean what you say." This is the way of the warrior.

Warrior Living

Be Here Now is the title of a book by Ram Dass. I have not read the book but the title speaks volumes. *Be here now*, is about living each moment fully, which demands consciousness awareness to the moment and mental discipline. It is frightening how much God and life I have given away by letting my thoughts drift into the future about how God might work in my life. It is just as frightening to think how much God and life I have given away by living into fear and anxiety. *Be here now.* How many people have I discounted by not being fully present to the moment, the conversation and their story? How many moments have I lost with my family when I have not been fully present with them?

This *now* is the only moment I have, given to me by God, to build or to give away to useless thoughts, to live into or to just get by. Certainly, mentally checking out is the easy road, even the coward's path. It takes guts to live into the present moment, especially when the present moment is painful. But who said living into warrior energy is easy? Certainly, not me.

For the Christian there is more to the present moment. There is the unseen world, the hope of the resurrection, the promise, the vision, and the dreams planted within our soul. We must learn to hold the promise yet be present to the moment. We must pursue our vision while finding the sacred in the journey. One without the other is not enough. In the journey pain and promise often coexist. This is the way of our humanity and our divinity given to us by God. Intentional living is about moving through the pain while keeping our inner vision on the promise. This comes with grace, perseverance and practice.

Be here now. I invite you take one simple task, perhaps washing dishes and simply give thanks to God for the moment. Be conscious of the sensation of warm water washing over your hands while giving thanks for your humanity and the senses you have been given. Let your task be a prayer.

If you are with your children, then be with them. Revel in their beauty, the features of their face, their unique personality, and the gift they are to you. See them as if for the first time. Let your eye contact be deep and sincere. This is the way of the warrior.

Warrior Prayer

Not all prayer is a cozy experience with God. Sometimes it is work, really hard work. There are times when getting into the presence of God is like walking upstream in a fast moving river. No matter what I do there seems to be forces within and without that fight against me. At such times my mind can't seem to focus on God for more than a minute. But in the midst of my struggle I am left with a choice, give myself to half hearted devotions or get into my guts and push through. Often pushing through means speaking the Lord's prayer with all my mental concentration over and over. It can be mentally exhausting. But many times the forces within and without that are resisting God have been broken by using this technique.

Prayer is powerful and often precedes the movement of God in our lives. We see this in the life of Jesus. I have experienced this same truth in my own life. Prayer precedes power. If we desire to see God's power in our lives we need to be people of prayer, especially when prayer is difficult.

Shadow Warrior

When the warrior energy is linked to a wound there is control, domination, greed, hatred and violence. We don't need to look very far to see the shadow warrior at work in our own lives and the lives around us.

A cunning shadow warrior can manipulate through words or play into his power by triggering a partner's fear. It can be covert stuff and just as damaging, taking the victim to the edge of instability. Using scripture to manipulate others is also about shadow warrior. There is nothing honorable about it. Remember, Satan sought to manipulate Jesus in the wilderness by using the word of God.

Most often, the man operating through the shadow warrior hasn't touched his own sense of inferiority, shame and self-hatred. Yes, at the core of his being he feels powerless, angry, out of control or weak. And so he compensates through control, domination or greed. Unfortunately, the victim of long-term and subtle abuse hasn't found their own sense of power either. It is a terrible cycle.

There is also a phenomena in the human psyche called projection. One form of projection is living through another person's accomplishments. A good example of this is professional sports. Let's face it, what guy doesn't want be the quarterback in some super bowl, playing his heart out and leading his team to victory. It is part of our hardwiring, given to us by God. We are designed to fight, to believe, to go to the edge and slay the dragon that seeks to destroy everything good in us. The problem is when we don't live out of a passionate relationship with God and from our masculine heart we begin to project that need onto others. Sound crazy? Next time you watch a football game on television take an inventory of the fans as the camera scans the crowd. What do you see? Guys living into their strength? I don't. I see people who have given away their power to professional athletes, living through their lives, hoping to touch something that is dormant within them. Don't get me wrong. I like sports just as I enjoy movies that inspire me. But that is where I draw the line. I have my own fight to fight. I do not need to live through another person's fight.

There is one more movement of the shadow warrior I need to bring to the light. As painful as this may sound I dare say that most of Christianity's efforts to evangelize arises out of shadow. Yes, out of our need to control, play God, and validate our own reality we seek to witness to everyone we meet, as if we know how and when God is going to touch a person's life. Jesus said, "No one comes to me unless drawn by the Father who sent me." John 6:44

I have no power within me to draw anyone to Jesus, no matter how hard I try. This truth is given to us by Jesus, which is so liberating, giving me the freedom to be who I am, a lover and servant of God.

Don't get me wrong. I do ache for the kingdom of God to come and to share the love and power of God through Jesus, but not on my terms. I am striving to evangelize by living into God, being present to every moment and seeking to be a blessing to everyone I meet. Words! well, I attempt to speak my truth when asked, not to sway them into my reality but out of integrity to God and myself. It is hard work, only because my ego or shadow seeks to put my agenda on people.

The illusion of evangelizing is that it takes you and I away from our real soul mission, and that is dwelling in the presence of God through Jesus Christ. Yes, this is the real quest, our own journey of transformation. When we are always seeking to change others there is no need to do the deep soul work the journey demands. This is right where the enemy wants us, focusing on others rather than our journey of union with God through Jesus. Remember, what we become brings power to what we do. If we become Christ then Christ will work through us. It is that simple.

Summary

"The Lord is a Warrior." Exodus 15:3 Created in the image of God, there is a warrior inside each of us. Once awakened, unleashed and aligned with the Spirit of the Lord a man becomes a powerful instrument of God's grace. Jesus lived as a warrior. We are called to do the same.

Awakening the warrior is much like a conversion experience. We must get to that place in our guts, unwavering and passionate, where we know we need this warrior energy more than we need our addictions, the hiding of our pain and the false self that arises out of the wound. Often this means rock bottom, but not necessarily. Then and only then, as we choose to break the destructive cycles within us and face shadow, will God open the sacred chamber of our soul and release the primal energy of the warrior within us. It is powerful stuff. It is real. Once released, it is our responsibility to live into that warrior energy. Strength begets strength. Weakness begets weakness. I have worked with several men who have tasted this warrior energy only to collapse in the heat of the battle. Again, strength begets strength. We must chose our strength.

I have been told that a Samurai keeps his fear on the tip of his sword, squarely in front of him as he charges into battle. Why? He knows that the vital energy of the warrior is released as he pierces his fear. It is the same for you and I. Each time I turn into my pain, face my fears, make the hard choices, an exhilarating surge of the warrior courses through my blood.

10 GRIEF

In the months that followed Kathryn became my prophet. Yes, she radiated Christ like I had never seen before, and through her God spoke words of wisdom as well as words that sliced bone and marrow, soul and spirit. Each word, no matter how painful, brought healing as shadow was brought to light.

We began therapy together. As Kathryn and I processed our journey with a therapist pain oozed from my psyche. Weeks into our journey the therapist touched upon my wilderness experiences. As I told her of my excursions something within me cracked open and I began to weep. Moments later I found myself unconsciously saying, "I never wanted to leave. I never wanted to leave!"

Buried grief, the silent killer of the masculine soul, is a slow and painful death of the inner man. Grief comes from a lost childhood, abuse, not living our soul mission or making poor choices. Our deepest self knows when we have been robbed or when we have robbed ourselves. We bury it. It is a survivor's choice. Overtime it ferments then festers only to be hardened over by anger. Own the anger, release it and often you will see a man weeping in grief.

By mid-summer I received word of a men's retreat in Albuquerque, New Mexico entitled, *The Day of the Warrior,* lead by Richard Rohr and Dr. Robert More. I journeyed to New Mexico with my heart wide open, ready to embrace the world of men, the world I had run from for so many years.

As our small group began the work of sharing our stories a window opened within me. I was not alone. Every man had a story. Our stories were different but there was a common thread that united us. We had suffered. There is something about suffering that can anchor men to God, to themselves and to each other. It is the great leveler which can dissolve the barriers that the ego creates through religion, race, politics and social status. I also began to understand that by the design of God, passed down through the ages, the primal masculine is released as men gather in sacred ways to share their stories of faith, speak their wounding and live into their courage to overcome obstacles. This primal masculine didn't come as a lightening bolt but rather as a soaking into my spirit through the laughter of other men, through the tears of grief and in the joy of simply being a man among men on a journey toward Christ. It was a new world, a world I desperately needed, a world that I liked.

One evening during the retreat, small workshops were offered by participants. As I sat down in a small circle of men I listened to Nathan speak with incredible insights on healing and the journey of union with God. I had no doubt he carried the gift of healing and more. Near the end of the session Nathan offered prayers for healing for anyone who wished. I watched him work with several other men, always asking permission to hold their hands while they prayed or asking questions so as not to violate their sanctity. I chose to trust him. As he held my hands he said a few things about my life then bluntly said, "You have damned yourself Brian."

I jerked my head up. His words pierced me because I knew they were true. In my anger and pain I had cut myself off from God and Jesus. I had fought until it nearly killed me, but the truth was, I had stumbled and allowed Satan to take up residence. It was hell, agony with seemingly no way out. That was why I was here.

I replied, "Not intentionally. I have been walking a dark road. I have stumbled badly."

Later in the retreat we gathered in our small groups as a man from Oregon lead us through a simple process of touching the hidden

112

grief. As we began the process I thought to myself, *'Okay God, where are we going with this?'* The process lasted about an hour, ending with my small group sharing in silence the grief that was written upon our faces and a few tears. For several minutes we simply gazed into the eyes of each man, sharing their grief and owning our own. A few tears began to leak out. It was good to let those tears flow. As the process concluded, I breathed a sigh of relief then thought to myself, *'that was good.'* Just then one of the men in my small group walked around our circle of seated men and stopped behind me. Without any words he wrapped his powerful forearms around my neck in a masculine embrace. Instantly, a stream of masculine strength flooded my entire being, unconsciously giving me permission to let go of the deep grief of the last twelve years.

Immediately, the searing pain and anguish of feeling separated from God, the spiritual oppression that came 24/7, the shame of being drawn to other women, the stress of my marriage and the pain of processing our crisis broke open. My body trembled, rocked in agony and heaved in grief. I was aware of little, except that my grief was uncontrollable and the man in my small group who had initiated my release kept his arm securely wrapped around my neck, silently imprinting upon me that in that moment I was held in the sacred masculine and that all would be well.

I continued to weep, really weep. The pain of being seemingly 'damned' and the grief that I had seemingly failed God and myself poured out of me like a river. About thirty minutes later and drained of every ounce of strength my grief seemed to subside. As I opened my eyes I saw a large group of men, men whom I had not connected with during the retreat circled around me, offering their masculine support, supporting me in prayer and choosing to be my wailing wall in my darkest hour. I took notice of the thirty or so men gathered around me, nodding my gratitude while knowing God had just indoctrinated me into the world of men.

That night in the downtown plaza of Albuquerque the men gathered for another process. The facilitator that had led the grief ritual opened the evening process by holding up a beautiful piece of southwest pottery in which we had placed a few grains of wheat which signified our dreams and hopes. As he spoke about the sacred masculine journey and choosing to follow Christ he raised the pottery as an offering to God, and then, without words or warning he violently smashed the piece of pottery onto the cement. Pieces of pottery flew everywhere as did the grains of wheat. I understood. So often the journey to Christ means a shattering of the ego and the dreams we have worked so hard for. I gathered one of the pieces of shard as a reminder of my journey. I still have it today. Soon after, the men began drumming. Some men danced. Like David before the Lord, I danced. In wild masculine strength, celebrating the breaking open of my pain and the hope of a new dawn, I danced.

11 THE WAY OF THE LOVER

In the quiet of the surrendered heart there is a longing this world cannot satisfy. Such yearning drives them into the remote places of the earth, seeking solace as they empty themselves before the risen Jesus. Such intense desire causes them to awake in the night, only to be consumed with a passion for God that is unlike they have ever known. This is the primal energy of the lover infused into the surrendered heart. It is the very foundation of our most wild and true self.

It is a paradox. I speak of our most wild and true self, drawing our sword, piercing the shadows, wilderness, and awakening the primal masculine, and yet here we are, calling forth the feminine qualities of the masculine soul. Such passionate love for God is at the core of our masculinity and yet, it is probably the most difficult for men to access. Richard Rohr said on one of my retreats, "If it doesn't involve blood, sweat, tears or sperm it isn't for men." We as men are about action, the warrior, sports, adventure and questing into the unknown. Some of us might even say the hell with feelings and being intuitive just get me a sword and a dragon to slay. And yes, this is true, except it is only part of who we are. If we are honest with ourselves, there is a part of us that hungers for the deep embrace of unconditional love and to be held in the arms of an all-loving God. So often we as men channel this deep desire or this love-hunger into the world of sexuality, choosing a woman's caress and the adventure of a woman's body over the deep and unconditional embrace of our God.

The Question

So where to begin? How do we embark upon this passionate journey of the heart and a deeper union with God? I believe it begins with a question just as Peter's work on earth began with Jesus asking him three times, "Do you love me?" Jesus knew the answer, but still, he wanted Peter to give voice to his true self and to own his deepest desires. We must do the same, that is, if we are serious about a passionate relationship with God. We must be willing to meet Jesus on the shores of our heart and allow him to ask us the tough question, a question that pierces soul and spirit and slices bone and marrow.

Recently at our small faith group I brought up the issue of trust, using the metaphor of Frodo in *The Lord of the Rings* standing on the edge of Mount Mordor with ring in hand unwilling to throw it into the fire. My fear and anxiety had become a part of my psyche and despite years of struggle I had been unwilling to simply trust God in the small and grand moments of my life. After sharing with the group we were invited into the woods to ponder our core issue. I walked through the woods then ended up at a pond on the property. There was a dock that jetted out into the water that symbolically resembled the ledge that Frodo stood upon with ring in hand. I smirked with a knowing of what God was asking of me. I grabbed a rock that represented the ring of dark power and walked out to the end of the dock, giving voice to my fears and anxieties that had plagued my spirit for so long.

God then took me back to the moment I had left the wilderness and embarked upon my journey with Kathryn. That was the day the seeds of fear and mistrust were planted in my spirit. I had never fully trusted God since. I held the rock for a long time, pondering what my life would be without fear and anxiety, then with all my heart, mind and soul I threw the rock into the water giving myself completely to God through Jesus, trusting that the way would open for me, that I would release my fear and anxiety. As I sat on the bank I whispered one word in prayer.

"My God and my all."

"My son."

So what would your question be? Or perhaps we should start with the simple question, "Do you want God?" I am serious, not the things of God, not to save the world, nor to convert the masses nor to just 'get to heaven.' I mean do you want God? It is a frightening question. I know many spiritual people who seemingly want God, the God who is wrapped up in their causes or tangled up in their religious traditions, scripture or whatever. So, I ask the question again. Do you want a passionate relationship with God? If the answer is yes then what do you need to lose, give away or metaphorically toss in the fires of Mordor? Finding the answer might come easily. Giving it away might be hell.

Inner Simplicity

With our question answered and our intent focused upon the heart of God the Holy Spirit will begin to clear away the debris to create sacred space within our psyche. This threshing of God within the human soul is one of the most powerful movements of the spiritual journey. God is now stripping the soul of the desires for worldly things, replaced by an incredible hunger for God that is expressed through aloneness, inner simplicity and contemplative prayer. We may walk into a room where the television is on and experience a heaviness of soul. Schedules and possibly the church board meeting may become a burden rather than a calling. Televised sports will become a distraction. This is the work of the Holy Spirit, setting us apart for Christ by creating an inner emptiness and simplicity of spirit, both which are needed to enter into deeper union with God. It is a powerful time. Like the caterpillar weaving a cocoon around itself, God is weaving a spiritual cocoon around us, drawing us away from the world so that we might experience the incredible joy of a more intimate relationship with God.

I experienced such a movement eighteen months after my conversion and following a two months solo cycling trip through Europe. I returned to Steamboat Springs and found lodging in an old chicken coop that had been renovated into a bunkhouse. There was no heat in this bunk house nor running water but there was solitude, which was what I craved the most. Those crisp winter nights in the Yampa Valley when the temperatures dropped well below the zero mark are fond memories. Each evening I curled up in my blankets, lit a candle and delved into the world of inner quiet and union with God. I knew nothing of the world of meditation, except a few suggestions I found in a book at church, to breathe, say a quiet prayer phrase and trust.

Most nights, as the presence of God descended, my consciousness subtly shifted to a growing awareness of God's presence moving into my heart and soul. There were times, with my mind still, that I let go of my prayer phrase completely and simply rested in the presence of God. This was a powerful experience, even frightening as sometimes I seemed to lose consciousness of my body and even my surroundings. More than once I playfully opened my eyes to see if I was still on planet earth. Each time, there I was, still in the chicken coop, watching my breath frost in the frigid air by candle light.

Accessing the Unconscious

In those early years with God I began to understand that the conscious mind must be calmed so our deeper self, that is, the unconscious mind, our heart and our soul can become available to the Holy Spirit. Then and only then can our deepest self enter into a sacred union with God. This is crucial. But before we speak about meditation techniques and accessing the unconscious it is important to understand techniques facilitate our desire for God. They are not a substitute nor are they a source of our power. No doubt there are benefits in them, but still, for the soul seeking God they are simply tools. So do not get hung up on the tools. Do not get hung up on accessing the unconscious either. Most likely we have all touched the deep waters within us and experienced a sense of oneness moving through us while playing sports, climbing a mountain, working or whatever.

Yes, accessing the unconsciousness is not limited to the inner world of meditation. Athletes have a term called the 'zone,' attained when they are fully in the moment and performing at peak levels. Musicians call it the 'muse,' and martial artists call it 'no mind.' Whatever term we give it, 'no mind,' the 'muse' or whatever, it is a phenomena that occurs when our conscious training gives way to our deeper self and we find ourselves performing through unconscious instinct rather than thought.

In the first *Star Wars* trilogy *Obi Wan* began to train *Luke* in the ways of the *force* by placing a shield over his eyes. This scene is about letting go of conscious thought and tapping into the primal forces of the unconscious self. Yes, I know this is a movie scene, but it is real. A friend who is a musician told me of an experience many years ago while rehearsing with his band. The band had invited an accomplished and classically trained musician to sit in with them. As they seemingly lost themselves to the moment they nodded to their guest to take the solo. As he began playing the written solo something grabbed hold of him and he launched into an improvised solo that stunned himself as well as the band members. As the song came to a close the band members came over and said, "Whoa, that was incredible." Miffed and even frightened their guest packed up his instrument and said something like, "I don't know what happened but I don't want any part of it." He then returned to his secure world of sheet music, therefore forfeiting the untapped power and creativity of the unconscious.

He had touched the 'muse,' that unconscious power that is unleashed as he passed through the veil of the conscious mind. It is real, a part of our human expression. I now understand why the Scottish played bagpipes as they marched off to war and the Native Americans beat their war drums. This is all about accessing the primal forces of the unconscious.

For the Christian this movement into the unconscious is a sacred corridor to a deeper relationship with God as well as an unleashing of our fullest potential as disciples of Jesus. Yet we fear it, really fear it. Perhaps because at some instinctive level we know that as we pass through the veil of our conscious mind we might touch our true potential in Christ. Isn't that the words spoken by Nelson Mandela, that we do not fear our weakness but our greatness? Yes, what if you and I really grasped our true potential in Jesus?

We also fear the unconscious because as we pass through the veil there is the possibility of encountering our greatest shadow. Most remember the second of the *Stars Wars* trilogy when *Yoda* leads young *Luke* into the dark cave to face his greatest nemesis *Darth Vadar*, only to discover that his greatest nemesis is within him, that there is a *Darth Vadar* within himself that he must first embrace and transform. Yes, we fear the unknown for good reason. It is a frightening place, and so most of Christianity has sealed the doors to our greatest potential in Christ Jesus. We stay in our secure world of religion or rigidity, hoping we never have to pull back the veil and look into the depths of our power and our shadow. We keep God in an intellectual box or skirt the whole thing through good works. All this is about fear of who we really are, fear of what might be asked of us and fear of how our life must change. But for those who hear the call, who long to venture into the uncharted waters of the unconscious, God calls and gently leads them to still waters so they might drink deeply of God and begin to realize their full potential in Christ, which of course, means calming the conscious mind so the world of the unconscious, our spirit, our heart and soul are opened to the Holy Spirit.

For many, calming the mind and accessing the unconscious will be a new language, one that demands we retrain our mind or perhaps unlearn what we have learned. Most martial artists, musicians and athletes agree that no mind, the muse or the zone isn't grasped by conscious thought, but rather is accessed through letting go, trusting the process and living into the moment. Guitarists must be almost unaware of what their fingers are doing on the neck of the guitar and free of their fear of failure. In short, they have let go of their conscious thought and their need to control the outcome, which allows them to fully enter into the moment so that their unconscious can guide them. It is an exhilarating experience.

As Christians seeking to go deep we must unlearn what our mind has been doing for most of our life, and that is, being in control. In some ways, the conscious mind must become the servant of the unconscious and the power of the Holy Spirit. Like the guitarist who is almost unaware of the movements of his fingers on the fret board, we must let God move through our psyche without judgement or thought. Yes, our prayer phrase is necessary to open the doors and keep our conscious mind on track, but at some point the mantra must give way to the Holy Spirit and the unconscious.

In accessing the unconscious there is an element of time and patience that must be honored. A person just doesn't access the unconscious and launch a powerful spinning back kick their first day in a martial arts *dojo*. They must start with the basics, train, concentrate and practice for years before they are able to integrate body and spirit into a fluid expression. Neither does a person just grab a guitar and start ripping off incredible solos. There are years of practice, learning scales and playing lead lines. Overtime, the conscious training begins to seep into body and spirit, therefore creating a platform from which the musician can launch into playing by instinct. It is the same for the spiritual journey. Going deep with God is a way of life, not a simple shift in prayer techniques. Yes, sometimes the Holy Spirit just comes. These are great moments. Still, we have work to do. We must learn to quiet our mind, calm our inner self and allow the Holy Spirit to move through the many layers of our psyche. It is not an easy task.

Many years ago I was leading a group of men during morning sessions at a retreat center in Canada. On the last day I led them to a remote overlook for a two hour vision quest. I then asked them to find a quiet place so they might enter into a more sacred union with God and all creation. Two hours later, as I called them back, their faces told me of their frustration. Most of them couldn't calm their mind for more than minute before it began racing to the 'next thing.' Such is the way of the conscious mind and thought patterns that become habitual and even addictive. For most it was a long two hours as they fought a mental and spiritual battle that played out in their own minds.

Guys, it isn't going to be easy. With our lives so complex, developing an inner simplicity is no easy task and like the parable of the pearl of great price, there is a cost in gaining such a profound treasure. Certainly, God is not going to just hand over the hidden treasures of the kingdom to those who simply put in time just as you or I would not hand over our car keys to our eight year old child. There is a wisdom in the struggle, a maturing of the soul that comes with perseverance. If your mind wanders be merciful to yourself. This weaving of charisma and discipline is not mastered overnight. Be patient. God sees all. The quiet of God will descend. Your day of consolation will come. Your life will be forever changed.

Meditation Techniques

The simplest of tools is the mantra, a prayer phrase, such as scripture or even the name of Jesus spoken internally to calm the conscious mind and create a pathway for the Holy Spirit into our unconscious self. I cannot say enough about calming the mind and practicing the presence of God through mental prayer. I have since learned that the science and medical world has divided our brain waves into four categories, Beta, Alpha, Theta and Delta. Most of us, in our daily activities, operate when our brain is functioning in Beta, that is, 12-30 Hz, meaning 12-30 cycles per second. The higher numbers leaning more toward anxiety if not neurosis. The second state, the Alpha, 7.8-12 Hz, is a common state of the brain achieved during prayer, meditation and relaxation. Most agree that healing occurs when the brain is in Alpha. The third category of the brain waves is the Theta stage, usually noted between 4-7 cycles per second. I have read that those who are gifted in the world of meditation can achieve this state. Finally, the Delta state, .2-4 Hz, which often occurs in deep sleep. I find it no accident that the Spirit of God often visits men and women in the deep of the night when their conscious minds have fallen asleep and their brains are operating at a much slower wave length. This is a teaching. If we continually operate in Beta or in the conscious mind we hinder the power of God moving into the deeper levels of our psyche, therefore forfeiting the incredible love, power and healing God has for us. This is just where the adversary wants us, busy in mind and without desire to go deep with God. Why? He knows as Christians go deep the living waters of God will pour through that soul, bringing healing, passion, vision, and a greater desire for God. John 7:37-38 reads: "Let anyone who is thirsty come to me, and let anyone who believes in me drink. As the scripture has said, "Out of a believer's heart shall flow rivers of living waters.'" The Greek translation reads belly as opposed to heart. In most traditions the belly is considered the place of the soul.

If the way of contemplation is new to you, I suggest starting with your usual devotion and ending with inner silence. As you move into inner silence simply let the prayer phrase facilitate surrender and trust. I have found it helpful to let my whole self pray the prayer phrase or to 'become' the prayer phrase, mind, body, and soul. I often experience a sensation God's love and energy enfolding me as well as an awareness of moving deeper into my psyche and spirit.

Years ago I led group of non-denominational Christians into this simple technique. Afterwards many of them said it was like being slain in the Spirit. For those unfamiliar with the term slain in the spirit it is a phenomena that can occur while laying on of hands. The person receiving the prayers can sometimes fall into an unconscious spiritual sleep. I have witnessed this phenomena many times in the three to four years while offering evening healing services. As best as I can understand it seems the energy of God flowing though the person is more than their conscious mind can handle so the Holy Spirit seems to take them into an unconscious spiritual sleep for reasons that are beyond my understanding. I can only imagine that the Holy Spirit is working deep in their spirit and unconscious mind to bring healing they could not consciously handle.

The breath is also a powerful medium of the Holy Spirit. Just to breathe in while saying the name of Jesus can calm the mind, heal wounds and bring balance to our life. For those not accustomed to praying with the breath I take you to the story of Jesus appearing to the disciples after his resurrection in the Gospel of John 20: 21 Jesus said to them again, "Peace be with you. As the Father has sent me, so I send you." When he had said this, he breathed on them and said, "Receive the Holy Spirit."

Prayerful, deep breathing is a natural bodily function, and yet over time, as emotional trauma takes hold, as fear settles into our spirit, and as anger finds a dwelling place in the heart region, our breathing becomes shallow, or what is called, chest breathing. Chest breathing robs our body of necessary oxygen and psychologically reinforces the mindset of fear.

So how do we breathe correctly? Let's watch the experts and perhaps remember when you and I were once experts ourselves, when we were infants, before the world's trauma became our own. Our belly rose and fell naturally as oxygen-rich air filled our lungs. This is the singer's breath, the baby's breath or the meditational breath that we have to relearn to reap its benefits. Many traditions recommend breathing in, holding the breath for about five seconds then exhaling through the mouth. I recommend deep natural breaths and let it evolve naturally. It seems simple and it is, except for the fact that fear and trauma has robbed us of our ability to breath deeply. Most of us chest breathe, which is incorrect. The chest should remain still as our bellies rise and fall naturally.

There have been many stories of people experiencing healing with just the breath. Imagine using the breath with the name of Jesus. Recently, a friend who works as a chaplain at a hospital was called in to work with a patient suffering from anxiety and high blood pressure. As my friend sat down to speak with the patient the doctor rushed in and explained she needed blood pressure drugs immediately. The patient grew more anxious because they had severely reacted to such drugs in recent visits. My friend approached the doctor and asked for a few minutes alone with the patient before he administered the drugs. He consented. Five minutes later he returned to find her blood pressure back to normal. The doctor asked, "What did you do?"

My friend responded. "We simply worked with the breath and said a few prayers."

The breath is a powerful medium to calm the spirit and open pathways for the Spirit of the Lord to move through us in ways we can't imagine or perhaps even recognize. It is one of those key survival skills necessary to hold the presence of God within us throughout our day and take us deeper into the silence of God in our times of devotion.

Another useful tool is visualization, which is simply imagining the Spirit of God filling our entire being as we breath in and say the name of Jesus. The greatest of commandments, to love God with all of our heart, soul, mind and strength seems to work well with visualization. As I mentally repeat, "I shall love the Lord my God with all of my heart," I visualize God's love and my love flowing between us like an invisible river. I then do the same for my mind, soul and my entire body. It is a powerful tool.

Finally, the technique I have depended upon much through my crisis is simply walking through the woods while repeating my prayer phrase, sometimes praying in cadence with my steps. Walking can calm the mind, therefore creating the space for God to bring healing and peace.

Through any of these tools coupled with a surrendered heart and a desire to love God we can open ourselves to the quiet of God. As the mind stills, these tools give way to the presence of God that now seems to flow into our inmost being like a gentle healing river. This is a place where there are no words, only love, surrender and rest. It is a place where God's power, guidance and love are anchored within. It is good medicine. Over time, as practicing the presence of God becomes more natural, our daily activities of work, washing dishes, martial arts training or whatever seems to flow into a prayerful expression of body, mind and spirit. Only then can we begin to understand that all is meditation or practicing the presence of God.

The Wilderness

For many men the way of the lover, sitting quiet and working with the breath will be uncharted waters. Take heart, God has prepared a sanctuary for men who prefer the wild and untamed path into God's heart. It is the wilderness, the expansive tracks of mountains and deserts, the quiet meadows, the deep forest and open plains that speaks to our heart in ways that no other place can.

There have been studies beginning with the German physicist Professor W.O. Schumann of the Technical University of Munich who in 1952 predicted that the earth and the atmosphere resonated with an electrical frequency which was documented a couple years later in 1954. In the simplest of language the earth and its atmosphere resonates at a frequency of 7.83 cycles per second and the main frequency produced by these oscillations is very close to the frequency of the alpha rhythms of our brain. This should come as no surprise. The earth was created by God. God's Spirit is infused in all creation. We as humans are part of the creation, intimately woven into the cycles of the earth and the cosmos. We don't have to be mystics to get this. If we could stand on a busy street corner in a city for an hour then be placed beside a quiet stream in the wilderness we would easily grasp the sense of healing that vibrates from the earth.

The way of the wilderness is coded into the human psyche, speaking a primordial language that calls us back to our soul in ways this human-created life cannot. As we shed the business of our life and sit quiet in a deer blind in the dawn hours of an October morning something within stirs. As we stand by the clear waters of a mountain lake or fish a pristine river or watch a golden wheat field sway in the breeze something beyond words moves within us. It is the Spirit of God, present in all creation, speaking through the wilderness. We know this language even if we don't know it as God's. This is our birthright and our gift, that we belong to the wilderness just as the wilderness belongs to us. So God calls, awakens and asks us to remember that the wilderness is our sanctuary, the place we must return too to find ourselves and our God. It is the place of letting go, calling forth and new birth.

It doesn't have to be some wild trek in the Alaskan Bush. The wilderness is closer than you know. Years ago, I was doing a wilderness program for a retreat center in the Northwest. At the end of the week, as we were sharing what treasures we would take with us, a woman said, "Everything you have taught us is in my back yard." She understood the creative energy of God is in all landscapes, even the smallest tracks of land. So wherever you are I invite you to wake up as dawn breaks the eastern horizon and sit still as the sun rises. Talk to God, listen, be still and surrender. This is the way of the lover.

Inner Listening

Every wilderness requires unique survival skills. The desert, with its scorching heat, demands a shift toward a more nocturnal schedule, resting in the cool caves during the heat of the day to keep the body hydrated. The Rocky Mountains command a respect for lightening strikes, an understanding of dramatic weather shifts and a wisdom concerning the threat of hypothermia. Without these basic skills a person may find themself in a life threatening situation.

The wilderness of our psyche is no different, perhaps even more foreboding, calling forth skills that will insure our survival. Inner listening, developed and honed through the path of the lover, is one of those key survival skills. Be it known, there is no going into the wilderness of our psyche until we have learned to yield to the subtle movements of the Holy Spirit. It just won't happen. It would be like sending a small child into the Alaskan Wilderness. God will not do it. So we must learn the gentle way, that is, receptive to the subtle movements of the Holy Spirit.

Moving with the Spirit of God is an art and discipline that is cultivated over years. Each of us must find our own path and the understanding of the voice within. But there are some universal truths that must be heeded. Inner listening comes through surrender, creating inner silence and a genuine desire to do God's will. I call this practicing the presence of God. Paul names it prayer without ceasing. Jesus says it this way, "I am the vine and you are the branches. Apart form me you can do nothing." John 15:5

An example of this charisma and discipline is given to us in the Gospel of Mark, chapter 1 verse 32. The account reads: "That evening, at sundown, they brought to him all who were sick or possessed with demons. And the whole city was gathered around the door. And he cured many who were sick with various diseases, and cast out many demons; and he would not permit the demons to speak, because they knew him."

To understand the power of this story we have to realize this is the beginning of his ministry. Imagine the exhilaration of having the power of God working through us like that. Most of us would be caught up in the emotional wave. But let's follow the story and see how Jesus, who is both warrior and lover, reacts. The next verse reads, "In the morning, while it was still very dark, he got up and went out to a deserted place, and there he prayed." We need to key into the words, *morning, very dark, deserted* and *prayed.* This not about action nor the warrior but about longing, desire for union, prayer and communion with his Father. This is where the lovers of God will be, in the deserted places during the morning hours, pouring out their hearts to God, hoping to satiate the hunger that burns within them like fire.

It is in this solitude that Jesus receives not only his daily bread, meaning spiritual food, but the word of God as well, which is a lamp unto his feet. And now that he has touched his power source and heard the still small voice he is ready to put it into action. Verse 36 reads, "And Simon and his companions hunted for him. When they found him, they said to him, "Everyone is searching for you." Obviously, the disciples are caught up in the drama, hunting for Jesus to tell him the whole town is asking for him. But Jesus, who had just spent maybe an hour or two with his Father, has heard a different voice than that of this world and so Jesus, in true warrior energy, says, "Let us go on to the neighboring towns, so that I may proclaim the message there also; for that is why I came."

This is a powerful teaching into our soul and the integrating of lover and warrior. If we are to wield sacred power in this world we must seek out those deserted places in the early morning hours. Without being truly anchored in God through surrender and silence of soul and without being tuned to the still small voice of God we wield God's word around like a reckless warrior, speaking out of guidance, judging others, pursuing our dreams or following the way of this world.

Inner listening is not easy. We each must forge our own path and find our unique understanding of the voice of God within. There are no formulas, only truths that ebb and flow with the Spirit of God. Be prepared to miss the mark or confuse your desires with the will of God. It just comes with the job description. Humanity is messy stuff. Desires run deep. More than once I have let my passions run wild and put my own agenda on God, confusing my own inner thinking with the voice of God. Inner listening is grace, art and practice. We are not going to get it right all the time. Instead, seek God with everything you have and foster a desire to do God's will. Create inner silence. Rest in God often. Resist business of mind through practicing the presence of God through mental prayer. The voice of God will emerge.

A Holy Hour

There is a sacred rhythm of body and soul in the early dawn and in the dusk hour. These movement of creation often instill a sense of quieting that opens our inner self to God. There is also a more obscure movement of the Spirit of God that most deem a nuisance but in which lovers of God experience intense joy. It is the early A.M. hours, when most of the world around us sleeps and yet we find ourselves awake.

Night time is for lovers. God is a lover. Sometimes God comes in the dark hours of the night, seeking souls who long to share deep and passionate intimacy with the Divine Lover. Clark Strand writes, "I discovered that numerous priestly, monastic and rabbinic schedules still preserve the 'Hour of God' as a special time for meditation. Carthusian monks rise to pray during that time and consider it the corner stone of their Spirituality." The Center Post, fall 2010.

So, in the deep of the night, when others of our household may be asleep, we may find ourselves awake, seemingly alone with our thoughts, our busy life, our fears and our mind that longs to race to the *next thing*. But, if we pause long enough we might hear a voice, quiet, longing and tender, inviting us to spend intimate time with the son of God. Yes, the spirit of God comes knocking upon the doors of our heart. Whether we physically rise up, light a candle and immerse our self in quiet devotion to God or lay upon our backs under the covers and give ourselves to God we must see these sacred moments as a movement of the Spirit of God calling us into a passionate prayer experience.

There is a critical moment though. I have missed this moment more than once as I have allowed my mind to engage in the worries of this world. Soon, the energy of such thoughts take hold as my mind becomes like a locomotive racing down the track of useless thoughts. But there have been other times, many of them since my conversion in Lubbock, when my soul has heeded the invitation of the Holy Spirit. More than once, after intense prayers, I have experienced healing dreams or the presence of God moving through my soul during the few hours of sleep after my prayers.

Psalm 103
Healing the Wound

"Bless the Lord O my soul, and all that is within me,
bless God's holy name.
Bless the Lord, O my soul and do not forget all God's benefits.
Who forgives all your iniquity, who heals all your diseases.
Who redeems your life from the Pit, who crowns you with steadfast love and mercy, who satisfies you with good as long as you live so that your youth is renewed like the eagles." Psalm 103: 1-5

In the healing of our soul there is no greater medicine than the word of God spoken into our soul, that quiet, powerful and healing voice that breaks chains, heals wounds, imparts courage and satisfies the hunger. This is the fruit of our desire for God expressed through silent devotion.

As our inner silence falls upon us and our love for God is released from the chambers of our inner-most self the Spirit of God begins to flow into the parched areas of our psyche, bringing pain into healing, releasing traumatic memories and creating a new vision of who we are in Christ. Without any conscious effort on our part God is healing the disconnect between our conscious mind and the world of the unconscious where psychological scar tissue has protected us from the raw and traumatic emotions that have worked underground. This is the buried anger, painful memories, fear, rejection, shame and hatred that plague our spirit, holds us captive, wreaks havoc in our lives and even destroys our physical health.

Overtime, as we grow into the way of contemplation the hard facial lines that have suppressed toxic emotions for decades soften with peace. Here the eyes, once hard with judgment and anxiety, now mirror the love of God poured out through Jesus. This is the place where Psalm 103, that is, the forgiveness of our sins, the healing of our diseases and the renewing of our youth, is realized within us. It is powerful medicine for the body, mind and soul. Eventually, as the soul continues to evolve in God a soul beauty takes hold. Our very presence begins to emanate the love of God poured out through Jesus. It is a beauty that surpasses any of this world.

Shadow Lover

Well, what can I say about the shadow lover that isn't plainly expressed in my life prior to awakening the warrior. I had become all lover, some of it was good, some of it was operating through the wounded boy, which is shadow.

When the primal energy of the lover is expressed through the wounded boy a man is often emotionally passive, lacks boundaries and is easily wounded. He is the classic 'nice guy,' who navigates through life avoiding conflict. Conflict triggers the wound and so he learns to skirt it by being nice. His Jesus is probably nice as well. Been there, done that, as the saying goes.

Without firm boundaries words cut deep which can create a victim consciousness. They are unwilling to accept the fact that they are participating in their own wounding and so they live in a world that says, change so I will feel safe and loved.

If the warrior is not brought online the wounded boy gains a stronger hold upon his psyche, which leads to greater dysfunction and imbalance. In the marriage bed, he loves to get love. Yes, the lover working through the wounded boy is about getting love, whether that be in his journey with God, relationship with women, service to others or whatever.

Such men are in need of the primal energy of the warrior, which they have most likely rejected until one day they have no choice. That is a blessed day, even if it is painful.

Closing

Jesus said, "Martha, Martha, you are worried and distracted by many things, there is need of only one thing. Mary has chosen the better part which will not be taken from her." Luke 10:41 That one thing! The way of the lover is about that one thing that Jesus speaks of, which can only come through a life of surrender, devotion and prayer to God. Choosing this one thing is about practicing the presence of God throughout our day through mental prayer and breath, holding that inner calm and peace that creates a dwelling place for the Spirit of the Lord. That one thing! A person of God is about that one thing! They carry within them a simplicity of spirit and that inner calm that gives clarity to the warrior.

"Do you have that one thing?" I ask myself that question throughout my day. It is a good question.

12 MARY

A leader raised his right hand that held a drum stick and began to slowly pound the large round drum in a simple downbeat. Deep resonate bass tones echoed off the wall of this simple structure where nearly eighty men had gathered for a five day men's retreat. Soon other men, all with their own stories of faith, wounding, healing and hopes began spontaneously drumming, calling forth the sacred masculine. I glanced around at the many men, knowing there was a timelessness to this sacred act of men gathering to share their stories and discover their strength. The fact that it was Christian was a comfort but there was something beyond my Christianity at work here, a sacredness that seemed to transcend all traditions.

As the drumming intensified I closed my eyes, listening, praying and waiting. The drumming took me deeper as I gathered my courage and focused my intent before God. A couple of minutes passed. As I exhaled I began to drum softly to the pulsating rhythm of the other drums. I then slowly opened my eyes, embracing all that was before me. It was my way of saying to God, "I am in. Whatever you have waiting for me I welcome." There was a release of emotion. I drummed harder.

As the drumming continued I was keenly aware that I was simply a link in the great chain of countless men who had carried and will carry the masculine torch. A reverence touched my soul as I realized that I now stood on the shoulders of men who had kept the sacred masculine alive through their lives. Through their struggle for God, their pursuit of integrity, the agony of doing the right thing under difficult circumstances and by protecting and providing for their families, they had kept the masculine fire burning for men like myself. I was now daunted by the awesome responsibility to take my place in this chain and become the man God desired me to be, to find my masculine soul for the sake of my marriage and my daughter and daughter to be, for the kingdom of God, and for the many men who would come after me.

As the leaders arrived the drumming intensified. A few men danced. Electricity filled the air as the primal masculine descended. I took notice of the men, most engrossed in the drumming, others looking as if they had been dropped off among some savage tribe. I understood both reactions. For me, it was like standing with my brothers on the front lines of some cosmic war, calling forth the warrior energy while waiting to charge into battle. That was why I came, to fight, to slay my demons and to seek God in a new way. As the drumming receded then stopped, a reverent silence fell upon us. My five day retreat began.

After the introduction we broke into small groups. This would be my home group, the men I would journey with the next five days, speaking my truth, listening to their stories and reflecting upon my own. I would be challenged by these men as well as held accountable. I was grateful for each of them. To my delight I was reacquainted with Nathan whom I had met during the prior men's retreat.

Each day I put my heart into the processes, teachings and simple rituals of awakening the masculine. There were moments of healing and the discovery of the masculine strength within. During free time Nathan and I shared about our journey, struggles, and our passion to be a servant of God. It is a rare gift to find someone to walk the road to Emmaus with. Nathan was that man. I could speak openly about my understanding of God and the way of the Christian mystic without fear of judgment or agenda. I gained much wisdom as I listened to his own story of transformation.

During our free time we spoke about prayer. To my surprise he mentioned his relationship with Mary, the Mother of our Lord, asking if I ever prayed to her. I played down my surprise and disagreement with the casual words that went something like, "No, Nathan, I belong to God through Jesus," then let it go. He then explained that Mary's place in the kingdom of God is just below the Holy Spirit and that she is a powerful vessel of healing to God's people.

I was shocked Nathan prayed to Mary, which in my mind was taboo. I was committed to my love for God through Jesus Christ, that was that, there was no room for anyone or anything else. He continued sharing that many times while praying for people's healing he had experienced the presence of Mary, especially when praying for spiritual healing. I appreciated his wisdom, although his words didn't really stick. I needed God. I needed Jesus. That was that!

By the eve of the last day I sat on the perimeter of a celebration, wondering what I had missed during the four days and wishing God had broken me open further. Yes, I had gained much, more than I knew but I was looking for a lightening bolt from heaven to break this spiritual oppression I had come to live with. But it wasn't the case and I found myself shutting down in frustration. Nathan noticed and came over, "What is going on for you?"

"I haven't found what I am looking for."

"The dawn will break, Brian. Trust."

That night I collapsed in my bunk only to be awakened around two A.M. with a sense of spiritual alarm. I lay on my back, breathing deeply, saying my prayers but drowning in the darkness, as if being entangled in a web of confusing evil thoughts and psychological pain. It is an ugly place. Reality becomes distorted, hope vanishes like the morning dew and the promises of God seem just a faded memory.

I continued to breathe and pray but the darkness pressed further, hijacking my thoughts into the realm of darkness. A sense of terror engulfed me as Satan's grip tightened upon my soul. I was going down and I knew it. As the oppression grew and my prayers seemed powerless my mind somehow traced back to Nathan's words about Mary. I could hardly believe his words, but still there was this hope, and of all the people I have met along my path, I have trusted Nathan the most. It was then, in the dark of that New Mexico night, that I whispered the simplest and humblest of prayers, "Mary, if you can truly be my Spiritual Mother, I ask you to take me as your son."

Instantly, light shattered the darkness as the love of God channeled through the feminine soul of Mary gathered the broken fragments of my psyche and simply held me in perfect love. It was a Mother's Love, a Divine Mother's Love that I had never known before. Tears streamed down my cheeks as I simply surrendered.

"Mary," I whispered over and over.

"My son."

For most of the night I lay there in prayerful tears, embracing Mary as my mother. As first light broke the eastern horizon I jumped out of bed and walked silently in the desert landscape in the cool October morning, knowing for this reason I had come to this retreat, to find Mary and begin integrating her powerful feminine love into my masculine journey with God through Jesus. It was worth the agony.

My Love is Deeper

The road out of hell is long. Still the fragments of my life lay like scattered pieces of shard upon the landscape of my soul. Upon my return to Michigan I was walking the beach praying the rosary. It was one of those days when all seemed black, hope was like a distant dream and pain was my daily bread. As I walked the deserted October beach the lullaby of gentle waves comforted my soul. I cried out to Mary, asking how am I to endure and of course, why? Her reply came, "God is leading you to your primal masculine."

There are many roads we must travel as we journey toward God. There is the road of joy, which I have known for many years. There is the road of blessings, both spiritual and material. There is also the road of suffering. This was the road I was now called to walk. It was difficult. In the midst of my pain I wanted to choose God, to live from my heart and trust that someday I would find my primal masculine in Christ, that I would be whole again and reap the honor and joy of a battle well fought. But for now, the road was steep. The chasm between Jesus and I was so deep it was almost unbearable to think about. But Mary's words brought comfort, that my pain was not in vain, that someday I would be whole and that God was using this pain to bring me to my primal masculine.

As my walk ended I laboriously climbed the steps leading to the bank overlooking Lake Michigan. My heart was still heavy. It was the depth of my wounds that I feared. My soul had been scarred by evil and was now polluted with the toxic emotions of anger, hatred and fear. No matter what I did I simply couldn't break those emotions loose. They were so deeply lodged within me that I feared living with them the rest of my life, which seemed unbearable. In hopelessness I buried my face in my hands and whispered, "Mary, my wounds are so deep."

"My Love is deeper!" came her reply.

Doing the Work

I continued my emotional work with a Christian counsellor, speaking of my pain as well as owning my choices and character flaws that precipitated the crisis. It was so obvious that I had become all lover until the path nearly destroyed me, following the path of the Christian mystics, seeking to find their wisdom and way of life in a modern context. For me God had been not in the world of men, nor in the world of work or even marriage, but in deep aloneness, emptiness of self and the way of the ascetic mystic. Obviously, this doesn't work in marriage and it especially doesn't work with family. But it was the only path I knew and I was hell bent on making it work.

I was learning initiation is about integration, which meant letting go of the mystic's path at this time. I later spoke with a good friend who has travelled a similar path as I, seeking God through the lover until it nearly destroyed him also. As I was sharing my wisdom of integration he asked me, "What ever happened to Francis of Assisi, Brian?"

"I killed him, Bill. For the sake of my salvation and my marriage I killed him!"

"No!" he responded. "You have got to be kidding!" Bill responded, obviously struck with disbelief.

"No! I am not. I killed him!"

It was metaphorical language but with deep truth. I had to kill that part of me to become a man. There was no way around it. So yes, I killed the Francis in me, but with a hope that someday God would invite me back into the world of deep contemplation as an integrated, initiated man. It was a painful death though, a shattering of my golden globe that assured me I was special. I was now just another man among men seeking to support my family. It was no surprise I had rejected this world so deeply, not only because I passionately sought God but also because being a man didn't validate the boy. Being a man is about doing the right thing without the need for validation. It is about steadiness of spirit, not running off to the next adventure and the next and the next. It is about responsibility to God and others and being true to my true self, not about ascension of self, no matter how noble the cause may be.

About this time my therapist suggested I read, *'Wild at Heart,'* by John Eldridge. I stopped by a Christian bookstore and began reading that night. I barely put the book down. It was a road map into my masculinity and affirming the emerging truth that God was in marriage and fatherhood, that there was great honor in being a man among men, that I could be *'Wild at Heart'* as a family man or in the wilderness.

About six months after my men's rite of passage retreat I reread *'Wild at Heart.'* There was a small passage in the book stating the physical geography should match the geography of the soul. A spirit of truth leapt within me as I read those words. The next morning while walking the white pine forest along the Boardman River, the whisper of God spoke into my heart, "Let's go back to the Grand Canyon."

I returned home filled with excitement. "Kathryn, God is calling me back to the Grand Canyon."

"What?"

I repeated the statement.

"I don't know if I can support that. Your path of deep quiet and alone time nearly burned you up. I don't believe it would be healthy for you to go back to a lifestyle that brought you so far down. At least not yet."

After several days of discernment I booked a red-eye flight then arranged a back country route that demanded previous experience in the Canyon.

Arrows

I was ready except for one last detail with a friend with whom I had a difficult verbal exchange with. Wanting to keep my emotions in front of me I asked if we could meet before I left for the Canyon. He agreed.

I had journeyed with this man for nearly a year. He knew the gritty details of my crisis and my hopes to someday create a program for men, which he supported. But at a meeting with clergy and other minsters he questioned my qualifications to someday lead men. It was a fair question, which I answered, an answer that eased his concerns but the fact that he supported me in private then questioned me among his peers caused a reaction of anger.

I began the conversation about my upcoming trip to the Canyon and wanting to be clear with him before I journeyed into the wilderness. I then said, "I've got to start out with saying that I know that I carry a father wound, a wound of rejection that is easily triggered so when you asked me that question I had a reaction of anger, mostly because it triggered my own fear of rejection but also because I wasn't certain why you were asking me in front of your peers."

For a moment there was silence, not a holy silence but an ugly silence as his face twitched and his lips tightened. I could see the unconscious wound slithering into his conscious mind, forming thoughts and battle strategies. *Oh God,* I thought. He immediately launched into a discourse that my passion for men's work was not a calling but just a path for my own transformation. To be amiable I agreed that was a possibility but stuck to my truth that someday God was calling me to gather men and invite them into the wilderness as well as on a journey of transformation. When he realized I wasn't going to budge to his way of thinking his anger flared further.

"Why are you going down to the Grand Canyon anyway?"

"Because I am called."

"No, it is because you cannot accept that God is asking to you to go back to your wife and daughter and live a simple existence. That is your problem. You are running from what God wants of you. You think you have a calling on your life. Your calling is to be married and raise children. Just accept it."

I knew where this was coming from, straight from the unconscious where evil dwells. It was an attack pure and simple on the very day before I was to leave for the Grand Canyon. In retrospect I should have excused myself right there and walked out but I played into the moment, which is a foolish thing to do, saying, "Excuse me, but how do you know what God is calling me to do? You know so little of my life." I then went on to speak about some of my awakenings in the wilderness to assure him that I was authentically called by God. As I finished he snapped back at me, "Everything you told me is from the devil. You have been deceived. Go home. Go live a simple existence with your family. Quit running."

I then stood up walked out of his office.

In the journey toward God, attacks will come, so often preceding or following a movement of God in our lives. A seasoned warrior is ready to draw his sword, meaning the word of God, or place his shield up to deflect the attack. To engage in this battle is to play into the enemies' scheme which robs us of our power and leaves us with a residue of heaviness in our soul.

The Canyon

It was strange being back in the wilderness. I walked timidly down the trail, questioning my wilderness savvy that had come so easily before the crisis. Some part of me even feared being alone in the wilderness. With so much disharmony in my soul I feared I would draw calamity to myself. The thought of a cougar attack seemed more possible as did a back country injury on a deserted route. I even questioned my choice of routes, wondering why I didn't choose a more travelled route as opposed to a route in which ropes were suggested but not necessary.

We create our own reality. To live into fear is to invite the presence of darkness and a spirit of chaos. To live into our wounds is to welcome relationships that are wounding and play into the victim. God meets us where we are, giving us free will that is played out through our thinking and our choices, all which have consequences and ramifications, both in the spiritual realm in the physical world. I couldn't have been more aware of this truth as I stumbled over small rocks and fretted about route finding.

The days were long. The trail moved slowly as I spoke my prayers, mostly the Jesus prayer and the rosary. Each night I collapsed on the desert floor beneath a starry sky, thankful for the day and the opportunity to continue my path of healing. About the third day, God whispered a word into my heart, inviting me to pray the rosary through-out the day with the knowing that Mary would carry me through the fire. I understood this meant facing darkness at some level, although I hardly seemed ready. But I began to pray like a warrior, speaking the Hail Mary non stop throughout the day.

The Canyon was spectacular, affording incredible views of endless red rock formations that jagged and spiraled in the desert. The trail was void of other travelers, which now seemed a delight. I kept at my prayer, sometimes speaking in cadence with my footsteps.

By early evening I descended into a wash with narrow rock walls around ten to fifteen feet high on each side. As I moved through the sandy trail I caught sight of fresh cougar tracks. My heart jumped.

Immediately I stopped, then searched the narrow ledges where a cat might perch. I slowly bent down, and grabbed a good sized rock for each hand. I would have preferred a strong walking stick but those just aren't available in the Canyon. If a confrontation came, rocks would have to do.

I slowly made my way through the wash, turning around every third or fourth step to protect my vulnerable backside, which is where a cougar is most likely to strike. A part of me wanted to walk fast through this narrow wash but that would have been foolish, signaling weakness to a predator. Fifteen minutes later I made it through the wash without sight or sense of any cougar. I kept my rocks in hand until arriving at my designated campsite. With a sense of relief I dropped my rocks, as I let my pack slide off my shoulders.

As I set up camp, choosing to sleep in my tent for safety reasons, a growing sense of an evil presence came over me. In my past this wouldn't have bothered me but I was still so fractured that I didn't have the confidence needed to stand against an evil presence. As I was pondering what to do a raven landed on a rock just feet away. I knew it was begging for food but still its presence really bothered me. It was not a good sign and in my mythology, ravens are a symbol of the underworld. I grabbed a few small stones and tossed it at the bird that flew fifteen feet away and then returned.

This went on for fifteen minutes or so, throwing stones to scare off the raven only to have it come back to beg for a hand out. But it wasn't the raven that bothered me but the growing evil that was pressing into my psyche. The raven was only a symbol, harmless of itself but growing in power through my fear. After ten minutes of psychological warfare and even though I was exhausted and even though the trail was to lead down a steep canyon wall in which ropes were recommended, I packed my belongings in a hurry and moved on, foolishly thinking I could outrun the evil presence. I traversed the steep canyon wall searching for where the trail descended a hundred feet into the wash below but for some reason I couldn't see any trail markings that lead me into the wash. I spent half an hour, searching back and forth. Finally, I gave up and went back to my old campsite where the raven was waiting for me. The raven caused another reaction of fear. With only minutes of daylight remaining I then turned around a second time in search of that trail. Again I was encumbered with my inability to find where the trail descended.

"Okay God, let's go back. There is no running."

I returned to the campsite and set up my tent. I crawled inside my tent and began my night time prayers. I decided to pray as much as I could through the night, knowing I needed to be connected to God, Jesus and Mary.

An hour passed, maybe two. Several times my head nodded as I drifted into a fitful sleep. Each time though I shook it off and resumed my prayers. Sometime later I fell into a deep sleep. When I awoke I felt a spirit of evil pressing upon me. It was strong, too strong. I tried to pray but to no avail. Spiritual panic began to creep into my psyche as I felt my soul descending into darkness, confusion and even damnation. I could feel the knowledge of God slipping from my psyche. It was weird. An overwhelming fear and sense that I was about to be separated from God forever gripped my soul. The madding confusion grew. The darkness intensified. I was losing the battle.

I cannot be certain how long this went on. Reality becomes distorted in the spiritual realm. I only knew sheer desperation came over me. With everything I had I cried out, "Mary, I don't want to die," over and over.

Soon in a dream, in the spirit realm, or with my naked eyes I cannot be certain, I only knew she came, standing before me, emanating incredible love and power. There was unspeakable beauty in her face as she simply gazed upon me. Somehow the robes around her chest seemed to open and her heart became visible to my sight. As I gazed upon her heart that was full of fire and divine love she simply said, "You live in my heart!"

In that instant she was gone, leaving me wide open, crying tears of love and relief, knowing I was safe in the heart of Mary.

13 THE WILD MAN

In the book, *Iron John,* written by Robert Bly, we are introduced to a king in dialogue with an adventurer. The adventurer inquires about possible quests. The king mentions a nearby forest in which men have been disappearing and so the adventurer and his dog set out to the forest. The young man and his dog explore the forest until they come to a pond. As they approach the pond a hand reaches up and grabs the dog. The adventurer responds, "This must be the place." The adventurer wisely leaves and gathers three or four other men with buckets and returns to the pond where they begin bucketing out the water. Over time, as they continue to bucket out the water, which represents the unconscious, they find a wild hairy man laying on the bottom. The Wild Man!

This story, first complied by the Grimm brothers around 1820, is rich with ritual, archetypes and the crucial elements of transformation. Yet it is much older. Almost 1800 years prior, Jesus ventures into the wilderness to find a wild man baptizing people in the Jordan River.

Take a moment and ponder this powerful drama which marks the emergence of Jesus into his power and mission. There is wilderness, the wild man, water and the blessing from God, woven together into a transformative and powerful experience. These elements of ritual are ancient and so deeply rooted in the human psyche that we cannot separate them from our own Christian journey. In fact, this moment is the conception of Christianity, and yet sadly, Christianity has seemingly done everything in its power to bind the wild man energy of Jesus and John the Baptist. For good reason. It is powerful and dangerous stuff.

Imagine seminarians being sent into the wilderness for ten days with nothing but themselves, simple provisions and their yearning for God. Imagine them facing their own humanity, weakness and confronting their personal demons. I can only imagine their Christianity would deepen. I can only imagine the the church would begin to shift toward a Christianity that fostered personal transformation.

What have we done to this profound rite of passage? Obviously, we have tamed it, intellectualized it, and confined it to knowing the Bible or administering the sacraments. It is no accident Jesus side-stepped the power structure of the temple to claim his power and mission.

So, is there wilderness in your life? I mean true wilderness, the unknown, risk and even a sense of trepidation. Is there mission and power? Do you carry God's blessing within you or are you left wondering who you really are? And what about the wild man? Is he bound by your fear or smothered by your Christianity? Perhaps it is time to unleash this part of your psyche, to meet Jesus and John in your own inner wilderness and discover your power and mission?

Transformation

In Matthew 14: 22, Mark 6:45 and John 6:16 Jesus sends his disciples rowing into the night and against the waves. In this account, "Into the night" is metaphorically a journey into our unconscious fears, which is true wilderness. "Against the waves" is symbolic of the struggle against the unconscious forces that drives our addictive, isolating, passive, abusive, fearful, violent, and hateful actions. Anyone who has begun a journey of recovery will tell you there are many layers of their dysfunction. Wounds run deep and seemingly come at us over and over and over like relentless waves.

Sending the disciples into the night and against the waves is well planned adventure by the Lord, significant in the fact that as we battle the layers of shame, rejection, emotional distance or addictive behaviors and struggle against dark spiritual forces within and without we can expect an endless assaults of waves and wind that seem to impede our progress. This is the sacred path of transformation and the design of God, that our spiritual journey is one that is beset with waves and impeded progress, knowing there is a wisdom in the struggle, a maturing of our soul and an anchoring of our truths as we struggle and struggle and struggle against the layers of our core issues that separate us from God and our true self. In short, Jesus isn't going to make this easy. He is too wise a Master to simply hand over the primal energies of God without a difficult and serious fight that can last for years if not a life time.

A Circle of Men

In the story of *Iron John* the men bucket out the water to reach the bottom of the pond where the wild and hairy man is laying. In the Gospel stories just mentioned Jesus sends his disciples on a seemingly impossible task. In both stories, the fact that men are gathered in a sacred quest is important. The truth is, we can't do this work alone. We need brothers to help us row into the night or bucket out our water. We need men to be strength when we cannot find it ourselves. We need men to metaphorically hold up the mirror so we can see our shadow, men who love us enough and are strong enough to ask the tough question and say, "Bullshit!" Excuse the colorful metaphor on this one but I believe it is needed here! Most often you and I cannot see our own shadow. That is just the way it is. We operate out of what we know and what has become familiar, not knowing that our familiar actions, thoughts, or ideology has emerged out of shadow, brokenness or dysfunction. That is why we need a safe but challenging circle to do our work! Yes, we need each other! This is one of the great movements in a man's life, the shedding of that boyish mentality that he is a hero and can go it alone.

Accessing the Wild Man

In the recent remake of the movie *Robin Hood*, starring Russel Crowe, the essence of the wild man is well captured during the final battle in which Robin *Longstride* is pitted against his nemesis *Sir Godfrey*. To set the scene, Robin *Longstride* believes *Godfrey* has just killed his love and so he attacks *Godfrey* with vengeance. The scene is well done and intense. During their fight *Godfrey* forces Robin *Longstride* into the English channel where he is pushed under and trapped by French ships. Satisfied, *Godfrey* then moves on. Just as death seems eminent *Longstride* explodes out of the water with a wild look in his eyes and his sword pulled back.

It is a classic wild-man scene with all the crucial ingredients, that is, water, the sword, meaning the warrior within all of us, and a situation in which the only way out is to dig deeper and call forth that raw primal masculine that lives inside of you and me.

About a year after my crisis I spoke with a client about men's work. He ended the conversation with an invitation to his men's group, which met every other week for three hours. I thanked him for his invitation but left it at that, thinking, *three hours, what in the world can men do for three hours together?* He pursued me, once a month or so, asking how I was doing and if I were interested. Each time I refused. The fact that it wasn't rooted in the Christian tradition scared me off. I had enough spiritual problems of my own. I didn't want to go deep with men who weren't on the same path as I. But he persisted and one night he called and said, "Brian, we are meeting at my house tomorrow night, come on over. If you don't like what you see you can leave at anytime."

It was a fair enough offer. Kathryn and I spoke about it. She encouraged me to go. I called Greg back and said I would be there. We gathered at 7:00 in the evening, formed a circle and began calling in the masculine energies. As we did a sense of reverence came over my soul, the same reverence that I had experienced during my first two men's retreats. There was also an electricity in the air;

these men were gathered to do their work, to own what needs to be owned, to make changes and to face shadow. As the evening progressed and the processes deepened I chose to do my work, to cut into my wounds, face my shame, and release my anger. As I did, the primal masculine surged through my spirit. It was exhilarating. As my process ended a man looked up and said, "Brian, your work is my work."

Your work is my work! That is the way of men's work, that when a man chooses to go deep and work, everyone in the circle benefits. As I left the meeting a surge of God, creativity and renewal flowed through my being. This is the fruit of facing shadow and bringing it to the light. It is exhilarating, like climbing a mountain or skiing untracked powder back in Steamboat.

The men's group continually invited me to enroll in their weekend training session entitled, New Warrior Training Adventure (NWTA). Having been through a five-day men's rite of passage I deflected the offer many times. They persisted. Sometime later, while facilitating a prayer session for men at a conference a man approached me and asked if I had ever attended the NWTA. I explained that I had not but the group I was involved with is encouraging me to go. He said, "I went through the weekend several months ago. It was the most difficult thing I have done in a long time. I strongly recommend it." When such invitations come around a second time I can be certain it is a God thing.

A week before my NWTA while sitting in prayer, God's voice spoke into my heart, "There are some things waiting for you down there." I breathed deeply, knowing God was going to cut into my heart. I was going for that reason, not just to get through the weekend, but to really do the weekend, to let God cut cleanly so that radical changes might take place in my life.

For the record and for those who choose to Google New Warrior Training Adventure you will discover that it is sponsored by the Mankind Project, (MKP). You will also find that some Christian organizations label MKP a cult and you can find all kinds of crazy things about it on the web. I can only speak my truth. I have never worked with such an incredible organization that honors individuality, practices integrity and offers such a committed program to support and honor men of all backgrounds. And I would not be the man I am without sharing the journey with them.

With that said, I arrived at the weekend with my inner sword drawn and ready for battle. From the start, it was obvious the thirty facilitators for us thirty-five participants came with their swords drawn also. I liked it. There was an element of risk, awakening the masculine and facing shadow. Throughout each process I opened myself to God and whatever lesson awaited me. There were tears of owning my poor choices in my search for God, there was a grief that I had injured my body over the years. By Saturday afternoon, the more intense processes began. I watched a couple of men who choose to cut deeply and face their core issues. It was daunting, perhaps even frightening. As I watched a strange dryness fell upon me. *Was I ready?* I wasn't sure. I feared going through the process and not getting into my guts. As a man finished his process they called for the next man. There was silence. I glanced around; nobody seemed eager. Some looked numb. I stepped forward. *Okay God. This is it,* I thought. As I took another step toward the facilitator and expressed my intent, the Spirit of God seemed to slice into my wounds. I breathed deeply. I thought to myself, *I came for this reason. I am only going to be here once. I am not going to hold back.*

Just as we were to begin the process I called stop.

"What is wrong?" my facilitator asked?

I would like to invite one of the leaders into this circle to work with me. Is that okay?"

They talked among themselves then replied, "Usually the leaders that oversee the weekend don't do this work but if it is important to you we can ask."

I was drawn to this man from the start. He was a wild card, the kind of guy you might expect to find in a bar or perhaps in the fishing industry in Alaska. He was full of life, though, and possessed an expression of the wild masculine that I desperately needed. He agreed.

As he stepped into the circle our eyes locked. I could see the wild masculine flashing like fire in his eyes. There was also a sense of playfulness that seemed to say, 'So you wanted to work with me, huh? Let's see what you've got!'

He asked me my core issue.

"SHAME!" I replied.

The process began. I engaged. I could feel my well-placed defense mechanisms crumbling as the skill of this facilitator and the hand of God began slicing into my wounds, emotionally stripping me to a raw nakedness. The process intensified. I struggled. The facilitator pushed back then cut deeper. There was a psychological ripping, wounds began to bleed and emotions rose to the surface. Reality and time seemed to blur as the past and the present blended into one cosmically charged moment. It was then the primal rage of the child and the pain of the last recent years released into an explosion of pain and anguish. My inner veil had been ripped in two. Psychological chains were breaking. I lashed out in anger then curled and wept out the grief, shame and fear that had worked underground throughout my life. It was painful. It was healing.

As the process ended a sacred calm fell upon me. I knew. I had faced what I had feared the most and now it was losing power over me. I stepped out of the circle to be with an elder. For a few moments we just sat together. He then brought me a glass of water and asked, "How are you?" Even though my body was spent of every ounce of physical strength I simply nodded that I was good because there were no words to say. I knew something powerful and transcendent had just transpired. There was no denying it. In the heat of the struggle and in the releasing of the primal rage of the child I had been taken deep into the unconscious world of my psyche, to the place of my fears and beyond, to the place of the wild man.

14 INTEGRATION

The first day my daughter and I attended a karate class we were taught a simple rising block from a well grounded horse stance. As I practiced the move over and over and as my thighs began to burn the instructor came behind each student and gave a front snap kick to the back of their legs just behind the knees. Compassionately, the instructor grabbed the uniform of those who were about to topple over due to a weak stance.

The lesson was clear, stay centered and grounded in my stance otherwise I am going down. For me, it wasn't just about the horse stance. It was a teaching about life; a balanced person is hard to take down. That is what it means to be initiated, integrated and live into our king energy. The king holds the warrior, the lover and the seer in balance. This is crucial. Too much warrior, lover or seer, and God will most likely give us a good *snap kick* to get our attention. A wise person listens, understands and pushes through to the root of the issue. A foolish man recklessly forges onward. We all know the consequences of not heeding one of God's snap kicks.

Family

By the end of my NWTA weekend profound changes had taken place within me. My heart burned to return home and bring this new energy and love into my family. I said farewell to the men whom I had journeyed with on the weekend, then sought out the man who had worked with me on my core issues. I cried as I stared into his eyes with gratitude and strength, unable to really express what this moment meant for me in my journey toward Christ, wholeness and healing.

That night Kathryn kept our daughters up so I could hug them good night. It was a deep embrace. For the first time in my life, I truly felt like a father and a husband, committed, passionate and with a reservoir of strength to give. I now understood the paradox of being true to myself yet given over to those that I love. For so many years, I had wrestled with this paradox of the wilderness, marriage, my relationship with God, fatherhood and a sense of calling on my life. Until now they had competed for space within my psyche but as God had taken me through the weekend and as the Spirit ripped through the layers of the false self a new expression of the inner man emerged, giving me the psychic space to hold opposites.

I told Kathryn I needed to reclaim my family name of Meagher. Upon our marriage we had agreed to take the name Christian, symbolically meaning a new creation in Christ. But just for the record, I had long since left my family name. When I had met Kathryn at Holden she had asked me my name, and I responded, "Brian."

"Brian what?" she asked.

"Just Brian."

She laughed and persisted in asking but I held fast. In my search for God and to emulate the mystics of the church, that is, John of the Cross, Francis of Assisi, Theresa of Avila and so on, I had run from my humanity into God, which of course meant running from my family of origin. I believed that if I climbed the spiritual ladder far enough I would never have to face the shame that I carried and so I ran. But that had now changed. The way of initiation and integration were working within me. I now saw greatness in my humanity and in my lineage. I could no longer be just Brian, nor Brian Christian but Brian Christian Meagher, son of God and son of Thomas and Alberta Meagher, married to Kathryn and father to Lydia and Sophia. It was a deep and profound shift for me, the beginning of my journey of integrating son of God and son of earth.

This weaving of opposites is a profound truth, reflected in the life of Jesus, nature and in other cultures. In short, truth needs compassion, earth needs heaven, the warrior needs the lover and humility must be coupled power. Richard Rohr said, "An initiated man can hold opposites." I didn't get this until God began to initiate me into a mature masculine psyche, grasping the concepts that an initiated man is powerless yet filled with God's power, wounded yet a warrior, compassionate yet speaks his truth, true to himself yet given over to those he loves.

The teachings of Jesus reflect the paradox of opposites as well, "In this world but not of it. The first shall be last and the last shall be first. If you want to find your life, lose it." The be-attitudes, considered a road map to the kingdom of God, is all about paradox and opposites. The cross is the ultimate symbol of opposites, grasped by those who can understand the mercy of God through the suffering of God's Beloved.

Jesus responding to the woman caught in adultery is paradox in action. The men who were seeking to stone her were uninitiated men, men who had not touched their own humanity, men who only sought the law without compassion, men who had projected their own self-hatred and condemnation upon this woman. Jesus rips their world into shreds, asking them, "Let anyone among you who is without sin be the first to throw a stone at her." John 8:7 Jesus is piercing their self-righteous spirit and unconscious hatred, calling them to consciousness by inviting them to embrace their own humanity. But he is not done yet. Jesus then turns to the woman with the words, "Neither do I condemn you. Go and sin no more," offering the woman compassion with truth. Those two statements spoken by Jesus reflect the balance of opposites, meaning one without the other is only a half-truth and half-truths lead to imbalance, addiction, obsessive thinking, rigidity and so on.

The relationship of opposites is also reflected in the Yin/Yang symbol. The symbol is circular and divided by a curved line which separates equal portions of black and white. The wisdom of integration is depicted by a smaller circle of white in the black section and vice versa. This represents the relationship of opposites which is necessary for wholeness and balance in our lives and in the universe, meaning earth needs heaven, day needs night, truth needs mercy, the masculine needs the feminine, the lover needs the warrior and so on.

Unguarded

Certainly the adversary prowls around like a lion, ready to devour the work of God, especially after the soul makes great leaps. This is probably the most vulnerable time, before our new truth has been anchored and integrated into our daily life. This is the responsibility of the inner warrior, to be alert, to defend the sacred and to recognize the advances of the enemy and counter with faith, strength and truth.

Our adversary is a cunning snake and will attack us in our weakest moment and in our deepest wounds, hoping to create discord within our soul and drive a wedge between us and God. It is war. We need to be on our guard. As Paul says in Ephesians 6:12 "For our struggle is not against enemies of blood and flesh, but against the rulers, against the authorities, against the cosmic powers of this present darkness, against the spiritual forces of evil in heavenly places." And so it is our responsibility to strip the enemy of his power in our lives by being true to God, placing our trust in God, practicing the presence of God, being grounded in scripture and facing our shadow.

About six weeks after my NWTA, Kathryn and I had an argument, about what, I can't even tell you and compared to other couples who really seem to argue and raise voices it was insignificant, perhaps a 1.5 on the rector scale as arguments go. But there was still a wounded and injured boy within me that was healing. In the heat of the moment I was caught off guard as old business about my crisis was dredged up into the present moment, thrusting me back to a time of great pain as well as emotional and spiritual instability. By the end of the argument it felt as if a psychological lance had been thrust into my heart, tearing through the healed layers of the wound, causing an avalanche of fear, shame and anger within me. As I drove to the job site, I called upon God and the primal masculine; but the toxic emotions kept cascading within me, taking me farther into the abyss and farther into the enemy's territory. By the time I reached the job site Kathryn called and sought to reconcile our differences but it was too late, the damage had been done.

As I hung up the phone the wild-man energy drained from my psyche and the spiritual oppression I had fought so hard to overcome gained power. I placed the phone down and then pressed on the gas pedal to continue the last mile to work. Not realizing my truck was in reverse the truck shot backwards. I slammed on the brakes then dropped my head on the steering wheel. The message was clear. I had collapsed, given into old patterns and fed the wound. I had played right into the enemy's scheme and knew it.

I lost my heart that day as depression swept over my soul, wondering if I could ever sustain a vibrant relationship with God in this world and in marriage. It wasn't about Kathryn, though, or about our argument, but about my inability to defend my sacred boundaries during conflict and trust God through conflict.

For the next several weeks I simply existed, without a heart, much like the Tin Man in *The Wizard of Oz*. I saw the effects of my failing ripple through my family and especially in my children who seemed to have an ultra-sensitive radar into their parents inner health. I feared the gains from my NWTA had completely drained from my soul, that for a brief moment I had tasted the primal masculine only to give it away. I had failed myself, the primal masculine and my God again and was now suffering the consequences of my choices.

By late June I journeyed back to Colorado for my annual solo in the mountains. I trekked into the Eagles' Nest Wilderness, set up camp and began to pray. There wasn't much juice in my prayers as I gave myself over to despair, but I prayed, one day, two and into the fifth day. There were glimmers of hope but nothing sustainable for me to go away with. The last night I prayed almost through the night, sleeping just a few hours before daybreak. As I woke in the early dawn and continued my prayers the whisper of God spoke one phrase, "I will open a door that no one can shut."

A Band of Warriors

I returned home with half a heart that was mingled with some hope. More than once I whispered in prayer, "You have asked to much of me God. I don't have it. I just can't climb out of this abyss."

"You'll see," came God's reply.

I received a call from my brothers about the next meeting. I gave a noncommittal answer. This is shadow at work, whose mission is to isolate, destroy and speak the lie that all is lost. Bound by pain, I was in shadow and living into this lie. Greg called, asking if I needed a ride to the meeting. I didn't want to go and probably would not have except the leader of that meeting arranged for us to take a large boat onto Traverse Bay where our meeting would be held.

Eight wild guys climbed aboard this boat as we set course for the waters on the far side of the bay. We anchored, called in the sacred masculine and began our meeting. During break some men dove off the cabin into the clear waters of Traverse Bay, screaming with delight as their heads popped up for air. God prodded, "Jump!" I hesitated. God prodded again, "JUMP!" I hesitated. God prodded a third time. I climbed on the railing, looked out on the vast waters of the bay and into the pristine waters below me. I whispered the simplest of prayers, calling forth the wild man then dove into Traverse Bay. The cool water washed over my body as I dove deep, cleansing me of my grief and the sense of loss. As I came up for air, I squealed with delight. I knew. From the depths of my psyche the wild man was emerging.

That night I learned the truth of why Peter jumped out of the boat to meet his Lord on the shores after Peter denied him three times. Peter knew in his soul two core truths, that the love of God through Jesus does not wax and wane with our failings or successes and that in Christ nothing is lost forever, not his love for Jesus nor his soul. When these truths are crystalized within us, we have a confidence that allows us to jump out of our boat and swim to our Master who is waiting with open heart, cooking our breakfast and ready to restore us to wholeness and integrity of self, no matter what we have done or how far we have fallen.

There is a great scene in the movie, *The Two Towers,* the second movie in *The Lord of the Rings* trilogy. This scene comes near the end at the battle of Helmsdeep which has been long and hard. The fortress is about to be breached. King Theoden of Rohan looks hopelessly at the gate that is being pushed through by the enemy and resigns to defeat. In the following scenes King Theoden's eyes grow vacant. Arigorn asks him a couple of questions about saving the women but he doesn't respond.

This is a profound scene as it depicts the truth that when the inner masculine crumbles and when the fight drains from our spirit, we can be certain the circumstances of our lives will crumble also. This is important. The battle is won or lost in our spirits not in the circumstances of our lives. The moment our inner warrior collapses is the moment the gates of our inner sanctuary will be breached. This is the moment we emotionally divorce our spouse even if our words don't say it. This is the moment when our heart is broken and when we choose to believe the lie that all is lost. I have seen pastors taken down by people in their churches who wield unconscious negative energy. I have watched these pastors wane through the battle until they simply throw up the white flag and let themselves be taken down. This is just what the enemy wants, to destroy our fight until we throw up the white flag upon our dreams, our marriage and our quest for the kingdom of God. There is nothing honorable about this moment.

In the movie, as the scene unfolds, Arigorn, who holds king energy, goes inward for a brief moment, calling upon the primal masculine. As he finds his true self he invites King Theoden to ride out and meet the enemy. It is a powerful scene and the first time I saw this scene God whispered into my heart, "That is a king!"

King Theoden is then swept up into the strength of Arigorn and rediscovers his king energy. This transformational moment portrays another spiritual truth, that is, if you and I live into our masculine heart we unconsciously give men permission to do the same. Yes, if you and I live into our primal masculine many will follow, many will follow.

Mentors

In the world of men, we are called to be mentors, to be the strong masculine for those who can't seem to find it within themselves at the time. But we cannot give what we do not have. If these primal energies are not awakened and operating within us we cannot lead another man to his strength. We can speak about the warrior, quote scripture and tell of God's love but our words will not carry transformational power.

I found this true as I plugged into my men's group and continued with my own work as well as facilitating other men through their own process. As we met in the circle and held our ceremonial staff, that wild masculine that had been awakened and reborn rose up within me, giving me the grace and skill to cut into another's wounded boy and call forth his primal masculine.

Masculinity bestows masculinity, but we cannot give what we don't have. For this reason, as God awakens the masculine within us, we have a responsibility to be that mentor or bridge to the masculine for other men or boys. It doesn't matter what arena we choose to work through, sports, outdoor skills, academics, church, or work we are called to be mentors, to empower others and to believe in them, which often comes with few words and a steady spirit. This isn't about doing their work for them or giving them some discourse on the meaning of life but simply being there, giving them your confidence through mistakes and failures.

I have learned through my own journey that a man needs two things when he is in the abyss. First, his pain needs to be validated. That equates to a couple of questions, such as, what is going on? Give me the core issues. If a man is ready to open up, he will speak. Just a note, the question, *give me the core issues* is a boundary statement that tells a man he doesn't have permission to ramble for hours about his crisis. The second thing a man needs is the primal masculine, that raw power of God that never quits and demands that we get up when we would rather lay in our wounds and die. It may come as a simple phrase, said with conviction and intense eye contact, such as, "You are going to get through this!" More is communicated in that moment than we will ever know.

Recently, I was asked to work with a young man who had his heart broken by the woman of his dreams. It was a *dejavu* moment, like looking into myself nearly twenty-nine years ago. For nearly an hour, he went on and on about this young woman and his pain. He was all mush. Several times I tried to pull him into the strength he knew as a high school football player but he wouldn't go there. He wanted only his pain, the role of the victim and the loss of his goddess. (Just a side note here, women who break our hearts often grow into a goddess-like figures.) I felt myself getting drained, which is a sure sign this wasn't a God thing. Finally I said, "Let's go outside." I grabbed my staff that I use when working with men, drew a circle in the ground and said, "If you really want to do some real work about this issue, I mean cut the bullshit, then step inside this circle and give it to me from your guts."

To my surprise he walked into the circle and grabbed the staff with a sense of strength. It was obvious he wanted the primal masculine he just couldn't reach for it himself. I pushed against the staff then said, "Okay, John, I want it straight. Tell me what is inside of you?"

He screamed out his pain, used lots of colorful metaphors then cried. After twenty minutes or so I asked him the simple question, "Are you going to get up or are you going to make love to your pain the rest of your life?" For a brief moment the warrior came online for John. He nearly knocked me over as he pushed against me and yelled, "I am going to get up!"

Again, when a man is in the belly of the whale he needs two things, his pain validated and the primal masculine. Give him those two things, and God and the person suffering will do the rest.

Shadow Counsel

In the story of David slaying Goliath, David approaches the men of Israel in the power of the Spirit. But King Saul, out of concern for David and knowing he is about to face a fierce enemy, counsels him to use his armor for battle, which David puts on. Wisely, David realizes his ability to move is compromised and so he sheds Saul's armor, and chooses to go to battle wearing only his authentic self.

This is about shadow counsel, that is, advice that is well-intended but contrary to the way of God. King Saul counseled David to fight the battle just the way King Saul would have, which is good advice for King Saul but not for David. This is shadow counseling, placing our agenda or reality on another person because that is what worked for us or that is what we believe needs to happen. We have all done it or had it done to us. Peter, out of deep love for Jesus, gave shadow-counsel to Jesus and we know how he responded to Peter. The worst shadow-counsel comes as we use scripture to place our agenda on another human being, which is exactly what Satan did in the desert to Jesus. He cunningly used scripture to give Jesus shadow counsel.

There is a cutting edge between being a true mentor versus a shadow mentor. One brings life, the other destroys. It is an awesome responsibility to wield power as we counsel others. In men's work we are instructed to ask questions so the man's sanctity is honored. Warrior listening is a must!

The Wounded Boy and The Wild Man

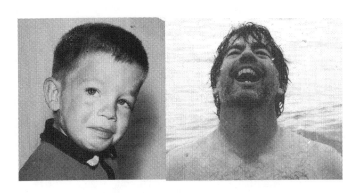

When I received this photo from my parents years ago Kathryn burst out with a laugh and said, "I know that look." Her nick-name for my wounded self was,"Boo." Of course, I had a completely different reaction upon seeing this photo. I wanted to burn it in our wood stove because this photo represented everything I had run from, the wounded boy, rejection, pain, lack of masculine strength and so forth. Fortunately, Kathryn prevented me from doing so.

Now to ask the obvious, when you look into the eyes of this wounded boy do you see anything that resembles the strength necessary to break addictions, face pain or navigate conflict with a spouse? And even more absurd, is there anything about this wounded boy that belongs in the marriage bed? Is it any wonder I ended up in such pain in my marriage and sexuality became such an issue? And what woman wants a wounded boy for a husband or a sexual partner?

Just to level the playing field, the wounded boy is universal. Whether he is pissed off, the center of his world, emotionally locked up, filled with shame, insecure or feeling rejected he is there, working beneath the surface, aching to be owned and integrated into a mature masculine psyche. He longs for his story to be told and his pain validated, but he also aches, I mean really aches for the wild man to come on line and make sense of his psychological world.

Recently, I was speaking to a woman about relational dynamics when she made the comment, "When I am in an argument with my partner it is like looking into the eyes of a nine year old boy." I knew exactly what she was saying. I have seen a similar look in the eyes of men as they process their wounds and feelings of shame. Their body slumps and their eyes go downward onto the carpet as if they are five years old and being scolded by their parents. When I see that look in men, I know their core issues of shame, rejection or insecurity is driving them at the moment. This moment is not to be judged or disdained but seen as a window into our psyche and an opportunity to do some real soul work. This is about integration, not running or fracturing ourselves further from realities that are working within us. Remember Luke 13:10 and the woman invited into the sanctuary with Jesus. When the wounded boy surfaces we need to gather our courage and invite him into the sanctuary with Jesus. This is the way of integration and the intimate connection between the wild man and the wounded boy. It is not enough just to embrace the wounded boy nor enough to awaken the wild man. They must psychologically embrace and become working partners in the path to wholeness. In short, the wounded boy leads us to the wild man and in return the wild man brings healing to the wounded boy.

Men's group is a great place to begin exploring and integrating the wild man and the wounded boy. I have done many of my own processes with my circle of men and have facilitated many. Processes don't have to be as intense as my NWTA although the ingredients are often similar, piercing the wound, embracing the wounded boy and then rising out of the destructive patterns of the boy through the wild man strength.

Most processes begin with awareness and seeing every subtle reaction of anger, shame, fear, hatred, greed or jealousy as a window into our wound and an invitation into the primal masculine.

I have always feared making mistakes in public. Perhaps you can relate, that gut reaction of terror upon realizing one has screwed up. Immediately, the defense mechanisms kick in. Mine have been in place for as long as I can remember. First, I see if anybody has noticed. If not, I conceal it, thankful the moment went unnoticed. My other defense is to diffuse it with humor and charisma; act like it wasn't a big deal, even though there is fright or shame within me. Either reaction is about protecting the boy and masking my true self. To bring this issue into men's work the processing might look like:

Facilitator: What do you want to happen, Brian?

Myself: I want to explore my gut reaction of terror each time I screw up.

Facilitator: Give me the story.

In men's work it is necessary to speak like a warrior, to the point and crisp. If the man processing begins to ramble the facilitator must be willing to cut cleanly and keep the man focused.

Facilitator: So when you make a mistake what's the reaction you are hiding through humor or concealment?

Myself: (a release of laughter) Oh man!

Facilitator: Oh man what?

Myself: Oh man I feel like an idiot.

Facilitator: I am not convinced. Where is the emotional charge with that? (The facilitator is pushing me to get into my guts.)

Myself: I said, I feel like an idiot. Do you hear me? I hate feeling like an idiot!

Facilitator: That's believable. So what are the emotions beneath your reaction?

Myself: Fear and shame.

Facilitator: I hear your fear and shame. They are welcomed in this circle. Where did you learn that making a mistake equates to shame and feeling like an idiot?

Myself: It is part of my personality. I also learned it through my childhood.

Facilitator: Can you recall scenes?

Myself: No, just a general feeling of terror every time I screwed up.

Faciliator: Is there an anger piece to this?

Myself: Yes

Facilitator: Who is the boy angry at?

Myself: My parents, possibly myself.

Anger is okay. It is part of the human journey. If anger is not dealt with in a safe manner it will work itself out sideways, in ways that harm ourselves, our significant other, our children, or our parents. This is not about blame either. It is about anger, an anger that comes when the sacred has been violated. Remember how Jesus responded when the sacred was violated.

There are many ways to violate a child's dignity. Shaming, abuse, discipline without dignity, physical abuse, over parenting, the absence of parent and so on. Even now, I hear parents say to their children when they make a mistake, "Shame on you!" Words and thoughts have power. This is nothing short of a curse.

Parenting is one of those great windows into our soul. Emotional charges come fast and furious. Stuff slips out of our mouths before we even know it. Even if we don't use words our tone of voice and our body language tell the real story. A story that is easily read and taken in by a young child.

This emotional charge in parenting is about unloading our baggage or shadow onto our children. Why? They are an easy target. For a short time in history we can exert power over them like no one else on earth. Recently, I have been pointing my finger at our girls when things get hot. I wasn't even aware of it until Kathryn called me out on it. Pointing my finger while disciplining my children is a window into my wounds and about unloading shadow onto an easy target. Sounds cowardly if you ask me, that is, unloading on my children. Can you imagine if God disciplined me like that?

"Brian! What the hell were you thinking down there? How many times have I told you? Can't you read the scriptures? Shame on you!"

When we as fathers unload our baggage on our children we are violating the sacred within them. Someday they will grab their whip and drive out the destructive messages that we as fathers have imparted to them. Why? Because we weren't willing to own our wound, take responsibility of our emotional reaction, follow the charge to its source and deal with it as a man. I have been that man too many times. I don't want to be that man any longer. I am learning discipline with dignity, consequences with compassion and emotions with boundaries, all emotions!

So let's continue with processing.

Facilitator: So each time you gloss over these emotions with humor who are you serving?

Myself: I don't get the question.

Facilitator: What part of yourself are you serving each time you hide your true reaction? Are you serving the man or the boy?

Myself: I am serving the wounded boy, protecting him from feeling the shame he carries. Feeding the false self.

Facilitator: So what are you going to do about it? It is your stuff. You are a grown man. Are you going to take back your power? Or are you going to live in your wounds the rest of your life and impart this baggage to your children?

Myself: I am going to own my stuff, claim my power as a man of God and live with integrity!

As stated earlier, in the processing of a wound it is important to touch the boy's grief as well as call forth the wild man strength. Once these two parts of the man have been brought forth the processing can go many ways. Sometimes just speaking the truth is enough. Other times we set up a physical and psychological drama that recreates the wounding. Such a process is called ritual space or psycho-drama, meaning, it is not real but can seem real to the psyche. Ritual work recreates the wounding drama, therefore retracing the wound while providing a pathway to overcome the message. This is an opportunity for intense healing.

A very simple example of a ritual might be having the facilitator speak the core message I internalized as a child, such as 'I feel like an idiot when I fail' then forcing me to push the facilitator out of the circle while we both are holding a ceremonial staff. This is a powerful tool as the wild man is often awakened through physical exertion. Physically pushing the man speaking the message is ritually pushing the message out of my psyche. I have seen such processes rip into a man's wound many times while creating an avenue for God to bring healing to the wound. It is powerful, to be used by a trained facilitator, most often during a retreat setting or with a skilled men's group.

As the wounded boy begins to heal, a healthy aspect of the child will take hold. This is good. The child within each of us holds wonder, knows the joy of play and enjoys good humor. Without this sense of wonder, play and laughter the rigors of life can drown us.

The First Commandment
and the Four Primal Energies of God

"You shall love the Lord your God with all of your heart-
　　　　　　the primal energy of the Lover.
"You shall love the Lord your God with all of your soul-
　　　　　　the primal energy of the King/Sovereign.
"You shall love the Lord your God with all of your mind-
　　　　　　the primal energy of the Seer
"You shall love the Lord your God with all of your strength-
　　　　　　the primal energy of the Warrior.

This commandment given to us by Jesus is more powerful than we will ever know. It is the journey of union with God, the road to wholeness, the way of integration and the path to our most powerful expression of our humanity. For within this commandment is the invitation to open these four energy centers, heart, soul, mind and strength to God so that the divine nature of God, lover, warrior, seer and king (sovereign for inclusive purposes) might express itself through our humanity.

Human Nature

We come into this world with a unique soul and personality that is hardwired into at least one of these primal energies. As said earlier, I was born into this world a lover, that is, sensitive, intuitive, drawn to the quiet and enjoyed my Catholic upbringing. I have memories of praying the Lord's prayer until sleep came as a growing boy. Some of us are natural warriors, we set our boundaries, are focused on our mission and speak our truth among our peers. The seer lives in the world of the mind, using logic, reasoning and the power of the intellect to guide them through life. These are the scientists, the mechanics, theologians, accountants, technicians and so forth. The fourth primal energy is that of the king. Men blessed with king energy often find themselves in leadership roles. They have been given the ability to call forth the warriors, to set vision in motion and to integrate the different gifts of their staff or employees to bring forth desired goals.

Throughout our lives we live into these different energies as circumstances call forth, yet so often we as men lean toward the one that best suits our personalities and our wounds. It is not surprising that upon my conversion in Lubbock I was drawn to the path of the lover. The way of the lover is my God-given gift but also best served my wounds. As years passed I became all lover. It was familiar, who I was, my identity and the way I gained validation.

I have a friend who is a scientist. Most of his world is tangled up in logical thinking, reasoning and scientific laws that govern the natural world. The intuitive world has little to no meaning to him. There is no doubt the intellect is my friend's God-given gift and yet it is so tangled up in his need for validation that he dares not threaten his secure world of facts and figures.

My friend is all intellect. I became all lover. Some become all warrior, living through sports, work or their passion to bring them purpose and validation. Eventually and by the grace and love of God we find ourselves at a dead-end road in which our familiar path that once brought validation and possible prosperity now brings wounding and even chaos. This is the Spirit of God at work, challenging us to move into a more integrated expression of our humanity. So often we resist because it isn't familiar. A common scenario is: Stan is all warrior. He is the go-to guy, gets things done and of course fathers his children just the same, with discipline, goals and a heavy hand. They begin to rebel, some of which is normal but the rebellion goes deeper. So Stan pushes, not knowing his warrior nature which has become oppressive over the years is the very reason they are rebelling until one day his daughter unconsciously and passive-aggressively comes home pregnant. He explodes. The chasm grows. He blames. She runs. He calls the church. They all pray for her. No doubt she has acted wrongly and is responsible for her actions. Yet, no one has the guts to sit Stan down and say, this crisis is also about you. Your daughter is crying out to be heard and to have her pain of living with an oppressive father-figure validated.

Integration is about becoming what we are not. It is about forging a new path through the unchartered areas of our psyche. It is not the safe road, but it is God's road, and sometimes God's way is painful. Leaving the wilderness many years ago was painful. I had become everything I had wanted in life. Years later and about the time the ministry was gaining momentum, God spoke those words into my heart at the bottom of the Grand Canyon. "In order for you to go any further in me, you must give up everything you have gained in me!" Again, I had become what I wanted, and thought I was ready to take the ministry to a national level. How could I have known that in the giving up all that I had gained in God the Lord would lead me to treasure beyond my imagination? Such is the way of integration.

The Seer

These four primal energies that I speak of have both a human expression as well as a divine expression. By our own efforts we could begin the integration process by choosing to live into these four primal energies. But the human expression of these energies is but chaff blowing in the wind compared to the divine expression of these energies. This truth is made clear in Luke's account of the two disciples on the road to Emmaus. As they are walking and discussing the death of Jesus the risen Lord approaches and enters into their dialogue. As Jesus speaks to them, the fire of God descends, burning within their hearts as the sacred mysteries of God are revealed to them. They now begin to grasp the scriptures in a new wisdom and power. Without this movement of the Spirit they would have groped in the darkness of their human faculties, trying to make sense of something that can only be grasped by the power of God.

Another profound example of the primal energy of the seer is found in 1 Kings 3:9 as Solomon prays for an understanding mind to govern the people of Israel. Six verses later we see the spirit of wisdom anchored in Solomon as he discerns between two women arguing over who was the rightful mother of a child. As they both professed ownership of the child Solomon asks for a sword and says divide the child in two. The real mother cries out, "No," and concedes ownership so her child might live. The woman who is lying says go ahead and divide the child. Solomon then discerns who is the real mother.

Wisdom is the penetrating light of the Holy Spirit that illuminates our minds. Without this anointing we are left on our own to discern the wisdom of God, which only leads to chaos. Scripture becomes tainted by our shadow and religion takes on the precepts of our humanity. Many young people take aptitude tests or heed the wisdom of professors or family to discover their gifts and possible careers, hoping they will discover their soul mission by use of their own intellect or the counsel of others. It simply can't be done. This doesn't mean they can't be successful as they put their talents to use. But being successful has nothing to do with soul mission and the Spirit of wisdom that brings revelation.

The spirit of wisdom also enables us to perceive the lessons beneath our woundings, that is, to understand why our plans may have failed. If we cannot grab hold of these spiritual truths we are spiritual, mentally or emotionally stuck in a cyclical pattern in which the lesson comes around and around and around. This is the merry-go-round of our dreams, financial crisis, marital struggles or whatever. We quote scripture, do self-help books, pray and attend church, but nothing changes.

Without the Spirit of God bringing wisdom we are like an acquaintance of mine back in Steamboat who was driving home at night in a blinding snow storm. Due to alcohol influence he unknowingly veered off the road into a snow bank. While stuck in the snow bank he kept his foot on the throttle which kept his rear wheels turning, therefore registering speed on his speedometer. And with snow flakes still pelting his windshield it created the illusion that he was still moving. And so he remained there, certain he was moving forward until a police officer walked up to the car and banged on the window.

Metaphorically, I have been that man who is believing I am going somewhere but in reality I am stuck in a snow bank, certain if I would just try harder the doors would open. Jesus says, "You know how to interpret the appearance of the sky, but you cannot interpret the signs of the times." Matthew 16:3 Simply put, without Divine wisdom working through us we cannot successfully navigate our way through the great labyrinth of life, nor can we grasp the lessons beneath our circumstances.

So where do we begin? How do we open ourselves to the divine expression of this primal energy? The answer can be found in the story of the disciples on the road to Emmaus. It wasn't until Jesus showed up and inflamed their hearts that their minds were opened to the wisdom of God. You probably know where I am going with this one but there is no circumventing this truth. Surrender and inner simplicity gives birth to the spirit of wisdom within us. Jesus said, "I thank you, Father, Lord of heaven and earth, because you have hidden these things from the intelligent and have revealed them to infants." Matthew 11:25

We study scripture, memorize the word, intellectualize God and mentally scheme how God is working in our lives, hoping to grasp Divine Wisdom that can only come through surrender and simplicity. Don't get me wrong; I love scripture and pray it daily. What I am saying is that we cannot attain Divine Wisdom through our human faculties, no matter how hard we try nor how complex we make God out to be.

Most of us know the teaching story out of the eastern tradition in which a young novice seeks out a wise elder to be instructed in the way of life. As they sat down for tea the elder began to pour water into the cup of the novice which soon began to overflow. The novice took notice and politely told the elder that the cup is already full. The wise elder smiled and said, "So it is with you. I cannot teach you until your inner self is emptied." Again, "I thank you, Father, Lord of heaven and earth, because you have hidden these things from the intelligent and have revealed them to infants."

Christian Mysticism

The path of silent devotion to God and the way of the seer can give birth to Christian Mysticism, given to those whose hearts are open and receptive to the flame of God that ignites an insatiable desire for God. This flame of love becomes a consuming fire that takes the soul deeper and deeper into the heart of God and into a sweetness of union that cannot be described. This union also gives birth to a profound understanding of the spiritual realm. These are the people who see with prophetic vision, carry gifts of healing and who hold the transformative power of Christ. They are subtly aware of the unseen forces of good and evil around and within them. They are often prayer warriors, working behind the scenes to bring forth God's kingdom. It is a powerful calling and one that is often feared or judged in western Christianity. Perhaps because the religious lines blur as God takes us deeper into the spiritual realm and into the world of the unconscious.

By the grace of God the mystic has journeyed into the unconscious, unleashing its power and facing the darkness therein. They have come to an understanding they are on a profound journey of union. The mindset of being 'saved' or getting to heaven has fallen from their conscious as they begin to understand the journey is far beyond their initial conversion. Their soul has been awakened by the Holy Spirit and is now embarked upon the great quest, a quest in which the soul must ascend through levels or dwellings in the kingdom of God. Each leap in God demands trials, tests and even facing Satan. With every leap greater blessings are bestowed.

St. Theresa of Avila in her work *Interior Castles,* uses the analogy of a castle to describe the levels of intimacy and prayer with God. According to St. Theresa there are seven levels, referred to as dwellings. Each dwelling involves both blessings and trials, agony and ecstasy. Proverbs 9 states; "Wisdom has built her house, she has hewn her seven pillars." Psalm 12: states, "The promises of the Lord are promises that are pure, silver refined in a furnace on the ground, purified seven times." And finally Proverbs 24:16 "Though they (the righteous) fall seven times, they will rise again."

Energy

Christian mystics live in the world of energy, the energy of God moving through them as they pray, the energy of God flowing through creation as they walk through the woods and the energy of those around them. Even my ten year old daughter, who is not ready to embrace the world of God at this time, experienced a sense of this energy at our karate class. Our instructor was leading us through a series of tai chi moves. Shortly into the exercise my daughter spoke out, "My hands feel funny."

"That is your '*ki,*' (pronounced chi) moving through your hands," replied our instructor. *Ki* basically means life force. In Christian terminology I would reframe *ki* as the breath of God. I have experienced this phenomena many times while doing slow martial art moves or while deep in contemplative prayer and of course more pronounced when I was engaged in active ministry of renewal and healing. I experience this energy as I walk through the woods, rising up from the earth in a song of praise to God. Psalm 19:1 states: "The heavens are telling the glory of God"

The mystic knows the energy of God is intimately woven into every fabric of all creation. The Psalms repeatedly speak of all creation singing God's praise. Paul writes about the creation groaning in Romans 8:22 The first four versus of Psalm 19 unfold the mystery of the cosmos and their voices that cannot be heard by human ears. This is the world of the mystic, who has crossed the veil into the unseen world.

I believe there is a mystic within all of us no matter how buried it may be beneath logical thinking, practicality or fear. I believe that is why the original *Star Wars* series gained such popularity. The character of *Obi Wan,* the ideal of becoming a *Jedi Knight,* facing *Darth Vadar* and the understanding of an all-powerful force that binds and penetrates every aspect of the universe played into a deep part of our psyche, a part that has been repressed for centuries by a rigid and fear-based religion. Yet, the story and the archetypes are so very Christian.

This path, kept alive by receptive women throughout the centuries, must be embraced by more men if the kingdom of God is to come here on earth. I believe God is calling men into this profound expression of their Christian walk just as the prophet Joel writes in chapter 2:28. "I will pour out my spirit on all flesh; your sons and your daughters shall prophesy, your old men shall dream dreams, and your young men shall see visions."

This flame though comes with a sword that leaves a wound, most often an unseen wound upon the soul. This wound in some mystical way is a sharing in the suffering of Christ, perhaps the thorn in the flesh as Paul writes about. But even with the inflicting of such a wound the joy and sweetness of such intimacy with God far surpasses the suffering.

Shadow Seeker

I use the word 'seeker' intentionally because those who seek God through their own intellect have not been lifted into the realm of the seer.

The person who leans heavily on the power of their intellect to guide him through life often becomes an emotional island within them self, isolated from their loved ones, their passion and their God. These are the men who can't emotionally connect with their spouses nor their children. They are imprisoned by the world of the intellect and rational thought. They know they should be connecting deeper with their loved ones but something within them just can't do it. They simply can't make the leap into the heart. Such men have probably intellectualized God as well. It is the safe road, a calculated detour around the heart that keeps God and the frightening world of emotions in a predictable box. There is no need to struggle when God is predictable, nor is there a reason to dig deeper into the heart for a new understanding of Christ. The world is safe, falsely safe.

I have processed with men who operate from their intellect. They categorize their wound, speak-self help language, quote scripture and even claim a new dawn but the inner landscape of their heart rarely changes. Healing the wound is messy and frightening, demanding the guts of the warrior and the grief of the lover. We can understand the wound through our intellect but we cannot do the deep work if we remain in our head.

Again, initiation is about integration. Integration is about giving away the old so the new man can emerge. It is about forging a path into the unknown places of our psyche so God can create the spiritual and psychological infrastructure to hold the energies of the lover, the warrior and the seer in balance. As God awakens and integrates these energies within us our life will begin to reflect the real and authentic Jesus, that is, a life that is rooted in love, power and wisdom. These are the key attributes of the three primal energies of God, the lover, the warrior and the seer expressed through an initiated man who holds the primal energy of the king/sovereign.

The Primal Energy of the King/Sovereign

Created in the image of God! It is not an intellectual-thing but a soul-thing that comes through a journey of surrender and the facing of the fiery trials that are given to us. Most agree the king energy comes online around 45 years of age or older. I dare say though, even if the king energy has come online, it is a long and perilous road to bring this energy to full realization within us. Many battles must be fought. Some must be lost. Others must lead to victory.

The first time God awakened the king energy within me was only a year after my crisis. I was still in immense emotional and spiritual pain. My king blessing came at night in a dream. In this dream I was following a very old king up a flight of stairs. Just as he began ascending he fell over backwards. Horror seized me because I knew this king was about to die which meant a further unraveling of my life. I then knelt close to him and pleaded with him not go. For a brief moment his strength returned. He then placed his open palm on my forehead and began to speak in an unknown language. In the dream I knew he was giving me his king's blessing.

In my limited understanding, the primal energy of the king was given, not because my life was perfect, but because God had awakened and rallied the warrior, the lover and the seer so that I might fight my real fight.

Presence

Then Jesus, knowing all that was about to happen to him, came forward and asked them, "Whom are you looking for?" They answered, "Jesus of Nazareth." Jesus replied, "I am he." When Jesus said to them, "I am he," they stepped back and fell to the ground. John 18: 4-6

This is about the power of presence, who Jesus was and the energy that he carried within him; so powerful that it caused his attackers to step back and fall to the ground. Now that is power, his very presence coupled with the words, *"I am he,"* was enough to overtake those seeking to kill him. And yet, he submitted to God's will.

The power of presence, it is our greatest resume and tells the real story of our journey with Christ. It is not that we have to be perfect but rather dwelling in the presence of God and God dwelling in us. This alone should be our greatest pursuit.

When our inner self radiates Christ, a power and a peace is communicated that is far beyond words, enough to dissolve conflict, bring peace and even evangelize. Often we don't need words, because our presence speaks volumes. There is a teaching story that speaks to this very issue. It goes like this:

"Once their was an old monk who had the gift of speaking of God. People traveled miles, days, and even months to listen to him speak of the love of God poured out through Jesus. One day a young novice set out to find his younger brother so that he might also listen to the wise elder. And so he travelled, found his brother and began the

journey back to the monastery. Upon his arrival he found the wise monk and introduced his younger brother to him. The wise monk smiled his acknowledgment but continued in his silence. The novice persisted saying, "Father, my younger brother has travelled a great distance to hear you speak. Please speak of God so that he might be encouraged." Again, the monk simply sat in silence. The novice pressed on. Finally, the monk looked up and said, "If my presence doesn't touch him how can I expect my words to touch him."

Author unknown

Paul wrote the same story in 1 Corinthians 13 with these words. "If I speak in the tongue of mortals and angels, but do not have love I am a noisy gong or a clanging cymbal. And if I have prophetic powers, and understand all mysteries and all knowledge, and if I have all faith, so as to remove mountains, but do not have love, I am nothing. If I give away all my possessions, and if I hand over my body so that I may boast, but do not have love, I gain nothing."

So I ask you; what energy do you bring to your family, work and community. Do your eyes mirror the love of God? Does your inner self speak of the peace that passes all understanding? Do you carry the transformative power of God? This is all about the presence of God within and true king energy..

Service

"Then he poured water into a basin and began to wash the feet of his disciples." John 13:4

Imagine any king or leader of a nation wrapping a towel around his/her waist and washing the feet of those under him/her. Absurd isn't it! But that is the true essence of a king as given to us by Jesus, that our journey of transformation is not about us but about giving glory to God and serving others! We are called to serve, not out of our need to be validated but out of love and responsibility to the kingdom, to be a blessing to others. This is the way of the king/ sovereign energy given to us by Jesus.

There is a powerful scene in the movie, *Return of the King*, which is the third movie in the *Lord of the Rings* trilogy. Just after the battle at Gondor, *Arigorn* is face to face with the ghostly-looking dead people that helped him fight. As Arigron releases them he turns around to find *Gandolf* standing off in the distance. Gandolf, the white wizard who holds transformative power, grasps the obvious, that Arigorn has awakened and realized the primal energy of the king, and so in respect and in knowing of the greatness within Arigorn, Gandolf nods his ackowledgement.

What makes this scene so powerful is that Gandolf didn't run over and lavish praises upon Arigorn. No! It came with a simple nod. When you are I are in our power and have journeyed beyond our need for validation we serve out of our strength, not our needs. This the way of the mature masculine psyche. Remember how Jesus responded in the Gospel of Mark 10:18 to the rich man who asked him, "Good Teacher, what must I do to inherit eternal life?" You can almost hear the contrived praise in the word "good." Jesus immediately deflects this false praise by saying, "Why do you call me good? No one is good but God."

We must do the deep work of healing the wound so we can serve out of our strength and not our needs. Remember, we cannot truly serve God and our wound at the same time. We must choose.

So, in your service to the kingdom what are you doing with your talents and time? Who is benefiting from your presence, wisdom and gifts. Whose feet are you to wash? This is not about going over-board neither. There is no honor in serving the masses while leaving the family stranded, that is wounded boy stuff and hero mentality. Perhaps we should begin at home. Who needs your strength, compassion and time? This is the way of Jesus, our servant king.

Forgiveness

"Father, forgive them for they know not what they do."

On a cross, pierced, deserted and in physical, emotional and spiritual torment Jesus spoke those words of forgiveness. Amazing isn't it. In such agony he still has the ability to see beyond their unconscious ignorance and release them of their debt. That is forgiveness, a forgiveness I can only imagine. But still, at some point in our pilgrimage we must begin to forgive those who have wounded us. I say 'begin' because forgiveness can be a process. There are many layers to the wound. Remember the story about the diabetic man who claimed he had no anger and had forgiven those who injured him? We dug a little deeper and found a tornado of rage.

In my own journey of forgiveness the wound had to be pierced before forgiveness could take root. No matter how much I had confessed forgiveness it simply couldn't happen until my anger and grief were pierced. This is where forgiveness becomes work. Often we have to reach into that ugly, chaotic mess within and release those toxic emotions, not once but many times. It is painful but necessary. As the wound lessens its grip, forgiveness begins to flow like a healing river within. Joy is soon to follow.

There is also another forgiveness we need to call to mind, which can be just as difficult as forgiving those who have wounded us, and that is of course, forgiveness of ourselves. Yes, to reach into our guilt and shame and say, "Lord, I am sorry for what I have done. I forgive myself just as you have forgiven me."

Courage

And going a little farther he threw himself on the ground and prayed, "My Father, if it is possible, let this cup pass from me; yet not what I want but what you want."

Imagine the son of God throwing himself on the ground, not kneeling, not collapsing but throwing! It is a daunting image to ponder. This moment is about agony of spirit and the courage to push through! Ever had one of those moments? When you knew that doing the right thing was going to cost you but you did it anyway. It was probably your greatest moment just as the Garden of Gethsemane was one of Jesus' greatest moment.

Holding King Energy

Love, wisdom and power channeled through our presence, actions, forgiveness, and courage are some of the traits that define a mature masculine psyche as given to us by Jesus. When we as men hold healthy king energy our world, that is, family, work, play, and other pursuits have an underlying ease to them that speaks of balance, power and love. Such men are a joy to be around and even contagious. Jesus was contagious.

Your world, my world and the world is in desperate need of king/ sovereign energy, men who are truly willing to journey into the wilderness of their heart and allow God to awaken and integrate these masculine energies. Our spouse and our children are crying out for the mature masculine in their lives, a person who can provide the spiritual and psychological platform for them to stand upon as they journey through life. You are the *Arigorn* in your world, the Christ figure that holds the family in balance. Your family is your kingdom given to you by God. If you do not fight then who will?

Closing

> "You shall love the Lord your God with all of your heart-
>   the primal energy of the Lover.
> "You shall love the Lord your God with all of your soul-
>   the primal energy of the King/Sovereign.
> "You shall love the Lord your God with all of your mind-
>   the primal energy of the Seer.
> "You shall love the Lord your God with all of your strength-
>   the primal energy of the Warrior.

This is the sacred journey of union with God, the road to wholeness, the way of integration and the path to our most powerful expression of our humanity. When these divine energies are awakened and integrated a man begins to mirror the true essence of Jesus to this world.

15 THE FIRE

Malachi 3:3 reads, "For God is like a refiner's fire and will sit as a refiner and purifier of silver."

In many Christian circles there was the story from an unknown source that surfaced about a silversmith refining silver. During the process, which demands high temperatures and brings the silver to a volatile state, the silversmith diligently kept his eye on the silver as impurities rose to the surface. As the critical moment approached an onlooker inquired when the silver was ready to be poured. The silversmith replied, "When I see my own image reflected in the silver."

The fire of God descending upon the soul is an intense and sacred path that demands the yielding spirit of the lover, the courage of the warrior and the wisdom of the seer, knowing our true self in Christ, created in the image of God, is being formed and fashioned through an agonizing process. It is a time of intense psychological or spiritual pain. Great care must be given to heed the wisdom of God so the work of the Holy Spirit may be completed.

Into the Fire

Nearly nineteen years had passed since Jesus invited me into the cave. Seven years had now passed since my crisis had broken open. For years I had pushed into God with everything I had, prayers, commitment, and action only to be met by an equal force of darkness within me. Yes, I had gained much, but still the battle raged. "How long Lord? How long?" It was daunting, even disheartening at times. My wilderness time was far longer than I could have imagined. More than once I had lost heart. More than once I had fought back the words "I quit" to God. More than once tears leaked from my eyes as I spoke the words, "You have asked too much of me God, too much."

"How long Lord? How long?"

My answer came in May 2010 when God spoke these words into my heart, "Mary is going to take you through the fire." Immediately, Mary's presence came upon me once gain as it did almost seven years ago during my men's rite of passage. Bathed in her love she left me with these words, "Jesus will be waiting for you as you pass through the fire."

My Mountain of the Lord

Several days later God called me up to a small hill near our house. It is a steep sandy hill with about 75 feet of vertical drop. As I stood at the base in prayer God spoke into my heart, "This is your mountain of victory. I want you to climb it each day." I began climbing, one step at a time, calling God's presence, claiming my strength in Jesus and focusing my spiritual vision upon the day when I would know victory in Christ.

As I stood on my mountain of victory I took several deep breaths, clinched my fists then snapped into a stance that I had learned in karate. It is a ready-stance which is used to summon strength before a series of moves. For a few minutes I grounded myself in this stance as the warrior energy surged within me. I then grabbed my walking stick thrust into the ground and said, "I am Brian Christian Meagher, son of God, disciple of Jesus Christ, redeemed, forgiven, loved and valued." For a few minutes and with deep breaths I let my proclamation to God and the universe sink into my spirit. Then with hands raised and still facing east toward the rising sun I began calling forth the primal energies of God.

It was my proclamation to the spirit world, both good and evil. I was staking my claim in God's kingdom, claiming God's victory and choosing to fight with everything I had.

In the days that followed the primal masculine really took hold. Each visit to my mountain centered me deeper into God and deeper into my masculine heart. I was on fire. Strength coursed through my blood. Kathryn and I were doing well also. My only concern was finances. Six moths ago I had begun to dissolve my tree and forestry business so I could devote all my energies into prayer and the writing of this book. It was a leap of faith, not one that Kathryn suggested or believed in. My heart was on fire though. The words burned with in me. I had to write. The writing was going slower than anticipated and even more unexpected was the fact that my tractor had not sold.

As I walked down the mountain I foolishly made some proclamation to God that I wouldn't stumble now, much like Peter's profession when he said he wouldn't deny Jesus. In the wake of my proclamation there was the smallest of voices that said, "We'll see."

In the next few days I chanced upon the story of Abraham and his son Isaac at the altar of sacrifice in my devotional. It is frightening story, not for the faint of heart. The reflection that followed spoke about going to the very edge, to a place where hope is shrouded, and yet, it is there we are called to trust. As I placed the book down an unsettled knowing came over my spirit.

About a week later I flipped through the growing pile of bills on the counter. Knowing our financial resources were dwindling, I went online to check our balance. As the screen popped up my jaw dropped. The balance of our account read just over ninety-one dollars. I panicked. That was my first mistake. I did not sit quietly nor pray but reacted in fear. The fear was rooted in what Kathryn's reaction would be, stemming from the fact that we had agreed not to withdraw from savings during the writing of this book. I had entered into this agreement with little thought, trusting God could and would sell my equipment as needed so it wouldn't be an issue. But my tractor had not sold.

In that moment I did not pray nor seek counsel with Kathryn nor my brothers but withdrew money out of a joint-account with my daughter to handle the bills until the tractor sold. It was my only option. The problem was I did this under the table and in the land of shadow, which was against everything I had thought crystalized the last seven years. If I would have read my own work on the chapter of the warrior I would have faced it head-on with Kathryn, but I skirted the issue because I feared painful discussions would rip into my wounds and crush my fragile hold on the kingdom, which it had done countless times before.

I prayed God would sell the tractor soon so I could repay the money and go on as usual. But the kingdom of God is about integrity one step at a time. To be out of integrity is to compromise our relationship with God. I knew this, have lived this and preached it but there I was, in shadow and one step out of integrity. The next day as I deposited the check I told God, "I don't have a choice. There are bills and the tractor has not sold."

A gentle voice said, "I would have told her." I should have heeded those words but something called fear of conflict or serving the wound overruled my better judgment and hardened my heart to that wisdom. Two days later we returned to her Mother's house on Lake Michigan to celebrate the end of the school year with our daughters. Ever since the taking out of money I had been on edge, which Kathryn picked up on. As we were working out a couple of interchanges, I sensed her shield going up. Words came with more of a charge. I tried to diffuse the conflict but to no avail. She then reached somewhere inside of her and said, "What about our finances? Where are we?"

It was a sword, perfectly aimed at my shadow, piercing that which I had concealed. How I wish it had not been drawn but the fact that it had told me I could not hide any longer. I took a breath and thought, *okay God, I screwed up, let's go into the fire.*

I told her that the balance went lower than I had expected so I had to withdraw money to meet the upcoming bills. First there was a fleeting moment of silence then a look of shock and horror upon Kathryn's face. Then there were words, many words. Her wisdom was sound, that I was depleting our family funds to pursue my dreams, that I was once again a lone ranger and forsaking my responsibilities as a family man. She asked why I resisted getting a part-time job while I wrote. Like I said, her wisdom was sound. It was the safe road. The road I would have taken ninety-nine percent of the time. The road I would have counseled any other man to walk. But the fire of God is not about the safe road. I had repeatedly prayed about work and repeatedly the inner voice said, "Write!"

For forty-five minutes we went around and around. There was no resolution. All the old wounds that I had hoped to protect ripped open as the trauma of emotional conflict deepened. She then asked, "Out of what account did you draw the money?"

This one blind-sided me. Fearing even deeper conflict I did the most cowardly thing I have ever done in my life. With one quick choice, I gave away the last dwindling reserves of my integrity and told her that I withdrew the money out of my IRA, which had been zeroed out years ago when I had a series of break-downs with my equipment. Yes, I lied. It was an ugly moment, one that I wish I could take back. But I own it, because that is what men's work is about, owning the fractured part of ourselves so God can make straight that which is out of joint. That is also what the fire of God is about, bringing forth the dross of our character for purification and healing. It is a painful process.

Before we go any further I need to jump into one of Paul's writings in Romans 7:15. "I do not understand my actions. For I do not do what I want, but I do the very thing I hate. Now if I do what I do not want, I agree that the law is good. But in fact it is no longer I that do it, but sin that dwells in me."

I agree with this passage except for the very last sentence because it defies a core principle of emotional and spiritual growth, and that is, taking responsibility for who I am. I don't mean to be disrespectful to Paul. He was a great apostle and chosen by God, but even apostles miss the mark now and then as we see in Peter's life when he wouldn't associate with the uncircumcised, which Paul writes about. So I need to put it on the line because an initiated man can hold within himself that he is both created in the image of God and a man in need of grace. One without the other is a half-truth, and so I say, it wasn't sin that caused me to lie. I lied. It is that simple. I lied because the inner man had failed within me. I lied to protect the boy and because I didn't trust God in that moment. I lied because I feared Kathryn's reaction. Like I said, it was an ugly moment, one which I would take back.

In silent tension, the kind that tears down hearts and rips open wounds, our dialogue ended. It was major for Kathryn, almost as bad as when my crisis broke open seven years ago. I then started toward the beach feeling like I had just been through a war, as did Kathryn, I am sure.

Two days later God convicted me about lying. I knew I had to come clean on this issue. I took a breath and asked, "Am I forgiven God?" Immediately a wave of God's presence washed over my spirit that left no doubt that I was forgiven which gave me the strength to face this issue. I told Kathryn. She was shocked. To be honest, I was also shocked. Understandably it was a major wounding and a breach of trust. We barely spoke. But even worse was the story written in her eyes, spirit and body language that she then voiced, "I have walked the long mile with you Brian, but I now draw the line."

I had fallen, terribly fallen and now the consequences were before me. I went for a long walk. There was comfort knowing Peter fell. Perhaps we must all fall at one time, but how I wished my fall had not injured Kathryn so deeply.

In the days that followed I experienced forgiveness like I had never known before. Several times I traced back to my wrong and brought it before the Lord but each time I was instructed that it has been removed and no longer existed in God nor myself. Psalm 103:12 states, "As far as the east is from the west, so far has God removed our transgressions from us." This is the power of God through the death and resurrection of Jesus Christ, that by his wounds we are healed. This is the gift of salvation that is freely bestowed upon those who seek God and the confidence we must carry, that we can enter God's courts with thanksgiving and praise no matter where we have been nor how bad we have fallen. We do need to own our sins and bring them before God and to the one we may have injured. This is our part of the equation, the accountability piece that calls us onward on the journey of integrity.

Lessons

A few days later, just as Kathryn and our girls were about to leave to pick up our new puppy, we had the same discussion about faith, work, depleting our funds with, of course, the same results. As I listened to her concerns, which were valid, and her arguments, which were sound, I thought, *maybe I am way off base. Perhaps I should have taken the middle road. Perhaps I was in deep waters without a life jacket, although to the best of my knowledge, I had been obedient to the voice of God.* Yet here I was, scared and with a marriage that was dissolving before my eyes, not to mention broke and with a book that I had scheduled to be done nearly a month ago. But this was the fire of God, a fire in which lessons were coming fast and furious. I needed to heed each lesson, face my own humanity and trust God, knowing a spirit of obedience is forged through fire. This was the test, the critical moment of the a long and perilous journey. To forsake the wisdom of God and to trust my own wisdom would have caused my soul immense pain and perhaps even the victory my soul ached for. Still, I could not dismiss Kathryn's wisdom which I would have given to any other man. Each time I listened to her words I thought to myself, *she is right, what am I doing?* So just after Kathryn and the girls left to pick up our puppy I laid it all out before God and cried out, "What am I missing God? What am I missing?"

"Nothing," came the inner voice of God.

Standing Alone

There is time when a man must stand alone and believe what God has spoken in the quiet of his soul even though the world and those he loves may not understand. It is a frightening time and even a dangerous time. We are all capable of being led astray by the evil one or by our own shadow and ego. That is why it is crucial to be integrating a passionate relationship with God and the inner work of bringing shadow to light. Until we can own our shadow, name it and begin the intense work of facing the pain beneath it, our discernment will most likely be tainted by the unconscious forces within. Even then, we are all human and all capable of being led astray. That is the risk you and I must take.

In the path of discernment, which can be shrouded by our own emotions and shadow, I dare say I would rather crash and burn seeking to be faithful to God then hold onto the security of my boat. In the twenty-eight years since Lubbock I have never experienced the transforming power of God while holding onto the security of my boat, that is, living into my fear. Just a word of caution though, living into our courage and piercing our fear is not permission to be reckless. Being reckless through adventure, investments and passions is the way of the boy hero, which can lead only to a fall. If we have not done our work, faced our wound, owned our shadow and articulated the way of the wounded boy within us, we need to be prudent about passions and the inner voice of God. But even then, as said earlier, there is the risk of our humanity clouding our spiritual vision.

Later that day God told me that He could sell the tractor tomorrow. I then understood there was a deep wisdom at work. Much like the story of Lazarus, Jesus could have arrived in time to heal Lazarus, but he didn't. He let him die. He let hope be crushed. Why? So a greater glory might be revealed. Jesus could have sold that tractor, made this fire easy and allowed me to finish the book in a timely fashion. But God didn't and now I needed to heed the wisdom in the circumstances and learn the soul-lessons that were placed before me.

The lessons through this fire were old lessons of trust, of facing my fears, of piercing shadow, and of awakening the primal masculine at new levels. I was called to trust, to obey and to seek God with everything I had. It was also a test, a test I had seemingly failed, but I have come to believe true failure is when I don't turn to God, own my shadow and learn through my mistakes. That was the failure of Judas and the redemption of Peter. Judas couldn't believe he would be forgiven and so he turned in shame and self condemnation and killed himself. Peter however, stripped off his clothing, jumped out of the boat and swam toward Jesus.

As I remained in quiet prayer, contemplating my lessons, a knowing came that my journey through this fire also played into Kathryn's own journey or rite of passage as well, that in some soul way we were in this fire together. It was a sobering reality. My lessons played into her lessons, even if it wasn't readily acknowledged. I had a responsibility to God and to Kathryn to be true, even if being true meant a wounding for Kathryn. It was painful though and most of me cried out, "If it is possible Lord let this cup pass." Yes, I would have preferred to be united in vision and understanding. But that wasn't the cup that was given to either of us.

I was also made aware that it was my responsibility to carry Kathryn in prayer. And so I did, asking God to place upon my shoulders her burdens. That evening, as I stood at the base of my mountain, I climbed, not for myself but for both of us.

Fear No Darkness

The fire of God continued to burn. Psycho-spiritual pain began to fracture my spirit again. Shadows were exposed. Impurities rose to the surface. "How Long Lord? How Long?" I asked in prayer. There was no answer. The silence of God can be brutal.

The chasm between Kathryn and I had widened. It was hell, every day, living in the tension. I began to train my body with a little more intensity and clean up my diet, choosing to shed a few extra pounds and increase muscle mass. It was a conscious choice, aimed at honing the warrior energy, keeping the mental edge sharp and staying focused in spirit. But even with my daily visits to my mountain and honing my body through martial arts training, my spirit grew weary from the intense emotional strain of the distance between Kathryn and myself. Each day my old patterns of connecting with women began to gain power. I could feel its dark power rising in my spirit as it sought to gain a stronghold in my psyche. *Oh God, not this battle again,* I thought.

A few days later while praying on the mountain God's presence came with three words, "FEAR NO DARKNESS!" These words came, not as an invitation but as a command. I took a breath, believing God was referring to an imminent spiritual battle. Later that morning Kathryn picked up on my stress and asked, "What is going on?"

"What?" I replied.

"What is going on? Something is not right."

Her question caught me off guard. I took a breath, tried to relax my inner self and deflect the issue by responding, 'I am just struggling with the pain between us and some issues with God."

My answer didn't settle well with her but she let it go. I then went for a long walk to seek God's guidance whether I should bring this battle into the marriage arena or take it to men's work. Our marriage was already so stressed I couldn't see the wisdom in bringing this issue to her and so I prayed and discerned for hours. My answer came in three words, "FEAR NO DARKNESS!"

I knew telling her was going to rip both our hearts in a thousand pieces. I didn't want that. But courage is about charging into that which we fear! And more than anything, I desired to please God and emerge from this fire an awakened man. Slowly, I walked the last mile to home. More than once I replayed Mary's words that, "Jesus will be waiting for you as you pass through the fire." It was that knowledge that gave me the strength to charge into the fire.

I told Kathryn. It was painful, sending us back seven years when this crisis first broke open. The next morning I climbed my mountain and wept with my face to the ground, asking, "How Long Lord? How Long?"

"One more step," came the reply.

I returned home knowing what that step would be. Years ago and as our relationship was rebuilding Kathryn approached me about connecting with women, asking of the details and what was going on. It was one of those fear-based moments for me. To tell the truth would have meant certain interrogation into my psyche, then possible counseling. I saw no reason to tear open my wounds and try to reveal this pattern that was linked to the spiritual battle I was fighting. So years ago, when approached by Kathryn, I had told her that it was gone, which was another lie and now it had to come to the light. Upon my return from the mountain Kathryn approached me on this issue. I told her the truth.

The painful interchange that followed took a chunk out of both our hearts. I left the house and stumbled toward my mountain, choosing to remain there in quiet contemplation, fearing our marriage had just been destroyed. I remained kneeling. Perhaps an hour passed, I couldn't be certain. But what did catch my attention was the movement of shadow across my body that was created by the tower that supported the power lines above me. It was symbolically a powerful message, that my kneeling position had begun in full shadow but was now half shadow. I remained there in prayer while the sun continued to move south, which caused the shadow to shrink on my body even further. As my body became immersed in full light I knew it was time to go home.

The Coyote

The next morning, after speaking with Greg from men's group about my current crisis, I began to drive home. There was an incredible relief in my spirit knowing that I had passed through the worst of the fire. I now understood why everything in shadow had to be brought to light. Darkness was losing power and a renewed spiritual energy was rising up within me. Yes, by the wisdom of God a path had been cleared for a spiritual breakthrough.

That night, after taking my children fishing and getting them to bed, I started toward my mountain. As I neared the base a coyote let out a soulful cry, much like a howl but with an edge. I jerked my head up to see but twilight had blurred shapes into unrecognizable shadow. For a brief moment I hesitated, pondering whether I was willing to risk walking into a pack of coyotes? The coyote continued to cry out. I listened intently. There was only one coyote. I relaxed a little.

For nearly a minute I stood motionless, hoping to catch a glimpse of this four-legged. The coyote was nowhere in sight, although the cry seemed to originate near the top of my mountain. I finally took a step, then two, keeping my eyes upon the hill for movement. Still nothing. I paused again. As I did an intuitive knowing came over me. This coyote was no accident. There was medicine in his presence. I could feel it in my spirit, that God had sent this coyote. It was a powerful moment, as if the veil between heaven and earth had momentarily ripped open, releasing the wildness of God that now shivered upon my body and coursed through my spirit.

I cautiously crested the mountain then looked about. The coyote was perhaps seventy yards out, although I couldn't see him. He continued to cry out, that soulful howl with a slight edge that penetrated into the depths of my psyche. I listened, then opened my spirit to this messenger of God. As I did the primal masculine surged through my spirit. His message was clear. It was a war cry, telling me the last battle lay before me and that I must prepare. I then thrust my walking stick into the ground, claimed my power in Jesus Christ and let out my own war cry, telling the coyote, "Yes I know. And yes, I am ready!"

Rebuilding Covenant

A few days later Kathryn attended a workshop that used many of the same principles used in mens' work. During the workshop she brought her pain into process with skilled facilitators. It was a pivotal moment for her as she worked out her pain in a safe process. That night she emotionally checked back into the marriage, of course with pain and anger. I welcomed the change. One long month had passed since this crisis had broken loose. The next morning a slight break in the clouds produced a full rainbow in the western sky.

A week later Kathryn and I stayed up late and journeyed to the core issues of our marriage. We spoke honestly about our pain, anger and woundings and why the marriage had been unsafe for both of us. It was an intense time, cracking open wounds that had festered since our first summer in Michigan. Racked in pain we faded off to sleep around midnight. At 3:42 in the morning we were startled by a large crash in our bedroom. We jumped out of bed and turned on the light. There on the floor lay her grandmother's antique mirror, which had fallen due to a hook in the back that had broken loose. The mirror wasn't shattered, although the crashing down of the mirror seemed beyond coincidence, that in some surreal way God was breaking open our illusions and our ego pain that had plagued our marriage from the onset, which I deemed necessary for true healing.

The next morning Kathryn returned from a bike ride with an unsettled and seemingly hopeless spirit concerning our marriage. I assured her I believed we were on the cusp of a new season in our journey and that we must see it through. With a failing hope she then confided that she had been angry with me since the beginning of our journey which had caused her to shut down. I then looked at her and said, "I want to hear about your anger."

Kathryn replied, "I don't really know how to share anger, neither do I know how to hold both love and anger. I also fear that if I share my anger you will draw away further." I assured her I would not. For a few moments she hesitated.

"Don't think Kathryn, just give it to me from your guts," I said. She then journeyed back to the beginning of our relationship and began to release the anger that had been buried for over eighteen years. I stood there with an open heart and simply listened. After she finished I told her that her anger was welcomed and justified.

The next morning and with a heart filled with grief I returned to my mountain. While the tears and grief poured out of my body God took me back to our first summer in Michigan, to a pivotal moment as we were walking down her mother's driveway. Nineteen years ago and immersed in pain, possibly about leaving the wilderness and the struggle of my new life, I had begun to share my grief with Kathryn, a grief that had come with vulnerable tears. I was expecting compassion but to my surprise Kathryn had shot some interrogating questions into my vulnerability. I was caught off guard. In that instant, as the charged discussion continued, I had unconsciously deemed our relationship unsafe and had shut down a part of my heart. It was a pivotal moment, seemingly insignificant, but with lasting consequences. From then on I had sought to navigate my marriage with a partial heart and a core belief that my marriage was emotionally unsafe, that if I were truly open I would be cut into pieces. From then on, shadow grew and toxic emotions took hold.

A Safe Container

In men's work we create a safe container, which is a core necessity if men are to do their work. A safe container assures each of us that our stories will never leave the circle, that there will be no judgment nor unwanted reflections after our work round. A safe container also keeps the work focused about the person doing the work so it doesn't cross over into blame. Without a safe container, it is impossible to do the deep work that men's work demands.

Ideally, but much more difficult is creating a safe container for the marriage where each partner is allowed to share their emotions and true self without fear of judgment or backlash. Like I said, easier said than done, especially in the marriage arena where our wounds seem to interact at unconscious levels. We have all been there, things get hot, wounds get triggered then comes the reactionary outbursts. Soon, the defense mechanism kick into gear. Yes, we have all been there. Such explosions are a window into our wounds of course, but over time these outbursts destroy emotional intimacy in the marriage. At some point we need to turn inward, own our stuff and stop spilling our unconscious baggage onto our partner. Only then can a safe container be built.

A Balance of Power

In the book of Genesis 1: 26 the text reads, "Then God said, 'Let us make humankind in our image, according to our likeness and let them have dominion over the fish of the sea, and over the birds of the air, and over the cattle, and over all the wild animals of the earth and over every creeping thing that creeps upon the earth.'

So God created humankind in his image, in the image of God he created them; male and female he created them.'"

In the context of balancing power in the marriage arena we need to key into the word "humankind" and the words "let them have dominion." The words "humankind" and "let them" speak of an equality of men and women which leads us to verse 27. "So God created humankind in God's image, in the image of God He created them; male and female God created them."

In the next chapter though, Genesis 2:18, the creation story is personalized as we are introduced to Adam who is alone and in need of a helper. The text reads, "So the Lord God caused a deep sleep to fall upon the man, and he slept; then he took one of the man's ribs and closed up its place with flesh. And the rib that the Lord God had taken from the man he made into a woman and brought her to the man. Then the man said, 'This at last is bones of my bones and flesh of my flesh; this one shall be called Woman, for out of Man this one was taken.'"

Now to state the obvious there is a disconnect between these two stories. The first story claims God created them male and female and in God's image and the second story claims woman was created by taking a rib from Adam. I don't mean to bring discord nor undermine the power of God's word. But if we take the Bible in a rigid and literal way there is a disconnect that needs to be addressed. I tend to believe this disconnect between these two stories is a subtle message from God not to worship the Bible but to allow the Spirit of the Lord to bring revelation through the scriptures through prayer, reading and a cultural understanding.

With that said, let's fast-forward to the New Testament and the stories of Jesus interacting with women. First let's use the story of

Luke 13:10 when Jesus invited the woman into the sanctuary. I don't know if we can have a cultural understanding of how radical this act was. I am certain Jesus was cutting into the rigid mindset of the Israelites about only men being welcomed into the sanctuary. As discussed earlier women were not allowed in the sanctuary with men, which perhaps reflects the story of Genesis 2:18 in which woman was created out of a man's rib and lesser than. And yet Jesus seemingly defies this wisdom by inviting her into the sanctuary with him, which is more in alignment with Genesis 1:26 in which God created male and female in God's own image.

Another profound example of this balance of power that I am working towards is in the story of the resurrection. Of the disciples that Jesus chose to be the herald of his resurrection, which is the most powerful event in the history of humanity, he gives the honor to Mary Magdalene.

Now, let's touch upon Ephesians 5 :22 in which Paul says, "Wives be subject to your husbands" and so on. Let's be brutally honest. I know many Christian women who are deeply devoted to God through Jesus and are strong in spirit. They are warriors, kick-butt women who seemingly take charge and get things done. This is the way God made them. It is in their personality and in the very fabric of their being and of course they have married their opposites. More than once, as the discussion of marriage dynamics comes up they are the first to pull out Paul's words in Ephesians and state that their spouses are the head of the house. I know their spouses. They are gentle of spirit and perhaps even meek, a meekness that is seemingly void of the primal masculine. I may be wrong and out of line here but I dare say I don't see their husbands as holding true power in the marriage system, no matter what words come from either of their mouths, which means there is a disconnect between their words and the reality they are living. This is called denial, perhaps created by the mindset of Christians who say all marriages must fall into this box.

Every marriage is a blending of two different people. We share core truths about marriage but each union must forge an untrodden path that honors both partners to grow into their authentic self in

Christ. So we need to look into our marriage and see who really holds power. If you are the one who has held power in your marriage do you have the guts to give your spouse the freedom to discover her God-given power? A man in touch with his power is not threatened by the strength of another. On the other hand, if you have farmed out your power to your wife or have denied your true self to keep a false sense of peace in the home do you have the guts to rise up and grab hold of your power? Giving back power or claiming power isn't easy but if the marriage is be the vehicle of transformation that God intended it to be, a balance of power is a necessity.

The Desert

August came. The 'fire' of God cooled. The lessons ceased. The presence of God seemed to flee also. The passion to write left my soul as well. A desire to work took hold. Two forestry jobs came in. It was good to work. It was strange though. A part of me feared I had perhaps failed.

In the weeks that passed my soul went through a barren wasteland. It was a lonely place, perhaps even a bitter place. Prayers were dry, like stale bread to a parched throat, if not painful. The spiritual battle intensified within me, faith and fear, shadow and light, God and Satan. It took all my mental effort to stay focused in prayers for more than two minutes.

"How long, Lord?" I cried. I was weary, tired and blinded to the wisdom of this barren wasteland. More than once the sense of slipping into shadow came over my soul. Sometime in October a coyote appeared in my dream as I found myself slipping off a cliff in the dream. There was medicine in his gaze, a plea not to give up the fight.

The Road to Victory

"Claim my victory. For you and your family. Claim my victory," came God's voice. For months now I had carried my family in prayer. God was asking to go one step deeper.

New Year's Eve came. I stayed up late in prayer. Near midnight my heart began to burn with the fire of God. Intense joy welled up in my heart as the energy of God poured through me. I cried. It was good. I had nearly forgotten the goodness of God. The following night, and the next, and the next, God came like a burning flame within my heart. I was certain the new dawn was coming. On the fifth visit and after hours of intimate prayer, God spoke these words, "I am ready to take you into the spiritual realm."

"Yes!" I spoke to myself. The new dawn was coming. I prayed into the early morning hours, believing the new dawn would come that night. I fell asleep with hope but the new dawn did not come and even worse was the fact that I awoke in spiritual oppression. God spoke clearly, "Be strong."

My timing is not God's timing. Perhaps you can relate. To me, "I am ready to take you into the spiritual realm, meant soon, tomorrow, the next day or perhaps a week. Obviously, "my soon" was not "God's soon."

Time wore me down. My wild man stumbled. My prayers faltered. Fear took hold as our finances dwindled. I began work as a substitute teacher. It was a strange twist of events. I checked in with God about my agony and fear. "Your fear is useless," came God's reply. I tried to grab hold of that line and live into it like a man. It was not happening though. My inner landscape grew darker. I stumbled further in my spirit. Evil tightened its noose around my spirit. A sense of drowning came over me. I cried out to God, "Will I stand?"

"You will stand!"

Two months passed. A dream came. In the dream I was kneeling in a bright room. A voice spoke, "I will accomplish everything I have told you." The next night in the world of dreams I found myself reading a sacred parchment. The words said, "Pray without ceasing.

Live into undying trust." And so I began an intentional journey of trust and prayer. It took all my mental, emotional, spiritual faculties to live into this command. Many times I fell short.

Kathryn and I repeatedly spoke about finances. They were painful discussions. Substitute teaching ended. "I need a job," I cried out to God. "I don't want to drag Kathryn farther into my hell."

"Your job is to trust and obey," came the reply.

That isn't going to go over well, I thought. I tried to explain my answer to Kathryn who was stilled veiled from my inner pilgrimage. Just as I had thought, it didn't go over very well. A few days later the thought of starting a program called "Survivor" for young adolescent boys came to me. A pastor jumped on board. We put the word out. Kathryn was relieved.

The Survivor program didn't draw enough kids. This took a chunk out of Kathryn's heart. We had a really heated discussion about finances, which was the same discussion we have had for eighteen months. "I need you to get a job," she demanded.

"Kathryn, I have prayed about it repeatedly. I am called to trust and obey."

"You mean getting a job when we are going broke isn't trusting and obeying God!" Again, her wisdom was sound and was the same advice I would have given any other man in any other circumstances. But I knew there was a wisdom at work that had to be heeded. Going into the spiritual realm and facing Satan is serious business. I had been there before. There is no room for compromise. Either I trust God fully or I forfeit my breakthrough.

Colorado

Our family journeyed to Colorado to visit family, prompted by the unexpected death of my brother-in-law last November. As we were packing God spoke these words, "You have work out there." I thought my "work" involved being present to my family members. I should have known. As we drove, a knowing came over me this journey to Colorado would be a threshold, that it would be intense and that I must face what must be faced and not crumble in spirit.

It was good to be in Colorado, to see family and go for hikes. I consciously chose to connect with all three of my brothers, to listen to their stories, give honor where honor was due and offer strength where strength was needed. The family gatherings were spirited and filled with laughter. It was good.

Several days into our stay my Dad challenged me about being fifty-two years of age with no retirement, living month to month and seemingly not providing for my family and so on. I understood that from any rational perspective my actions and choices looked irresponsible, but still, it took a chunk out of my heart and cut into my father-wound. I shared a little of my journey with my father and the responsibilities given to me by God, that I had a calling on my life and was asked to travel an unconventional road. But the words didn't seem to connect. The conversation went on for over an hour and ended like most of my conversation ended with Kathryn, painful and wishing some things were never said.

Later that day Kathryn approached me. We began to have the same conversation, with of course the same results. It was like being caught between a rock and a hard place. There was no where to go. I could acquiesce to Kathryn's wisdom or hold the wisdom of God and take the hit. I chose to take the hit, just as I had done for the last eighteen months. Soon, our dialogue became tainted with awkward silence. Finally, with tears running down her cheeks she said, "I have lost all faith in you, Brian."

Immediately, the wound inside of me lashed out in fury, seeking to gain a stronghold within my psyche. Yes, it was a battle between the wounded boy and the wild man. To give into the boy was to give power to the wound and create an opening for evil to take hold. Yes, I could feel the hot of breath of Satan upon my neck, just waiting for me to break.

In strained silence we began our journey back from Colorado. I was raw, wondering when God and I would get to the bottom of all this. This fire seemed cruel, beyond what deemed necessary. There was wisdom I was sure, although it was veiled from my eyes. I only knew I had to get through it, to be true to God and trust all would be well.

That night, in some hotel in Grand Island, Nebraska, I found myself awake at two A.M., which is a frequent occurrence. I prayed intensely. Tears flowed freely down my cheeks as I released my pain. For a year and a half our marriage had been strained, really strained. It was hell.

God then took me back to a pivotal moment in my journey. Twenty-six years ago and while living in Steamboat I had been awakened in the dark of the night with the knowing of an angelic presence in my room. At the moment I was quite intrigued and wanted to look upon my visitor but was somehow prevented by a power greater than myself. The angel then spoke the words, "It is time to have faith like the ancient times," then left. That was it, short, to the point, leaving me pondering what faith like the ancient times meant. I understood little and still do. I was certain though there would be tests, trials and dark nights. This was one of them.

"It is time to have faith like the ancient times," I said to myself over and over as I lay in that quiet hotel room in Nebraska, listening to the gentle rhythmic breathing of my loved ones. Long into that night I cried as I thought of Abraham willing to put Isaac on the altar. This last eighteen months I had put my marriage on the altar, trusting God would see us through. I had been tested, not once but over and over. I had gone to the edge and had been true to the voice of God as I understood it, even at the cost of possibly losing my marriage.

"Father, am I about to lose everything?" I asked.

"No, you are about to gain everything."

Soon, Mary's presence came as she held me in her deep embrace. For a long time I just prayed. Near the five O'clock hour she spoke these words, "My son, it is finished!"

I cried deeply. I understood. I had endured the fire. "It is finished," I said to myself. "It is finished!"

16 VICTORY

"You will conquer. The conquering spirit is never crushed. Keep a brave and trusting heart. Face all your difficulties in the spirit of Conquest. Rise to greater heights than you have known before. Remember, where I am is Victory. Forces of evil, within and without you, flee at my Presence. Win me and all is won. All"
From God Calling, May 20th reflection.

I returned to Michigan ready. Yes, I was ready and knew it. I no longer feared going into the spiritual realm. I no longer doubted whether I would stand or fall. I had endured the fire. I was ready! God knew and the devil knew it. I was ready. I kept vigilant in prayer. The doors didn't open. A week passed, then another. God's wisdom said, "Be still," and so I waited some more.

"The kingdom of heaven will be like this. Ten bridesmaids took their lamps and went out to meet the bridegroom. Five of them were foolish and five of them were wise. When the foolish took their lamps, they took no oil with them; but the wise took flasks of oil with their lamps. As the bridegroom was delayed, all of them became drowsy and slept. But at midnight there was a shout. 'Look, here is the bridegroom! Come and meet him.' Then all the bridesmaids got up and trimmed their lamps. The foolish said to the wise, 'Give us some of your oil, for our lamps are going out.' But the wise replied, 'No! There will not be enough for you and for us; you had better go to the dealers and buy some for yourselves.' And while they went to buy it, the bridegroom came, and those who were ready went with him into the wedding banquet; and the door was shut. Later the other bridesmaids came also, saying, "Lord, Lord, open to us,' But he replied, 'Truly I tell you, I do not know you.' Keep awake therefore, for you do not know the day nor the hour." Matthew 25:1-13

This is about waiting, which can be the most difficult of tasks given to us by Jesus. When we know the work is done, when we have completed all that has been asked of us and still the door does not open. It does not matter the arena-employment, healing for ourselves or loved ones, ministry, marriage, or whatever; the fact is, waiting can be agonizing. So we are called to wait upon the Lord, to be still in spirit, steady in our heart and patient in our agony, trusting there is a wisdom in which we cannot see, that God is working through people and circumstances that are beyond our sight.

One month passed then two. During this time God impressed upon me the lesson of living in the presence of God, which meant releasing my fears and living fully in the moment. That is where God is, in the *now*. The moment I let my mind fret regarding tomorrow the power and joy of God slipped from my consciousness. I was learning the lesson of trust at new levels. It was exhilarating. I experienced the freedom of God, the joy of being human and the power of the now. I was also learning not to judge the moment but simply embrace the moment, that God was in the moment.

Certainly, the human ego searches for the next thing, that next buzz that will validate and give our lives purpose and meaning. We have all played into it, the next big ministry event, sporting event or whatever. It is a big lie. Consumerism and our economy is built upon the way of the ego and the craving of the next thing. So much for, "In God we trust," which is printed upon our dollar bill.

But when God becomes our meaning and our purpose, our world is turned upside down. There is no more chasing the next thing. There is only God and the now. This is the way of the kingdom of God.

These lessons were coming hard into my soul. Of course, like all lessons, they come with hard work and patience. I would grab hold of it, then with the slightest of worry, slip into fear. Instantly, I could feel the kingdom of God slip from my consciousness. Then the downward spiral began, that is, until I cried stop and re-centered myself.

As a few weeks passed I inquired in prayer about the new dawn. God's whisper came, "I have chosen the very hour." A sense of joy came over me. My only concern was having the time and space that going into the spiritual realm demands. I needed a cave. God spoke, "Trust me."

Near the end of October, nearly three months after our return from Colorado, my dad phoned, asking if my family would like their eleven year old Mercedes Benz for a family car. Kathryn and the kids shouted, "Yes."

My dad asked, "Should I ship it out to you?"

"NO!" I stated, with a little more emotion than was necessary. I knew. "I would prefer to pick it up," I replied.

"That would be fine. We are leaving for Tucson. It will be here waiting for you."

As I packed Kathryn encouraged me to take several days for myself. Two years had passed since I had spent alone-time in the wilderness. I caught a flight to Denver. My sister shuttled me to Colorado Springs. As I opened the door of my parents' home and walked downstairs to the spare bedroom God spoke these words into my soul, "You will know when it is time to leave. Trust me with your whole being."

I had heard those words, "You will know when it is time to leave" before in my journey. They were spoken on the second day of a two week trek into Canyon Lands. I left Canyon Lands forty days later. *This is it,* I thought to myself, the moment I had been waiting for and trained for. Yes, I had trained over twenty-one years for this moment. I was ready though. God told me I was ready, that was enough. I trembled at the words, "Trust me with your whole being." I had not heard those words before. Obviously, this wasn't going to be a picnic.

The next morning I began a slow ascent up the Barr Trail at the base of Pikes Peak, praying my prayers with cadence to my steps. The skies were autumn-blue crisp. Pikes Peak was graced with a dusting of snow. Temperatures would climb into the mid-sixties. It was Colorado perfect.

My soul went into vision quest mode, focused and prayerful. Sleep came intermittently as I prayed into the night. I ate little. Three grace-filled days passed. Prayers were deep. Knowing Kathryn was on call at work in several days I checked in with God about departure day. I heard, "Every detail is in my hands. Trust me with your whole being."

That morning I continued my prayers in the quiet of the bedroom, my prayers deepened as God's Spirit washed over me, renewing my soul and giving me vision as to the work God would ask of me after this quest. Just as my prayers ended the phone rang. I checked the incoming number.

"Hi Kathryn," I said.

"Hi. When are you coming home?" she asked.

I hesitated. "Kathryn, when I arrived God told me that I would know when it is time to leave."

Understandably, there was an awkward silence. "So you don't know when you are coming home," she said in a voice I barely recognized.

"No."

"Brian, some of your quests have been a month or more. What am I supposed to do? What about being on-call this weekend? Who is going to watch the kids if I get called in? What about running this house and helping with the kids and the dog?"

"I know," I said. "It is a difficult moment and a faith thing. I would like to come home tomorrow but I can't leave yet."

"So what am I going to do this weekend if you are not home?"

"I will call Liz," I said.

The phone call ended. "Oh God, how can you ask this of us after all we have been through?"

"Trust me with your whole being!"

I called Liz. She said she would gladly help out. As I hung up the phone I heard once again, "Every detail is my hands."

"Amen," I whispered to myself then set out for Barr Trail.

Each day I grew stronger in God and each day Kathryn grew more distant. She was falling, really falling, into despair about me, my choices and our marriage. It was understandable. Our marriage journey had been unconventional, which had been amplified this last twenty months. In many ways her journey had been more difficult than mine. I was given the fire and the vision. She held on out of love for me. Now that love was being shaken, if not destroyed.

Being fourteen hundred miles apart my only course of action was to trust and pray. It was the great test of trust and living into the moment. And when I did, I experienced incredible joy and peace, even though circumstances dictated otherwise.

On the eighth day I began a very slow ascent up Barr Trail, praying "Holy, holy, holy is the Lord God Almighty." I prayed this with every step, with my whole being and without stopping. Shortly into my ascent clouds descended upon Pikes Peak. Thunder rolled off the mountain. A thrill of excitement coursed through my spirit. I turned a corner of the trail then set my course for a small peak.

Hours later I reached the summit, found a flat spot then fell to my knees in worship. It was good. I remained there for about an hour then began my descent. I returned to the parking lot just after dinner hour. Fearful, I called Kathryn. She answered the phone. Her voice told the story. Every muscle in my body tensed as she spoke of possible divorce or living together as friends and co-raising our children. It was brutal. The conversation lasted about fifteen minutes. As I hung up I wondered if she would take off her ring that night.

I sat quiet in the car for a while, breathing deeply and retracing my steps that had lead me here. It was crazy. I tried to calm myself as a battle sought to gain a stronghold in my psyche. Fear and faith, like two wolves fighting for the *Alpha* position, had positioned themselves for a battle within my spirit.

There is a Cherokee Legend that speaks of this very battle. Perhaps you know it or have lived through such a battle yourself. It goes like this: "An old Cherokee was teaching his grandson about life saying, 'A fight is going on inside me. It is a terrible fight and it is between two wolves. One is evil, he is anger, envy, sorrow, regret, greed, arrogance, self-pity, guilt, resentment, inferiority, lies, false pride, superiority, and ego.' He continued, 'The other is good. He is joy, peace, love, hope, serenity, humility, kindness, benevolence, empathy, generosity, truth, compassion, and faith. The same fight is going on inside you-and inside every other person, too.'

The grandson thought about it for a minute and then asked his grandfather, 'Which wolf will win?'

The old Cherokee simply replied, 'The one I feed'."

As I sat in the car I couldn't have been more aware of this battle. Before me was the wide dark road that sought to pull me into despair, anger, fear, mistrust, and of course self-pity. There was also the temptation to pack my bags and seek to heal my marriage of my own doing. It was the logical and seemingly responsible thing to do. But deeper down there was a voice, a voice that once again invited me to put my entire trust in God. I had a choice, to trust or not to trust. It was that simple. I retraced many of my pivotal moments with God to reassure myself that my hearing of God's voice within was authentic. That was the core issue. Do I believe in God's spoken word within my heart or give room for doubt, fear and self-wisdom. Jesus had told me many times that God would heal my marriage. Now I had to believe it even though Kathryn had thrown the word divorce into our relationship. Yes, two wolves were fighting.

I returned to my parents' house. I prayed into the night, fell asleep for a couple of hours then woke at midnight. Upon my waking I sat up in my usual meditation posture and began my devotions to God. But there was an unsettledness in my spirit that beckoned me on my knees. I then wrapped my blanket around my body, got on my knees, held up my hands and began to worship God. Not long after, a growing presence of evil began to fill the room. I tensed up. I had fought many battles in the spiritual realm, but not face to face when I was awake and conscious. Instantly, Mary's voice, no longer sweet and tender but with a fierceness I had never known, said me to "BE BOLD! BE BOLD!"

For a brief moment I closed my eyes and went inward, seeking to grasp the meaning of Mary's words. "Be bold," I said to myself, "Be bold." Within a split second the realization came that being bold is about claiming my identity and power in God. I opened my eyes, stared into the darkness and said, "The same power that lives inside of Jesus Christ lives inside of me." Yes, this is what it means to be bold. I said it again and again. As I did, the primal power of God shot through my soul and psyche. I focused my body, mind, and soul and peered hard into the evil that was manifesting before me. My jaw clenched as the warrior energy coursed through me like I had never known before. There was no fear nor shrinking back within me. I was here to fight. The evil presence came closer. I stayed kneeling and peered harder into it, eager for battle. Just then, Mary's voice spoke, "Grab the sword, the same sword that Jesus used in the desert when he faced Satan." I did not see a sword but in faith I reached down and symbolically grabbed the same sword that Jesus used in the desert.

Instantly a bolt of electricity shot through my entire being. With both hands holding this unseen sword I screamed the warrior's cry as my spirit lunged at the evil. Instinctively, my arms slashed back and forth as an unconscious growling came from the depths of my being. It was war, a war I had been anticipating for nearly twenty-one years. Time blurred. I was conscious of little, except that every part of my being, body, mind and soul, was at war. I never let up as God's power surged within me. The evil weakened. I continued to slash into the evil presence. Finally the evil fled. Instantly, I collapsed face first on the carpet and began to weep uncontrollably.

"I did it God." I said several times, hardly believing this moment had come to pass.

"Yes, you did it."

When I finally regained my composure I asked God, "Am I done?"

"No," came God's voice. "Call to you the heavenly hosts and make war on the strongholds of evil upon my earth."

The instant I consented to God's command I sensed, but could not see, a powerful force of God's angels gathering around me. There was great joy and a sense of celebration. As we were gathering I spoke out, "Jesus, you need to lead me and this army."

"No, you must lead them, came the voice of Jesus. "I fought this battle two thousand years ago. Now you must fight."

It was a moment of great awakening. The kingdom of God rests upon the shoulders of men and women who are willing to go into the great wilderness to make the kingdom of God their own. It is a paradox. Christians are waiting for Jesus to return, and yet, Jesus is waiting for us to claim who we are in him, that we are created in the image of God, born for greatness, born to love, surrender, and of course, born to fight. Yes, it is our transformation that will bring God's power and love to this earth.

In the realm of the spirit I journeyed across the face of this earth, claiming God's victory and power. It was not a battle but more of a ritualizing of the victory that had just been won. When my spirit returned to my body I knew I was done. I laid back down and spent a couple of more hours in prayer to God.

Near the four O'clock hour and anticipating God's outpouring upon my soul I gave myself to sleep. I woke a couple of hours later troubled in spirit. God did not come, which meant another day in Colorado, which meant more stress between Kathryn and me. "Oh God, after last night I was expecting you to come and to send me back to Michigan." There was no reply. I sat up to pray but it was useless. I couldn't shake my anxiety. About sun up I dressed and went for a long walk, speaking my Jesus prayer, hoping to find some sense of peace. "I can't shake this anxiety God. I just can't," I said while walking. I kept walking and praying but my efforts were useless. After two hours, I asked in prayer, "Should I return to the mountain I was at yesterday?"

God's voice came, "What you seek is not on the mountain. It is within you. Go back to where you battled last night."

I returned to my parents' home, wrapped the blanket around my shoulders and began to meditate. God's voice spoke, "Be still." I knew what God was asking of me, to be still in spirit, to trust in the moment and to release my fear. A half hour or so passed without any success.

"Will I be here long?" I asked.

"As long as it takes," came God's reply.

Oh dear, I thought.

Sometime later I found the grace to surrender as the presence of God descended. God's voice came again, "Forgive Kathryn." As I consented to God's command, grace flowed through my spirit as the gift of release came over my spirit. I cried deeply. "Let go of your anger, fear, rage and hatred." I did. God's voice came again, "Forgive yourself." Again, as I obeyed there was a huge release within me. "Give away your shame, self condemnation and self judgement." More tears came. "Give away all judgement of others." I did that also.

"I feel like I am preparing to die," I said.

'You are preparing to meet God," came my Mary's voice.

"Forgive all who have injured you." Instantly, my mind went through a litany of the people whom I had felt injured by. I forgave each one. "Bless all your family members." I began with Kathryn and my daughters then thought my parents and each of my siblings, giving each a blessing of love and gratitude for being in my life. There was a pause.

"Am I done?" I asked. My answer came in an instant as I found myself kneeling in the presence of the Holy One. Yes, before me was the brilliant presence of the Holy One, although I saw no shape or form. But I knew where I was and in whose presence I was kneeling before. There was no one else but myself and the Holy One. I did not experience fear, only love, acceptance and a sense that I belonged to God. As I remained kneeling a voice spoke to me, "Come closer." A sense of fear and reverence came over me as I began to move forward on my knees. "No, not like that. Come forward," said the voice. As I obeyed that command I moved very close to the Holy One, still kneeling. "Drink deeply," came the voice. I opened every energy center within my soul and spirit and simply drank of God's perfect love. While I was there it was made known to me that I would be given permission to return to this Holy Place many times in my life and that my soul would journey into the spiritual realm as it had the first eight years of my walk with God. Joy came over me.

As I remained kneeling before the Holy One and knowing I was being drawn back to earth I asked if I could see Jesus and Mary. Immediately, the presence of Jesus and Mary came into this inner sanctuary, although I could not see their form. I fell to my face and wept with gratitude while saying, "Thank you," repeatedly. Soon, I found myself moving away from the Holy One.

"It is time to go home," came God's voice. I then found myself fully in my parents home.

During the quiet hours of driving a burden was lifted from my soul. I felt like *Frodo* in the *Lord of the Rings* after the ring and fallen into the fires of *Mordor*. Yes, the burden was gone. A wound remained though. I prayed the wound would heal completely. But the test was over. God and I had become friends. I no longer feared failing God or my humanity. Nor did I fear Kathryn's humanity. It was that freedom that allowed me to reflect upon the last two years with more of an open heart and an open mind. It was obvious I had made some mistakes along the path. I did not heed Kathryn's wisdom on the onset of writing this book. I should have worked part-time like she suggested. I had been so eager and passionate to get the book written that I forsook the obvious, at least to Kathryn, that the journey to completion might be longer than expected. But it wasn't the writing process that took two years, but rather the journey of transformation, healing and purification.

I called Kathryn. Again, her voice and spirit was far away. "I need to tell you I am sorry. I did not heed your wisdom about working part-time upon the onset of writing this book. I missed that one and I am sorry. I let my passion and desire to serve God squelch your wisdom."

"Thank you," she replied.

"I have not been a good team player in our marriage either. I see that plainly. For this I am sorry."

I returned home the next evening. There was peace. In the next few days the presence of God descended upon Kathryn and me. Healing came. Several days later while sharing breakfast Kathryn looked up and said, "We made it through."

"Yes, Kathryn, we made it through."

A day later I told Kathryn about Colorado Springs. There was more peace.

17 EPILOGUE

So here we are, at the end of the story. Thank you for taking a journey with me. I pray my story is an invitation into your story as well.

It is time. I cannot emphasize that enough. You are the one who must grab hold of God's power and wield it upon this earth. No one else can do it for you. You are the one.

At such moments we are left with a choice, a choice that has profound ramifications upon our soul, our loved ones and the kingdom of God. I invite you to be still in spirit. Ponder what legacy you want to leave behind. There are roads before us. We must choose. To say, "Yes" to God is to welcome a joy that can never be expressed in words. It is also to welcome a sword, a sword that will pierce our shadows and cut into our wounds. Certainly, the word of the Lord is a two edged sword. Yes, it cuts into our wounds but it also heals, and in the healing we will discover a strength we knew not. That is the journey.

I take a moment to speak to those who may be in the twilight of their earthly journey. Perhaps you feel as if you have missed the Lord's calling upon your life and now time is running short. But I say to you, if you have but one breath, there is time. That is the truth Jesus spoke about in the parable of the workers in the Gospel of Matthew chapter 20, that those who worked only one hour received the same pay as those who worked the entire day. Yes, there is time. Give yourself completely to God, call forth your masculine soul and face the shadows that have kept you from living. In doing so, the kingdom of God is further manifested here on earth, and an unseen bridge is built for the next man.

So, for those who choose to make the kingdom of God their own I take this moment to honor you and your story. How I wish we could sit in a circle and share our stories. It is unlikely we will meet while on this earth. But we will meet in the kingdom of God. And on that day we sill sit at the king's table and share our stories of the wounds we suffered, the mountains we climbed and the dragons we slew. And we will dance. Yes, in wild joy before the Lord we will dance. And it will be good.

Until then, I invite you to surrender your all to God, trust, and let your life be a prayer. Do your work. Yes, find a circle of men you trust where you can face your shadows, cry out your pain and awaken the wild man within you. And when it hurts and you feel like you can't take another step, reach deep within, draw your sword and fight with everything you have. The kingdom of God will come. And it will be good.

Amen.

Until we meet,
Your brother, Brian Christian Meagher,
Wild Lover of God

Made in the USA
Charleston, SC
10 April 2012

ABSOLUTELY NECESSARY

First printed by:
RR Donnelley
4101 Winfield Road
Warrenville, IL 60555

Library of Congress Control Number: 2014915337

Contact Ross Shafer:
www.RossShafer.com

Contact Michael Burger:
www.MichaelBurgerTV.com

ISBN: 978-0-692-27999-1

Printed in the United States of America

ABSOLUTELY NECESSARY

HOW TO KEEP YOURSELF
IN HIGH DEMAND

ROSS SHAFER
MICHAEL BURGER

CONTENTS

ACKNOWLEDGMENTS

From Ross: In writing a book about staying relevant and necessary, I find that I must acknowledge and thank everyone I ever met who made me feel "necessary." My life has been informed by the kids I met in school, the parents of my neighborhood friends, my teachers and coaches, the fellow football players who collided into me at full speed yet offered me a hand off the turf, all of the employers who validated my worth by hiring a disruptive wiseacre, the comedians who challenged me to rewrite my jokes and then laughed out loud at the result, the TV stars who became my mentors, the companies who had the confidence to pay for my advice, and most of all to my family who kept loving my notions even when they were obviously lame (a Stereo/Pet Shop?). To my mother Lois and my father Chuck, I think of how much fun you two had every day. To my two brothers, Clell and Scott. While we haven't been geographically close, my heart is never far from you. To my sons Adam and Ryan, I must tell you, I feel like I won the lottery. You are far better men than I was at your age and I'm so gratified by your character, kindness, and sense of honor to others. To my daughter Lauren (Lolo), yes, you are smarter than I am. You are funnier than I am. And you possess a natural empathy for others that instantly makes you endearing. Never change, girl. And finally to my wife Leah. When I was a young boy, I often dreamt of marrying a beautiful princess who was smart, funny, and thought of me as her one-and-only knight in shining armor. You have made that dream come true every day. You are all absolutely necessary to my life!

From Michael: Unlike Ross who's written six books, this is my first. I would be remiss if I didn't start off by thanking my friend, business partner and co-author of this very book, Ross Shafer. Without his encouragement, inspiration, wisdom and contribution, this book would be...half as long. Seriously I could not have done this without him. And speaking of people who have made a difference, I would like to mention Richard Lawrence, Harry Friedman, Rick Rosner, and Bob Noah. All you need to know is they define the phrase, "one of the good guys." Additionally, many thanks for the encouragement and inspiration I have received from family, friends, and a group of people who probably never get thanked. My audiences. From the early days of stand-up to my keynote audiences today in the corporate world, I appreciate all of you who come up to say you were either moved, motivated, or inspired. Well, I have news for you, you have done the very same for me. Thank you.

INTRODUCTION

Who Should Read This Book?

We wrote this book to be read by both leaders, team members, and/or associates. We want leaders to absorb this material as a tool for remaining an important agent of growth. We want team members/associates to use this material to become regarded as people whose ideas and opinions must be taken seriously.

For Team Members/Associates: We know that any person, regardless of title, has the opportunity to become extremely valuable. But to be an "absolutely necessary" member of the team you must show management that you have an endless flow of ideas that will either (1) make a lot of money or (2) save a lot of money. By example, the idea of a hotel promoting a luxurious hotel bed Westin's Heavenly Bed went largely unnoticed by the entire hospitality business industry for almost 1,300 years until one young man at Starwood Hotels showed his leaders how a good "heavenly" type bed could be a highly profitable brand differentiator. From that moment forward, it was "absolutely necessary" that savvy competitors followed suit.

Any team member, at any level, can become invaluable if you know how to properly introduce your ideas. Regularly speaking up, with good research and authentic enthusiasm, are the worthwhile risks for achieving greatness. We will show you how to get your true worth noticed.

For Leaders: The leaders who are in high demand have the ability to see into the future. Some say they can "see around corners." They notice trends that will elevate their organization to a higher level. They also notice market shifts that can render an organization irrelevant. Then, they act upon those trends before their competitors. We will show you how to make consistently better decisions.

Ross Shafer here.
I have known Michael Burger since the days when we were both stand-up comedians and later, network TV hosts. As irony would have it, we even hosted different iterations of the same game show "(Match Game)." I hosted that show it from 1990-1991 and Michael hosted "Match Game" '98. At one of Michael's birthday parties, he introduced me to a gorgeous and funny woman named Leah. Leah and I have been happily married ever since. Thank you Michael! As lifelong entrepreneurs, (and after our television careers morphed into other business pursuits,) Michael and I would often get together to analyze why some of our television shows (our "products") were successful…and why others were so bad you can't even see them in reruns! We agreed that "remaining relevant to the collective herd of viewers" was the common denominator. But how could we crystalize that forensic conclusion into a predictive behavior? About the same time, I spoke at

an IT meeting and heard a software engineer ask, "What can I do today so I will be indispensable tomorrow?" That simple plea hit Michael and I like a lightning bolt. Yes, being "absolutely necessary" is how we all want others to perceive us. As individuals and as companies, we all want to feel so important that our ideas and skills are forever valuable.

What you will read here are the insights and tales of people and companies who were either considered "absolutely necessary" (can't live without you) or expendable (glad you're gone). These insights were gleaned during hundreds of conference calls with clients, personal conversations at our client's headquarters, and feedback from the many corporate speaking engagements we do every year. Whether you are a team member/associate hoping for a promotion or a CEO hoping to take your company public, we hope you'll find this book absolutely necessary to you.

Michael Burger here.

True, Ross and I have known each other for over 20 years, both starting out in the comedy world. I didn't know Ross in the '80s when he was doing stand-up, however I was a big fan of his act and would often use his best stuff as my closer. Our TV shows may have come and gone, but the challenge to stay relevant and "absolutely necessary" (to those that hire us) remained ever present. That's what struck both of us so clearly, regardless of our occupations. I don't care if it's hosting a TV show, managing a hedge fund, or making that little thing that does that amazing little thing I saw on The Discovery Channel show "How it's Made." (Is it just me?)

Or, can you kill an entire afternoon watching that show?) The people and companies that succeed have figured out how to make themselves necessary to others. As much as I love the world of show business (I was lucky enough to host over 4,000 hours of television), I was fascinated with the business of show business. I realized early on that innovation was necessary for survival. As Ross would say, if you don't like change you're going to hate extinction. So Ross and I didn't give up; we got busy noticing the connection between the broadcast world and the corporate world. We studied why some companies fail miserably, while others experience wild success. Incidentally, one of my first attempts at staying relevant in the '80s was to get my real estate license. I took the test and passed... but here's the punch line. The day I received my license from the California Department of Real Estate, the headline of the Los Angeles Times was that mortgage interest rates hit 19%!!! How's that for timing? Yeah, I really don't miss the '80s.

Ross mentioned that we spend countless hours on the phone with our clients. We hear firsthand what keeps them up at night. But we love it. It is not uncommon for either of us to step into a random hotel conference room just to hear what a visiting expert or renowned CEO has to say. We sustain our value to our organization by staying alert to what happens on the front line—doing the heavy lifting before someone asks us to do it. I've been in more conference rooms and onstage so many times I don't leave the house until a CEO says, "Ladies and gentlemen, please welcome Michael Burger!" In fact, I've been on so many business related flights that when I get home I pull a chair up next to a window and wait for someone to bring me warm nuts.

You Will See Sidebars in This Book:

Aside from being pals and business partners for 20 years, we co-founded The Relevant Report® (www.RelevantReport. com). The Relevant Report is a video blog we launched as a way to inspire individuals and companies. We use the site to share the ideas and cool practices of both organizations and individuals. The Relevant Reports also serve as direct shots of personal development. These short video blogs are not only fun— but a jolt of inspiration you can use as a "meeting opener" or as a private motivator. To that end, we will sprinkle a few of our reports throughout the book as a sort of "station break" to give you a breather, to grab a cup of coffee, and force you to think about a company other than yours. If you have the electronic version of this book, you will be able to view some of the Relevant Reports online, by just clicking on the link.

The first Relevant Report you will stumble upon is about a company who was courageous enough to face the reality of a changing market— and in particular customer buying habits; causing them to completely flip their business model upside down. Now, they are making more money than ever.

ONE

REALITY SHOULD BE YOUR BEST FRIEND

For Team Members/Associates: If you go to work and perform your job adequately, you will get paid and you will go home. But to become an invaluable asset to your company, first you must get noticed as someone who is exceptional. To become an "absolutely necessary" resource, you must transcend what people normally expect from you. You will become extremely important if you keep your eyes wide open to the changing realities of your position. Is your position necessary? Will your position be combined with another job? If so, do you have the skills to do both jobs? Beyond doing the job you were hired to do, you will raise your worth to the company by studying the realities of your company's market position: Is your company #1 in your market? Are you merging with #3? Are you going out of business? What are your competitors doing that you should be doing? What are your competitors doing so poorly that you can take their market share?

Coasting into complacency while the world changes around you could cause you and your company to disappear in a cloud of irrelevance. When you a spot a trend that threatens your job, be ready to adjust. Learn what you need to know before you are told your skills are no longer relevant. Don't be the last one to know when your company enters Chapter 11 bankruptcy. As our tech guru friend Scott Klososky often says, "Reality watchers drive their companies with the high beams on."

For Leaders: The future of your company will be dependent upon how well you adapt to changing market conditions and trends. When revenues drop, don't assume it's a cycle that will automatically reverse itself to the upside. You may be subject to profit blindness—the condition that occurs when you've made a lot of money one way and are reticent to change. The market always dictates the next big swing away from conventional wisdom. It's your job to notice when *reality* might torpedo your ascent to greatness.

How Did This Happen?

Have you ever had a boyfriend or girlfriend who suddenly dumped you? It was impossible to understand, right? Didn't make sense. How could this happen? It seemed like you were so happy together last week. And now, your partner is seeing someone else? Come to think of it, maybe there were subtle clues along the way. "How could you forget our anniversary?" "You are a total slob," "You insulted my family," "You are too lazy," "You never do enough things right," or the deal-breaker, "I don't love you anymore."

Even though you hear the evidence, you can't help but think there must be something you can do to turn the clock back to "the good old days."

In a relationship, if the other person tells you, "Our relationship is like doing push-ups on your knees, it's just not working out." Working on your career or running a company is no different. Believe the reality in front of you rather than acting on some delusion rattling around in your mind.

Denial can be a paralyzing factor that has the power to reject reality.

When your business is failing before your eyes, it is impossible to believe your once great company is currently in trouble.

You say to yourself, "This does not make sense. We have worked too hard at this."

How could you have made so much money in the past yet now your market share is being devoured by competitors? Or worse, your customers have changed their buying habits and you are not a good fit anymore. What do you do? React quickly if your profits are being threatened.

It Can't Be Us, Right!?

When leaders have faith in their mission, their people, their ethics, their products, and their history, it's almost human nature to blame either outside influences or internal obstacles.

"The economy is killing us."

"Government regulations are making it impossible
    to compete."

"Our competitors are undercutting us."

"Management is making the wrong decisions."

"We can't attract the right people."

"We don't have enough marketing money."

"If we had a bigger plant we could increase capacity."

Here's what we know. Your problems are not a secret. Good news—and bad—travels fast, especially within your industry. But you should know that your competitors are in dark rooms after hours complaining about the exact same factors that plague you. You should also know that whining and assigning the blame for your misfortunes is a shameful waste of time and energy. You cannot whine your way to more profits. Instead, the successful teams we've witnessed tend to adopt *this* attitude:

No Blame.

No Excuses.

No Surrender.

No Limits.

We are not saying your fears are imagined.

Your feelings are probably 100% accurate. But you can't do much about them today, can you? So, stop lamenting and start chanting, "These are the economic circumstances we are facing...so let's be inventive. Let's win with the resources and people we have."

Then, it is up to leadership to agree upon a going-forward plan—and create practical tactics and deadlines to wage war against realistic obstacles.

This CEO Managed Reality Very Well

In 2005, young Jon Vrabley was one of several vice presidents at Huttig Building Products, headquartered in St. Louis, Missouri. They served what seemed to be an endless supply of new housing starts

As you no doubt know, in 2006, the mortgage crisis caused the bottom to fall out of the U.S. housing market. Huttig was a direct casualty. Huttig's revenues went from $1.1 billion to almost half that. A worried board of directors asked for ideas. Vrabely had the courage to tell senior leaders that Huttig's current strategy would kill the 125 year old company. He backed up his claim with a step by step plan to turn it around. The board was so impressed they immediately replaced their long-time CEO with 41-year old Jon Vrabely.

As the housing market continued to plummet, Vrabely had no fear about terminating old strategies. He wrote off two projects that represented a $16.1 million dollar investment because they were draining cash. He closed 18 of their 45 distribution centers. With a heavy heart, he let go nearly half of the workforce.

Yet, while he was cutting costs at Huttig, Vrabely also knew his competitors were hurting. So, Huttig aggressively went after his competitor's best talent, their product lines, and their market share. Since 2011, Huttig has added approximately 200 people, sales have risen 8.1%, and the company is generating positive earnings.

Jon Vrabely is the model of a leader who faced reality—defied convention—and wasn't afraid to insist his board of directors listen to the dire truth.

RELEVANT REPORT

By Michael Burger

How to Adapt to Unforeseen Markets Shifts

You work hard. You try to stay relevant. But sometimes dramatic market shifts are out of your control. Rather than live in denial, or think "this will pass." You must face reality and quickly adjust your business model to stay necessary—particularly to the people who give you their money. Today we will visit The Border Store in Westminster, California, or at least we can visit for a little while. This wallpaper store is closing in a couple of days. Sad? Not at all. The reasons for closure are an inspiring story.

The store started at a flea market for roughly four years. They followed by renting a retail storefront, ran it for 15 years and during that time they also started a website. Over the years, in-store sales went down... and internet sales went up. Owners Lisa and Michael Arnell told me, "It just made financial sense that when 80% of our income is from the internet and 20% is walk-in, we didn't need the added expenses." So they decided to face reality and close their brick-and-mortar store. By doing so they actually saved money. A lot of money. They saved $30,000 in rent, $20,000 in advertising, and $15,000 in staffing. So how in the world do people buy wallpaper online when you can't see it or touch it? And, aren't a lot of patterns similar? Yes, but this couple was very smart. Along the way they created original border designs that can't be found anywhere else. Forty percent of their sales come from their proprietary private label.

So the lesson is this. If your customers have changed the way they want to buy from you, DON'T QUESTION THEM! Be humble and follow THEIR wisdom. Be empathetic and follow THEIR needs. And for the sake of your business be smart and FOLLOW THEIR MONEY. The good news is Lisa and Michael's online business is thriving because they are available online 24/7 365, defining themselves as a perpetually valued company.

LINK: http://youtu.be/Q38X6bMX1Aw

A Surprising Reality: Big Often Fears Small

There is a tendency to think that larger organizations have the competitive advantage. It's not always true. In the home improvement sector, we've had conversations with leaders at Home Depot and Lowe's. They are not as worried about each other as they are about the smaller home town retailers like Ace Hardware, Do-It-Best, and True Value. Why? Smaller community retailers have the relationship advantage. They can see and talk to everyone who comes through their doors.

The same is true with Neiman Marcus. They are not worried about Nordstrom or Macy's as their primary market share thieves. The large department stores are more wary of the more nimble online retailers who can spot a trend quickly and react within the same day.

As you probably know, Sears has announced plans to spin off Lands' End and sell its auto centers, a deal that one analyst estimates could be worth as much as $2.5 billion. But the company has about $2.8 billion in long-term debt. They have closed some stores and downsized operations in the wake of e-commerce threats from online retailers who don't have Sears' brick and mortar investment. However, there is one bright light in the Sears story. True to the concept of small being able to compete with big, the Sears Home Store outlets are extremely profitable. The Sears Home Store concept has a smaller in-store inventory but can still access the full range of Sears products. It's a shining model of how community-based businesses can still remain competitive.

Nimble entrepreneurialism is sometimes very scarce in a large organization.

Because when you are a "giant," you have scale. You can allegedly negotiate lower prices from vendors; thus increasing your profit margins. But giants also tend to commit to large scale plans and large scale expenses. When you hear of a company like Sam's Club laying off 2,300 workers or Macy's laying off 2,500 team members, you get a sense of how scale doesn't inherently protect you from losing money.

There Are No Perfect Organizations

Our team of consultants has the unique opportunity to study hundreds of organizations each year. Some are multi-billion dollar companies. Others are mom-and-pop operations. Some make a lot of money. Others are struggling to keep the lights on. But they all have one thing in common.

None of them are totally satisfied.

There is no perfect company. There can't be. Our economy is too evolutionary. You will always covet what your competitors have, and they will covet what you have. You will never get everything you want—when you want it. You will never be 100% relevant; and if you are, it will be temporary because circumstances change.

Knowing that perfection is the goal then we have to stay on the path to get there. The path is fraught with dead ends and U-turns. Curse the heavens if you like, but then calm down, accept reality, and react quickly to your changing landscape.

Learn from the triumphs and mistakes of other organizations.

• ——— RELEVANT REPORT ——— •

By Michael Burger

Legacy Companies Can Beat the Competition When They Remain Relevant

While we want you to obsess over what your competition is doing, you don't have to abandon your legacy brand if you can reinvent yourself in a relevant way. Here's an example.

In a world of electronic tablets and interactive games, how can a 100-year-old, non-tech company that manufactures a simple red wagon possibly thrive, let alone survive? Yep, I'm talking about The Radio Flyer wagon. I've had one of these since I was too young to climb into it by myself. Today the company that makes this wagon is rolling along just fine thank you very much. And here's how this nearly century old company is doing it. By innovating! A decade ago, wagons accounted for virtually all of its sales. Now, they drive less than one-third. Radio Flyer and its CEO Robert Pasin (also known as the CWO, Chief Wagon Officer) say they keep innovating with new scooters. Like one for girls called the Groove Glider—it comes with an iPod speaker and holder for your smartphone—or the Shockwave for boys made with flexible shocks in the rear that give riders the feeling of jumping extra high.

Ouch, I feel old writing this. Let me pause here and rant for a second. If you're old enough to remember the 60s—and if you really lived those 60s you probably don't remember them, as the joke goes—you know toys of that era were the best. I'm speaking from experience. No, I didn't have an iPod at the tender age of 6, but I did have real lawn darts with real steel tips on board—that you could toss at the Fourth of July picnic and accidentally hit your Uncle Bud in his calf. True story. What do today's kids have? Nerf Darts! Oh, look out for the foam! Come on! In my day the toys came apart, heads fell off, parts and pieces wound up in your mouth. I can't speak for you, but I'd swallow them. No big deal. I turned out alright; I ate a whole platoon of GI Joe's one summer. Talk about going on maneuvers. I'm fine; in fact, that's how we got our fiber. No lead paint in the toys today? Really, I used to lick my Etch a Sketch. I grew up in a house that by today's standards was dangerous. It wasn't baby-proofed in any way. The coffee table corners were sharp, the wall plugs were exposed, the stove was hot and my parents smoked. There, I said it. My dad smoked a pipe, my mom puffed cigarettes. Yet somehow I turned out okay. Say it with me, somehow we turned out alright!

Our parents didn't love us less, they just weren't sold the bill of goods that said kids can't fail. Talk about not being ready for the real world—give a kid a trophy for just showing up and see what happens when he loses his first job in the real world!

How did we ever survive? I'll tell you how!! We had parenting! Mom told me not to put that egg beater in my mouth and a few turns of the handle later I learned.

OK, sorry about that detour but it felt good to vent. Back to why Radio Flyer still matters.

You see, we live in a nation where customers demand innovation. Think about it, Starbucks no longer just sells coffee; Mc-

Donalds no longer just sells burgers. In the words of Pasin, "We had no choice but to innovate. It's paid off. Radio Flyer sales have doubled to almost $90 million over the past eight years. With Radio Flyer's 100th anniversary just a handful of years away, CEO Pasin is asked what the company might be making 100 years from now. He says with a smile, "One thing I know for sure, we'll still be making wagons."

Here's the point—don't give up your legacy and brand. But, like Radio Flyer has done, roll into new categories and put a twist on the old ones. CEO Pasin said they've had the tough conversations internally about the company's future. Should it become a different kind of company that opts to push the coolness factor and layer on techno chic, or should it rely more on its heritage, its nostalgia factor and, truth be told, its square-ness?

"I honestly don't believe that Radio Flyer needs to become hip to extend its brand," says Bob Friedland, former Toys "R" Us publicist who is now a consultant at Kaplow PR, "To extend the brand, they should rely heavily on the nostalgia factor." And CEO Pasin agrees. Nostalgia comes first. "Who doesn't remember, as a kid, sitting in a little red wagon with the wind in your hair, the sun in your face and someone you love pulling you forward?" asks Pasin. "We're all about love, warm memories and smiles."

Look, if you're lucky enough to have a company with that kind of history and legacy, then leverage that nostalgia and loyal following you have into staying relevant. And speaking as someone who has 20, OK 30, in his rear view mirror...something things do get better with age, right?

LINK: http://youtu.be/jkO2z06N9MQ

What <u>Can</u> You Control?

If you agree that making excuses is a worthless pursuit; and you have limited resources to combat the unfriendly realities that stalk you; you realize that you can't control the overall global economy, or who is pulling the strings in government—then what are you supposed to do? The answer is in the next chapter.

TWO
STAY OBSESSED WITH YOUR COMPETITION

For Team Members/Associates: If you want to remain absolutely necessary, you must not only pay close attention to the subtle intricacies of *your* job but also be hyper-wary of your competition's advantage(s). You are not playing this game in a vacuum. There are other companies that sell what you sell. You must know how their prices and fees compare to yours. You must know the "value proposition story" they are telling—and how their story stacks up against yours. You cannot compete if you don't know what you are competing against.

Once you know your competitor's perceived advantage(s), then you can craft an offensive and defensive tactics. In TV and movie acting, each cast member is required to know the other cast members' spoken lines so that (1) the actor can anticipate when it is his/her turn to speak and (2) the actor can jump in and recite the other person's line to save the show, if need be. Trial lawyers use a similar tactic. They never ask a witness a question unless they already know the answer.

For Leaders: It is mandatory to be obsessive about your competition. Ah, but what about those executives who teach their teams, "Don't worry about our competition. Just keep your nose down and focus on what we do here"? Those execs are trying to generate money in a vacuum. Maybe they think they are so smart they can manipulate the universe at their whim.

Well, if ignoring your competition is a good strategy, then why does every high school, college, and professional coach study so much game film of their opposition? They are looking for weaknesses. They want to use their competitor's weakness against them. You can't be competitive if you don't study your competition.

While you may not be able to control government regulatory policy or the global economy, you can still take control of knowing your competition.

Due Diligence

We have a good friend who often calls to float by us a cool new app idea he's dreamt up. The ideas always seem plausible—until a quick search on the App Store reveals that his ideas have already been developed. It never occurred to him to check the competitive landscape.

The bad news is that the barriers-to-entry into your industry are almost non-restrictive (especially in e-commerce) so new competitors can literally surface overnight. Your next competitor may be somebody working in a garage with a computer.

The good news is that it's easier than ever to "watch your competitor's game film." You can keep a keen eye on them with a little thing we like to call The Internet! The Internet is a never-closed resource for studying the competitors you know—as well as the nascent up-and-comers.

There is no excuse for you to be ill informed about who is vying for your dollars. Look them up on Twitter. Join their Facebook page. Do they Instagram? Are they on Tumblr? Subscribe to their RSS feeds. Sign up to get their press releases. Do they post YouTube videos? Do their customers add comments to their online "forum?" What about commercials, infomercials they might post on Vimeo? You should be reading the dozens of industry-specific blogs that comment on or review your competition. All this is necessary if you don't want to be blindsided by an innovation or inventive practice you missed. Incidentally, you should expect that your competition is doing the same things to study you and your organization.

That said, any information you uncover will be meaningless if you don't do anything about it.

Your "must-practice" is to digest every one of your competitor's strengths and weaknesses, and then take action.

Obsessed About Dog Food?

We have a client who makes private label animal feed for large retailers. (For those of you who don't know what "private label" means, the short explanation is that a manufacturer makes a product that retailers can then label with their own brand name. For example, Wal Mart sells dog food under the private label of *Ol' Roy* but they don't manufacture it. *Ol' Roy* is made by a dog food manufacturer; who may sell *Ol' Roy* under a different name to a different retailer.)

Our client wanted to tap into the larger wholesale customers who normally bought animal feed from the two largest manufacturers. To preserve anonymity let's just call these manufacturing giants Fidocrates and Dogorello.

We suggested our client needed to do some *business counter intelligence* and discover the strengths and weaknesses of these larger competitors.

Our client took action. They joined their competitor's Facebook pages, monitored their Twitter feeds, scoped out their press releases, and regularly received their RSS feeds. It didn't take long for our client to get a clear picture of what their competitors were doing well—and what they were doing *not* so well.

In our client's due diligence, they also discovered a lot of new customer contact information like email addresses and phone numbers. Armed with specifics, our client offered plane tickets and hotel rooms to these potential new customers—if they would just come out and visit the plant. And, do you know what happened? Sixty-two buyers showed up. Once these potential new customers saw the squeaky clean manufacturing facility and met the friendly staff, these new customers wrote significant orders on the spot.

Why did these new customers so willingly fly five hours to see how dog food was made? The feedback was embarrassingly obvious, "The other companies never invited us. So when you paid some attention to us, how could we refuse?"

If you want to take business away from a competitor, you have to be obsessed about them enough to dig deep for *business counter intelligence*—and then act upon their weaknesses.

THREE
BE A PERIPHERAL VISIONARY

For Team Members/Associates: Having peripheral vision might be the fastest route for you to get noticed. But wait, what is a Peripheral Visionary? The Oxford English Dictionary defines peripheral vision as, "Side vision; what is seen on the side by the eye when looking straight ahead." To our way of thinking (and the way we operate when consulting) we encourage you to look straight ahead at your own job while keeping your eyes wide for what's lurking on either side of your specific charge. Looking for what? Looking for fresh ideas that will appear revolutionary when applied to *your* job or your industry. When you apply these previously unexplored, fresh ideas, you could be perceived as a "visionary." Visionaries are *always* noticed by management.

Let's say you work in the software industry. We want you to pay attention to what's happening in every industry

EXCEPT software. We would even encourage you to start going to the wrong meetings! If you only go to software meetings and conventions you are missing 99% of the world's innovative practices. How do you start doing this? Get up early one morning. We should say, get up early on your day off. Drive to your nearest large hotel, walk into the lobby and check out the "Today's Meetings" board. There are meetings going on every single day. NOTE: Dress well enough that your attire won't stand out as odd for a business meeting. Scour the hotel lobby 'events board' for a meeting that looks like it might have an interesting topic. Now, with confidence and your note pad, walk in. Don't freak out! You don't need a badge. In fact, if anyone ever asks to see your badge, you say, "I don't have a badge. I just wanted to audit this session." 99.9% of the time you will be welcome. You will hear new trends, research, and business practices you've never heard before—for free.

If the folks won't let you in the meeting, walk down the hall and slip into a different meeting. There is no law against attending meetings.

For Leaders: Please read what we wrote to your team members above. The same applies to you. Your job is to bring fresh and innovative ideas to your organization. But you do not have to reinvent or spend thousands of hours brainstorming new ideas. Borrow ideas from other industries. You will be stunned how many inspiring new thoughts are being implemented in other industries. First, you must train your brain.

A Comedian's Thought Process

We both started out as stand-up comedians. The discipline of writing jokes turned out to be the perfect skill set for noticing what most people ignore.

The anatomy of a joke has two parts: (1) Lead the audience down one path and then (2) Make a sharp right turn that the audience didn't see coming.

The result is an emotional surprise. When surprised (in a fun way), most humans laugh involuntarily. Here are some examples:

Ross: "I was driving my wife home from work and I thought I would impress her with my automotive intellect, 'Honey, you feel that slight shimmy on the right side? It's nothing to worry about. It's probably just the inner tie rod end or a ball joint. Either way I can replace it myself.' She said, 'No, you forgot to release the parking brake.'"

Michael: "I love Costco, you can get anything there: 48 cans of Bush's Baked Beans, 2,400 Q-Tips... you can even get flu shots now...you gotta get 12 of them though..."

If the joke works well, the audience doesn't see the punch line coming until the last couple of words. As comedians, it is natural for us to look for the unexpected solutions. Often, the biggest laugh comes from a simple punch line. You've no doubt experienced an involuntary laugh at work when you made a discovery that the solution was actually much simpler than you first thought. You laughed because you overlooked the obvious. We like to say, "The answer is usually hiding in plain sight." Now, let's describe some simple tactics for spotting (previously unseen) trends.

A Peripheral Trend We Noticed and Cross-Pollinated

A few years ago, we attended a national retail grocery store convention where a startling sociological study was released. The multi-million dollar survey revealed that by 4 p.m. every day, almost half of you still haven't decided what you want for dinner. You call home and ask your spouse, "What do you want for dinner tonight?" and your spouse says, "I can't think about that right now. It's four. I'm not even hungry." That's why your grocery store has been so successful selling you those hot, rotisserie-style chickens. It's a quick fix for those of you with growling stomachs and limited time. You simply can't be bothered with one more decision.

There's more. About 18% of the food you buy at the grocery store doesn't even make it back home. You're eating pre-packaged sandwiches and finger foods in your car—probably noshing some nourishment on the way to an appointment or your child's third activity of the day. The usefulness of "car food" will be revealed as you are installing tire chains on a snowy night. If the blizzard worsens you will be able to mine your seat crevices for enough Cheetos and Animal Crackers to see you through the winter.

Most people would hear something like that and laugh, not recognizing this behavior as a significant buying habit shift. Smart companies not only recognize new behavior—but find a way to leverage into the trend.

We are in the business of spotting and leveraging trends.

So when we heard the "Our-family-can't-plan-dinner-two-hours-before-we-eat-it" research, we immediately called one of our clients (a premium restaurant chain) and persuaded them to start running their radio advertising at 3:30pm with the message, *"If you haven't decided what you want for dinner tonight (and we don't think you have) then let us do the cooking for you."* The result was a several million-dollar increase in five weeks. Our client leveraged into the trend.

7-Eleven is a smart company. If you fail to think of them as a popular dining experience, you would be wrong. In 2013, 7-Eleven franchise stores grew revenues over $1 billion last year by selling a broader range of "emergency foods." You rarely go there as a planned shopping experience, right? I'm doing a grilled balsamic London broil for dinner tonight; what Slurpee shall I pair with that?

Look what else they did. Microwavable sandwiches were replaced with made-to-order deli sandwiches and other hot ready-to-eat items. For 40 years, 7-Eleven has been the quick stop for convenient last-minute purchases. But now, they are leveraging into this burgeoning "good meal" trend.

More Solutions Hiding in Plain Sight

It is rumored that a young Starbucks barista suggested they stop greeting customers with, "Can I help you?" Her idea was to say, "What can we get started for you?" It's a brilliant way of reimagining the old cliché. Her rationale was that by asking, "What can we get started for you?" she was now your partner in a cup of coffee—giving the buyer all of the control. By showing respect for a person's coffee preference, the barista is now projecting a service mentality rather than a tired old cliché. We thought that was such a powerful 'shift in perspective' that we have encouraged the folks at AutoZone Stores to greet the customers with, "What are you working on today?" That kind of greeting engages the customer right away.

Here are a few more examples:

- A major airline wanted to figure out how to make their routes more profitable by filling the cargo holds of their narrow-body planes. We suggested they partner with Amazon and eBay. Utilizing their frequent short distance routes, this air carrier could offer 'same day delivery' of Amazon's top 200 items for a small additional fee. How did we think of that? We simply noticed who had the most deliveries of items that might fit in small planes.

- At one meeting, we heard Dr. Peter Diamandis (founder of the XPRIZE Foundation) talk about offering $10 million dollars to any team who could develop commercial space flight for those of us who are not astronauts. Diamandis was convinced the $10 million prize was the incentive necessary to solve this problem. He was wrong. What he discovered was that the money wasn't the incentive at all. It turned out that teams vying for the prize would spend up to $100 million to build a space ship. The *real* prize was actually bragging rights to be the first to offer commercial space travel. The lesson for leaders is that money is rarely the top motivator. What can you do that would provide bragging rights instead of cash?

- A woman (whom we'll call Margy) unexpectedly lost her $200,000/year software job and didn't know what she was going to do for work. She had held a senior position and knew job hunting would be arduous; especially to find another high level job. To keep herself busy, she started a dog-sitting business in her home town of Calgary, Alberta, Canada. Within a year, she more than eclipsed her former salary. She now has a thriving business. How did she do it—especially since the competition was already established in the dog-sitting business? When Margy would show up at a client's home for the pre-sitting interview, she would immediately start asking the dog questions like, "Where are your toys?" "Do you want to go outside?" "Do you like to be scratched here?"— virtually ignoring the owners. She would get hired on the spot. And, she would get paid double the going rate. Margy learned a skill at her previous job that she took into her dog-sitting business. Margy explains, "I was always hyper-conscious about who the *real* customer was. Early on, I determined the dog was the *real* customer—not the owner. The dog had to like me and want to be around me." She found that the owners were astounded that she cared so much for their pet. They often gave her bonuses. Margy also knew how to sustain ongoing business. Each month, Margy would give the owner a small photo scrapbook. The photographs were of the dog playing and having fun when the owners weren't around.

RELEVANT REPORT
By Ross Shafer

Why You Should Hold Expensive Meetings

This is a note for leaders...and for you team members who want to make a case for your indispensability.

Suggest something counterintuitive to get everyone's attention. Bear with me on this...

I am submitting this report from the Bahamas...Nassau... Paradise Island...the Atlantis Hotel to be specific. Just a few years ago it was unheard of for an organization or company to hold a meeting at an exotic resort like this. Why? Because it looked too ostentatious – too much like you were showing off. But times have changed. Think carefully about where you want to hold your meetings – because the impression you project means a lot to your associates, their families, your suppliers, or any user groups you are trying to impress. Want to get people talking about the meeting? Take a look at what there is to do here. Kids can't believe they are in a water slide surrounded by sharks. Spouses—men and women— love the high end shopping. And who doesn't want to be able to tell their friends they saw an eight-foot manta ray?

See, the point is, if you try to make it more of a memorable experience for your attendees, go a little upscale. Give them a W Hotel experience. Give them a Hard Rock Hotel experience. Or, give them an exotic destination resort experience like this one. If you try to save money by being too cheap, your attendees will remember you in all the WRONG WAYS.

LINK: https://www.youtube.com/watch?v=NHLSQiGuSWQ

Assign a Chief Trending Officer

When we talk about you becoming a Peripheral Visionary, it's understandable for you to push back with, "But I'm already buried in the minutiae of my job. How can I tackle anything else?" Then, give that assignment to someone who wants to prove him/herself. Why not call this person your "chief trending officer"? (We think we invented this term.) It makes sense to make someone accountable for spotting trends. Your chief trending officer doesn't have to be a full time position. But when you designate that assignment, at least someone is out there watching for trends the rest of you don't notice.

What does this person do? How often do they do it? At first, make it bi-monthly. Every two months, this person should report on areas that might affect your business. Trends and innovations happen all the time. The report could sprout from news clipping, Facebook posts, or watching YouTube videos. For which kinds of trends should this person sound the alarm?

- Hiring trends. What skills are hot right now? What do the top talent candidates expect from an organization (healthcare, gym, nap pods, etc.)?

- Which companies are named "most admired" and "the best companies to work for," and why?

- What new start-up companies are runaway successes on Wall Street? What services or products are they providing?

- When you search Google, Yahoo, Bing, or your choice of

search engine, what or who pops up in your industry? Do you see a current non-competitor trying to get a foothold in your industry?

RELEVANT REPORT

By Michael Burger

Leveraging an Old Trend...for a New Audience

I get my hair cut locally at the Dean Anthony salon in Long Beach, California—a salon that is somewhat unique in the "barber business." They've leveraged their business into the growing personal care and grooming market for men. Did you know that the men's grooming market will hit $33 billion in sales by 2015? How's that for a trend you didn't see coming? Men are paying more attention to how they look. The trend is being driven by male role models—from the world of sports to film personalities. As gender boundaries blur, global firms are focusing on finding new ways of making money from this untapped male market. Companies are leveraging into trend with cosmetics and beauty products designed exclusively for men.

Take Dean Anthony. The salon is doing many little things right to grab men's business and attention. For starters, men get their hair cut in private alcoves with flat screen TVs imbedded in the mirrors. Research says, men prefer privacy to the open room—avoiding the "I can see and hear everything you're saying" problem. I can tell you from personal experience getting the "Just A Touch Of Gray" sauce applied on my noggin in a wide open room for others to judge my vanity is at best uncomfortable.

Update: I've stopped rinsing. Go gray or go home! Guys, it's very tough to pull that off. You can spot the look of a dye job across a busy interstate. It's that odd color not found in nature. A shade somewhere between the color of a holiday side dish and the overspray on a Radio Flyer wagon. That reddish/magenta hue? Yeah, that can only mean, that ain't factory equipment. I again digress...The salon offers complementary beer and wine, with the smiles from the beautiful and handsome team members just as quenching.

There's a full time aesthetician on staff to remove hair from most anywhere, and guys get the complimentary facial and hot towel treatment in their service. Dean Anthony saw a trend in the men's grooming business and leveraged into it. The fact that his business is growing is proof that he was smart to act on the trend.

LINK: http://youtu.be/ymnd1GV_KQI

Heed This Warning:

The accelerated pace of the economy dictates that whoever recognizes—and responds to—a market trend-shift first, wins. The trends we are talking about cover relevant product and service offerings, manufacturing methods, sales territory management, web-driven supply chains, big data, digital marketing, and ultimately customer or client buying habits. We can *never* forget about leveraging into what the end user wants—and how they want it. Regardless of your high level go-to-market strategy and tactics, the end user's decisions will always prevail. And, if you don't give them what they want, in the way they want it, at the price they are willing to pay, they will find alternatives to what you sell.

FOUR
COURSE CORRECT WITH HUMILITY

For Team Members/Associates: If you truly want to become a necessary cog in your company wheel, you must be willing to put your pride aside and change your direction with humility. Sometimes a course correction will be obvious to you. Other times, management will change the course for you. However, you will become invaluable if you can anticipate a necessary change before the boss has come to that conclusion. Your daily routine should include trying to identify non-productive strategies and tactics. (Strategy is the idea. Tactics are the actions.) When you are certain you have something worth mentioning to the boss, back up your ideas with evidence. Don't walk in with, "I've got a hunch." Hunches and feelings are worthless to management. You cement your value by presenting details and

financial consequences. The key word there is financial. You
will always have the ear of management if you can reduce
your conversation to actual loss and reasonable, potential
profit. You might approach the boss with, "Here is what
will happen if we travel along the current path. Here is
what will happen if we change X by doing Y."

Management craves people who are looking out for the
company's best interest (because most don't). Management
tends to promote people with forward-thinking skills. Learn
to stay "eyes wide open" so you can sharpen the peripheral
vision we talked about in chapter 3.

For Leaders: Nimble course-correcting is one of your
prime directives. Constantly study the results of your strategy and tactics. If your decision isn't producing acceptable
results, jettison your pride and say farewell to your hard-
fought ideas. Admit the mistake and move on. Oh, and learn
from the failures of other competitors in your industry...
failures that didn't cost *you* any money. Some of you might
have a hard time changing old behaviors—especially when
you have been "married to an idea" for a long time.

The Great Cell Phone Tragedy

Your children cannot imagine a world without cell phones.

Let's go back to 1988. How many of you baby boomers
had a cell phone back then? By now you've probably owned
6-10 different cell phones because the technology changed
so quickly.

Michael Note: My first cell phone was a Motorola. It had a 10-pound base unit you had to lug around…it looked like I was on battle maneuvers. I think it was also a dollar a minute for a call. Ah, the not so good ol' days, right?

Aggressive cell phone manufacturers were constantly course correcting. By the mid-1990's, Motorola's Star-TAC flip cell phone not only looked like a Star Trek Communicator but that particular model virtually owned the entire cell phone market. At that point, Motorola's analog devices were so reliable that AT&T came to them and asked Motorola if they would make a digital cellular phone for AT&T. Motorola balked because they were convinced that digital voice quality was substandard to analog. Not only were Motorola's engineers so sure of themselves (we wanted to say "cocky) they made it known that (and we are paraphrasing here), "If we don't make a digital phone, it won't get made." AT&T left the Motorola meeting and contacted a newbie in the cell phone business— Nokia. Nokia was thrilled to be tapped to make the digital phone. By 2000, Nokia became the worldwide market share leader and analog hasn't been heard from since.

Look at the timeline. Marvel at how little time passes between each major innovation.

- 1994: Motorola dominates global cell market with a 32.5% share, versus Nokia's 21%, according to Gartner.

- Mid-1990s: The first digital wireless networks are built in Europe, but Motorola is slow to ditch analog for digital technology.

- 1996: Motorola launches StarTAC, the first of its signature clamshell phone range with a lid that hinges open. Their lead continues to outdistance Nokia and others.

- 2000: Motorola's market share is 13% and it hovers in the mid-teen range for years. By comparison, Nokia (developer of the digital cell phone) had a 31% market share.

- 2004: Late in the year Motorola launches Razr, an ultra-thin phone that becomes a design icon. Cool as it was, it didn't overtake Nokia. Nokia sold 130 million units this year and became the world's best selling phone.

- 2006: In July, Motorola announced they had sold 50 million Razr phones. CEO Ed Zander promises 500 million. But market becomes so glutted with Razrs, by year-end Motorola is giving them away for free. Motorola market share peaks around 23%.

- 2007: Activist investor Carl Icahn starts pushing Motorola to split up, buy back shares and fire its CEO. 2007: Apple Inc. sells its first iPhone. Motorola ends year with a 9% share.

Don't Limit Future Revenues by Celebrating Yesterday's Profits

Nokia had pulled off a coup. They introduced a brilliant digital phone and killed the giant Motorola. But then they took a three-year nap while Apple's iPhone enchanted customers.

Nokia's sales pitch must have been something like, "Ours is the lowest price phone." Apple unabashedly sold the notion, "Yes, our phone is expensive—and you can only get it with AT&T service—but look at what you can do with our phone."

In an effort to resurrect their once glorious cell phone market share, in September 2010, Nokia hired an innovative thinker, Stephen Elop, as their new CEO. Known as a swift tactician, Elop studied the landscape. In February 2011, his intended-to-be-internal company memo spread into a widely-circulated missive. In the brief excerpts below you will experience how Elop pulled no punches.

"What happened at Nokia? We fell behind, we missed big trends, and we lost time. At that time, we thought we were making the right decisions; but, with the benefit of hindsight, we now find ourselves years behind."

"The first iPhone shipped in 2007, and we still don't have a product that is close to their experience. Android came on the scene just over 2 years ago, and this week they took our leadership position in smart phone volumes. Unbelievable."

"I believe we have lacked accountability and leadership to align and direct the company through these disruptive times. We had a series of misses. We haven't been delivering innovation fast enough. We're not collaborating internally."

How would you like to wake up to an email like that waiting in your inbox? Would you have been motivated? We have asked that very question to some of our audiences. Not only was his missive interpreted as anti-motivating, the CEO spent more time shaming and assigning blame than he did trying to get everyone excited about a meaningful change.

To our minds, Elop forgot job #1 for affecting change. You have to get Buy-in from the entire team before new leaps in culture and innovation can happen. In the next chapter, we will go into detail about getting company-wide Buy-in.

The argument could be made that management style doesn't matter as long as market share and profits were restored. During Elop's three-year tenure at Nokia revenues fell 40%. Profits dropped 95%. Market share went from 34% to 3.4%. And market capitalization plummeted $13 billion. Oops.

Sad, right? Nokia fell from grace at a time when the cell phone business was actually accelerating.

Nokia Should Have Hired <u>This</u> Woman

Now, compare what happened at Nokia with what happened at Welch Allyn—a 95-year-old company. That name Welch Allyn probably isn't a household name to you but they are the market leader in medical devices. When you go to a doctor's office you are probably face-to-face with a Welch Allyn stethoscope, among other devices. Does their company logo look familiar? It will the next you visit your doc.

Welch\Allyn®

Dr. Henry Cloud writes in his excellent book "Necessary Endings" that organizations only recognize the need to change when they see that their future is hopeless if they continue on the same path. Welch Allyn had a leader who saw a hopeless future, believed in reality, and moved quickly to create a new future.

Welch Allyn's business credo has worked brilliantly for almost a century. It says, "Be always kind and true." That's a fine tradition of niceness and integrity. And it's been extremely profitable. So why change anything? Dr. Cloud tells the story of the dramatic changes Julie Shimer proposed when she took over as CEO.

What Shimer noticed immediately was that each medical device was running on its own operating system. By comparison, all of Apple's devices use the same operating system, and all devices can be updated simultaneously. Shimer realized correctly that Welch Allyn was on a hopeless path unless they could create a single diagnostic platform for all Welch Allyn devices. She was lobbying for "a standard ecosytem"—the same model Stephen Elop complained was missing at Nokia. Shimer compared the medical devices to Apple's iPod, iPhone and the iPad. In her vision, no matter what Welch Allyn medical device a doctor might be using, the interface looked and worked the same as on all other Welch Allyn devices. What's crazy is that Shimer was the only person in the medical device field to make this connection. She was calling for the end of a 95-year disjointed development process. So now, with the extreme focus on better managing the health care industry, Shimer has made sure that Welch Allyn is poised to lead the market for many, many years.

Your Turn

The lesson for all organizations is this: If you can see into the future and you suspect that your process, product, or service could become extinct, you need to stand up, believe reality, and admit to all that your future is on a hopeless path. Show the evidence. Get people behind you (for their sake) and encourage fresh solutions—; regardless of how hard the pill is to swallow. Oh and the next time you go in for your annual physical casually ask your doctor, "Just wondering if you will be taking my temp with the Welch Allyn SureTemp Plus 690 Electronic Thermometer?" We predict you'll get a little more respect.

FIVE
PREMEDITATE GOOD DECISIONS

For Team Members/Associates: To be highly valued by your organization, you must always be ready to make a good decision. Fear of deciding—or stalling, hoping the boss will forget—is not an option for anyone who aspires to be an absolutely necessary asset. Luckily, you can actually make many good decisions in advance. How? By predicting the obstacles—and deciding upon your action—before the obstacle becomes an actual roadblock. Better decisions lead to being given greater responsibility and authority. Better decisions impress leadership.

In this chapter, we will outline ways for you to make consistently better decisions.

For Leaders: As you know, leadership, at its core, is being able to make good decisions every day. Sometimes the onus falls directly on you. Other times, it is your ability to delegate the decision to your trusted team members. Regardless, the proverbial "buck" stops at your responsible feet. Leaders win, keep, and lose spectacular jobs on the quality of their decisions. So why not take the guesswork out of the decision-making process?

Here's how.

What Does Artificial Intelligence Teach Us?

If you own an iPhone, Siri is the virtual "person" who can recognize your voice and answer your basic questions. Siri's artificial intelligence is the result of countless hours of input matched to likely answers. Siri is programmed to make premeditated decisions.

In the Internet technology world, IT programmers call it "Structured Query Language" or "SQL," which is just fancy language the computer uses to communicate. The computer stores responses and procedures ("rules") so that your computer can internally monitor your computer activity until a certain procedure is violated or you want something on-demand. The "rule" then triggers an alert for corrective action. Programmers construct these workflow logic rules to make sure you can do your job correctly.

Aside from Siri's artificial intelligence response, let's say you want to order a new lampshade online but you forgot to enter the state in which you live. The e-commerce software program won't allow you to advance to the Payment Page until you fill in the proper state field. The software stands in your way of completing the order because it knows the product cannot be shipped to you without a full address. That's a logical workflow "rule."

Effective leaders create business behavioral rules that will stop the decision making process before they get themselves into trouble.

Leaders Need Stored Procedures and Rules

What if you had a software program that could help you make better, more informed decisions? You would type in the facts and the software would quickly analyze the outcomes. Actually, many of these software programs already exist.

Here is a short list of decision-making programs you can explore on the web:

www.Loomio.org
www.d-sight.com
www.transparentchoice.com
www.makeitrational.com
www.superdecisions.com
www.1000minds.com

One such company, Logical Decisions Inc., (www.logicaldecisions.com) has a variety of software applications that have been used to predict the possible outcomes of long term Air Force technology applications. LD software has helped to locate the best site to build a reservoir and plant pipelines. LD software has also been employed to determine the financial stability of insurance investments. Fact-based decision-making helps eliminate the emotional influencers that can sometimes derail so many mission-critical business decisions.

No doubt you made many decisions based upon your "gut feeling." You might have even made the right decisions along the way. But think about how poor decisions nearly brought our global financial community to full collapse.

We Assumed These People Were Actually Smart

In 2008, some of the smartest people on Wall Street caused an economic meltdown that had catastrophic consequences for the global credit markets, a brutal U.S. housing collapse, and an announcement that the United States was in an official recession. As a result, Lehman Brothers became the largest bank failure in U.S. history.

According to TheStreet.com, "The key problem the Federal Reserve addressed throughout 2008 was keeping overnight funding between funds liquid. Any breakdown in liquidity on hand by banks in a single day could have quickly spread across the system and created a panic."

The "panic" he is referring to would have occurred if millions of Americans had gone to their ATMs and their savings account money was no longer available.

How does something like that happen—especially when the most brilliant minds in the country were supposedly standing watch and aware of such contingencies?

Simple. The lending safeguards were based on a rising

real estate market. The predictions about the true state of the economy were wrong. And, several giant companies had been fudging the rules. In 2006-2008, if you wanted to buy a home in the U.S., no down payment was required. Banks were lending up to 110% of a home's list price. This formula works fine as long as home prices keep rising. But when home prices outstripped a person's ability to make the payments, the market dropped like a stone.

A veritable "perfect storm" of risk surfaced.

By comparison, Canada had plenty of inflexible safe-guards. If you wanted to buy a home, you were expected to pay a 20% down payment. Canada didn't suffer a housing collapse because they had wise qualifying rules in effect.

Establish Protocol and Parameters for Wise Decisions

You can 'lighten the load of leadership' by establishing protocol for certain recurring, predictable decisions. Protocol defines, "This is what we do when A, B, or C happens." When you internally publish such protocol, you've sent a wave of comfort through your company that assures safe procedures are followed.

We suggest applying protocol to emergencies as well. On a nuclear submarine, when the ship's PA system bellows, "Code Red," the crew would likely snap into a rehearsed procedure like this:

1. Shut down all fuel lines.
2. Lock appropriate bulkhead doors.

3. Evacuate personnel from area of danger.

4. Assess all systems.

5. Account for all personnel.

6. Report damage.

7. Initiate repair procedures.

Every team member, manager, and company should learn from this.

Assigning a protocol to certain eventualities takes the guesswork out of decision making—especially when you have exceeded safe, operational boundaries.

As we saw, it doesn't matter how experienced or smart the leaders, if procedures exceed preset safeguards (i.e., diminishing revenues, market share, expense control, etc.), a catastrophe can occur.

Operational boundaries?

Yes, every TV series we've been associated with has written a "show bible." The show bible helps a TV producer decide if a story or a character's actions fall within the boundaries of believability. If a character or a storyline doesn't make sense within the bible's rules, the idea is dismissed.

Speaking of bibles, every religious belief has a written set of guidelines. These guidelines define which behaviors are considered acceptable and which are not acceptable behaviors. There are always moral and ethical boundaries tied to either a good or bad choice.

What do you do if "outside market factors" exceed your boundaries? That's what happened to Jon Vrabley at Huttig Building Materials when the housing market was in free fall.

Vrabley and his team had to keep readjusting their pain tolerance boundaries, "We braced ourselves for big decisions in advance. If revenue dropped to $750 million, we knew we needed to close certain distribution centers. If revenue dropped below $600 million, we knew we needed to close an additional number of distribution centers. It was really rough but we took the surprise and panic out of the decisions."

Make a comprehensive list of every possible decision scenario you can imagine. Then, don't rely on your own memory. Talk about the various scenarios with your trusted team members. Agree, if you can, with the best course of action for each eventuality.

"If our product causes an injury, we will _____ "

"If a customer wants a refund, we will _____ "

"If a member of our team fails a drug test, we will _____ "

"If we pursue a merger or acquisition, it must first pass these tests _____ "

"Our pricing decisions are based upon _____ "

"When our market share drops below ____% , we will do this _____ "

...and so on. Make the list long and comprehensive.

As rudimentary as it seems, having these predetermined

decisions in place makes an organization move more quickly in response to changing market conditions. These are decisions based upon facts.

The C-Suite Loves Facts

When you have a great idea, don't barge into the CEO's office armed only with a "brilliant" idea.

Bring the facts.

Bring supporting evidence to show that your idea is not only valid, but that the numbers make sense. (Wait, we hear an argument coming).

Diehards would tell us, "Experience and enthusiasm are the soul of an idea." They will look to Malcolm Gladwell's best-selling book *Blink* as support for that thinking. Gladwell makes a case for decades of experience imbuing us with honed instincts; instincts that make it easy to make judgment calls. If you are still in business today based upon your gut instincts, good for you. But, using 'the gut method' runs the risk of making decisions based upon what happened in the past (forensic)—not your relevant future (predictive). The way customers previously bought—or the way previous team members viewed the workplace—may have nothing to do with how they buy or behave in the future.

Finally, Don't Overthink

Jim Barksdale, the man who created Netscape and then sold the company to AOL in 1998 for 4.2 billion, loved to reduce decision-making to a process everyone could understand. His decision-making credo when he was dealing with a mistake was to address the mistake and then let it go.

Jim Barksdale's Three Rules of Business

* Rule 1: If you see a snake, don't call committees, don't call your buddies, don't get a meeting together; just kill the snake.

* Rule 2: Don't go back and play with dead snakes. We haven't got time to go back and revisit decisions.

* Rule 3: All opportunities start out looking like snakes. So look at problems as opportunities.

RELEVANT REPORT

By Ross Shafer

I'm a Big Fan of Under-thinking Decisions

Some decisions are so simple we tend to overlook the obvious. An example of this happened to me in Carlsbad, California, at the Park Hyatt Aviara hotel. First, let me say I was checked into a standard room (not a suite or club floor with any privileges). I ordered breakfast from room service—eggs, ham and toast. Within 18 minutes, a nice young woman delivered my breakfast. I was impressed; but what happened next, blew me away. The young woman, whose name was Roxanna, said, "How do you like your toast? Light? Medium? Dark?" I said, "What do you mean?" Then, she reached under the cart and pulled out a full size toaster! She was going to toast my bread on the spot. She said, "We want your toast to be fresh and to your specifications." Oddly, I DO have toast specifications (lightly toasted please). But, I'd never had a choice before. Thankfully, she let me take a picture to show others. Look, I spend about 200 nights a year in hotels and I have NEVER seen anything like this – bringing a toaster to your room?! Thank you Park Hyatt! Oh and one more thing. You know that awkward moment when they hand you the check and it says delivery charge, gratuity, service charge…and a space for an extra gratuity. At the Park Hyatt, Roxanna said, "The bill is in the envelope. No need to sign it. No need to add a gratuity." This hotel blew me away and eliminated the final awkward moment. I hope if you are ever in Carlsbad you will stay at the Park Hyatt Aviara. But I'll warn you "towel thieves" up front—the toaster will not fit in your carry-on.

LINK: https://www.youtube.com/watch?v=8B7KbQX9ndA

SIX
KNOW HOW TO GET BUY-IN FOR YOUR IDEAS

For Team Members/Associates: People in high-demand don't argue for the sake of arguing or because they are afraid of change. People of value to the organization are enthusiastic agents for change—not buzz kills. If your boss presents an idea to restructure a department or a plan to redefine the corporate mission—or any other major shift for that matter—he/she knows they cannot get that change done alone. That's where *you* come in. Be willing to support change—assuming the change doesn't go against your integrity, morality, or governmental laws. Show that you are not fazed by something that may inconvenience you. Further, show that you are happy to contribute in any way to help the cause. Your flexibility will be valued by management and will not be forgotten when the reorganization is fleshed out.

Play ball whenever you can.

For Leaders: You know that you cannot execute change alone. You may see the urgent need to exchange old habits for something better, but now your job is get others to see it your way. Put hubris on the shelf and make humility your battle plan. A politician can hatch a brilliant strategy to create more jobs and reduce government spending but if Congress and the people don't vote for it, the plan dies. You need buy-in from enough people to ensure that your ideas build the momentum required to succeed. This is not different from when you try to sell a new product or new service to a customer. You must convince the customer that your product or service is better than what they have already become accustomed to buying.

Change Has to Include a Well-articulated, Logical Reason to Live

As persuasive as you might be, your personal desire to change something usually isn't enough to be convincing. You need to give change a reason to live. And to make people care about your idea, you need to make the reason(s) about *them*. Your argument for change has to be personal, emotional, real, and reasonable. The overall tone should be, "This change is urgent."

The Personal, Emotional and Very Real Argument

In the case of Welch Allyn, CEO Julie Shimer made the current path of her company a dire reality. She made a plea to her people that if they didn't convert their varied products to a common ecosystem (ala Apple), Welch Allyn would be signing its own death warrant. She crafted an articulate and very likely scenario whereby the company would become irrelevant if they didn't change. The consequences meant revenues and market share would shrink to the point of causing massive layoffs—plus serious threats to health care and retirement incomes. Shimer was convinced that extinction was a scary reality.

Shimer's description of the consequences made the situation real. She made it personal and emotional. Her research showed her findings were real. Most significant, Shimer made an authentic argument. She was able to clearly map out a timeline whereby everyone could see the end was near unless something drastic was done quickly.

The final plea was also urgent. Once you address the problems of, "Why did this happen?" "What will be affected?" you need to be able to step in with the solutions to the questions, "How do we fix this?" and "When do we start?"

● ————————— ●

Michael Note: *In 1994, I hosted a morning talk show called Mike and Maty. It aired on the ABC network and was produced by Disney. I worked with a brilliant executive by the name of Mary Kellogg who reported to Michael Eisner and developed shows for the company. She was responsible for the original Regis Philbin and Kathy Lee talk show. What made her especially brilliant was how she responded when challenged by someone who disagreed with her. She wouldn't lash out defensively. Instead, she would calmly say to her opponent, "Make me smarter on that" or "why should we do such and such?" The beauty of the line, "Make me smarter" is that it doesn't insult your adversary and yet it makes them prove their point.*

●————————●

Being Other-Centered Softens Push-Back

Human nature predicts resistance should be expected. Why do you think that happens— even when change is so good for us? We think it's because it takes a long time to get comfortable with learning a routine. None of us want to do our jobs badly. Change has a learning curve and we would prefer to sustain competency—or better yet—expertise. Change disrupts everyone's world by bringing with it an unfamiliar playbook.

So, before you un-holster your guns and start blazing away at the problem, make sure you know, "Who will get hurt by this proposal?" Think about the consequences to other people. Much like pre-meditating your decisions ahead of time, do the same for managing people during change.

Make a list of all the foreseeable objections and develop an articulate argument to combat each main point. Keep going back to the personal and emotional benefits for change. Make sure to make the change about *them*. Recognize that change will not be easy. Assure everyone that the successful transition to "new" will take diligence and discipline. Be encouraging that the rewards will be worth the effort. Close your argument by answering the #1 question on *their* minds, "What's in it for me?" That's how other-centered leaders get things done. You cannot motivate change until you hit the hot buttons of the people who will carry the water for you.

Ask yourself these questions:

"This is going to impact society in a way that changes our brand promise forever."

"We can improve the customer experience to make us the clear provider of choice."

"We will finally have the ability to compete with the top two competitors."

"We have the solutions you've all been asking for."

"We now have the resources to care for all of you the way we've always dreamed."

RELEVANT REPORT

By Ross Shafer

How to Double Your Revenue

Getting buy-in can work really well when you are able to construct a sensible financial argument for making a big change. Glenn Beattie is an American success story who executed this strategy perfectly. Glenn wanted to own a Denny's restaurant but barely scraped together enough money to buy a franchise— one that was struggling. The next hurdle was convincing the Denny's franchise organization that he was the right person to turn this unit around. The restaurant was located in Phoenix, Arizona. Glenn knew taking over this business wasn't a risk. He knew he could spike revenue when he noticed something the previous owner had completely ignored. What did he see? The restaurant was located in a largely Hispanic neighborhood but the restaurant didn't have any Spanish-speaking servers. Patrons had to point at the pictures on the menu to order what they wanted. When Glenn took over, he immediately hired a bilingual staff...and doubled the business from $1 million to $2 million in under a year. Today, Glenn owns almost 40 Denny's restaurants. He also has two basic rules for his managers: (1) Be nice, (2) Say YES! Glenn told me about a customer who came in with an IHOP coupon to get pancakes for $2.99. Glenn immediately said, "YES!" because his logic was that IHOP had paid to bring a customer to HIS door. If you want to capitalize on your market, notice the obvious. Have the courage to leverage into basic logic...and you might just get rich.

LINK: https://www.youtube.com/watch?v=25qpDFbneiA

Buy-In is More Effective by Attaching Urgency

Once you have outlined the consequences of what happens when you follow the path of complacency, it is imperative to underscore the importance of urgent action. Be clear that you are in a Code Red situation. Make it widely known that the reason for a quantum change is because, "this is an emergency." Urgency will only make sense if the team believes your situation requires emergency action. If you don't create a true sense of urgency, your team will remain complacent and worse—they won't feel the need to contribute.

Nokia's Stephen Elop completely dismissed the powerful requirement of providing an emotional and personal motive for their market-share-loss emergency. Instead, Elop tried to shame his team into accepting change. Imagine your spouse collapses from an obvious heart attack. While standing over your blue-faced choking mate you say, "I told you smoking and fried foods was going to cause this. Now, we have to call an ambulance. But before I dial 9-1-1, you tell me—to my face—that I was right and that you understand you might die from this!"

Don't Settle for Acceptance—Award Medals for Contributions

Getting acceptance for your ideas doesn't guarantee your audience will become "engaged" in your plan. It likely means they are thinking, "Change is happening with or without me, so I'll just do what I can do."

But if you sincerely ask them to actively contribute to the changes, you stand a better chance for a smoother transition. The best case would be where team members feel like their opinions matter. People must feel they are integral to the changes. How do you pull that off? First, you have to really want their help. Ask for their feedback on your ideas and plans. Earnestly consult with them frequently so they believe you are listening. To some, it may seem like extra work. The wise ones will see this kind of participation as a "seat at the table"—a way to prove themselves as worthy contributors who will be tapped for future advice.

As a leader, watch carefully which team members emerge as your "fans of change." These are the people who get excited about being a part of the process. They want to be able to say, "I was there when this all went down." Eager participation is invaluable. You need to reward their vigor with eye contact and ongoing encouragement. When a team member suggests a viable alternative that evokes an "ah ha" moment, publicly embrace that idea so the rest of the team sees you are a flexible thinker. If you can let go of *your* ideas in lieu of something better, your people will lock arms in a quiet army who stand ready to champion your next change effort.

SEVEN
MASTER TECHNOLOGY

For Team Members/Associates: If you want to become the "go to" person in your company, discover how you can use technology to create an ongoing digital revenue stream. Secondly, show leadership how to save more money from technology tools. Do those two things and you will indeed be, invaluable.

For Leadership: The future of your company will be dependent upon how well you leverage technology tools. One such tool is employing big data. According to brilliant technology author, speaker, and consultant, Scott Klososky, "The companies with the most big data on customers will win the top line revenue war. The companies with the most big data on performance will be able to improve the bottom line through efficiency. The companies with the most big data on talent will be able to capture, manage, and retain the best people."

What is Technology Mastery?

You can't duck and dodge your way around technology any longer. The organizations that are aggressive about having a technology toolbox are winning market share. Luckily for you, today's business technology keeps getting easier, better and more secure. It's not enough to accept technology, it's "absolutely necessary" to master it. Technology mastery will be your competitive advantage. _

So what is technology mastery, exactly?

We found the most comprehensive definition from Klososky, who says, "Technology Mastery is when an organization is expert at what they do - and then they add the ability advances to become world class with how they apply technology." He is convinced that every operational element in your organization is touched by technology. Therefore, you must be savvy in applying technology at every level to achieve top tier status in your industry.

Klososky's firm, Future Point of View, consults with all sizes of organizations in all manner of industries. His experience has shown him that, "...it doesn't matter how good you are at your niche, you also have to be expert at applying technology to retain your edge. Your mastery of technology will determine if you win or lose."

Klososky wants leaders to think of technology as a practical toolbox filled with ways to connect with consumers. Scott and his team are brilliant at everything from social media to big data to online learning. He sees all three of those disciplines as mutually dependent. His message to leaders reaches farther than just discussing the "plumbing" requirements of IT (i.e., routers, networks, intra-mail, etc). He wants your organization to acknowledge the profitability of knowing how today's consumers *use* technology to connect with *you*. As Klososky points out, "Look at how technology changed travel agencies. In the first three years Expedia was active, two-thirds of all travel agencies went out of business. Why? Expedia made it possible for airlines to connect with consumers. Technology gets you closer to your customers."

Digital Marketing

How do you decide which marketing channel to use? Think about generational habits and exposure. The mature and baby boomer generations grew up on traditional marketing so they will respond to it. However, younger generations like millennials respond to digital marketing choices. In the early days of the internet the boss would come to the IT department with demands like, "Build us a website," or "We need an e-commerce store," and "We need faster bandwidth." Those edicts evolved into, "Shouldn't we be tweeting something?"

What Can You Do Today That Will Make You Even More Necessary Tomorrow?

Today, IT is not just about website plumbing and faster download speeds. If you want to be an invaluable resource for your company, learn how to create a revenue engine with digital marketing. Strong digital marketing can actually replace the sales force in some companies. In other companies, digital marketing will support the sales team in ways that drive revenue in previously unthinkable ways.

If you want to think about your digital strategy as a checklist, Klososky encourages you to think of your digital assets like this:

"I like to tell clients they have five components in their digital marketing toolkit. First, your web site is The Destination. Second, your social properties (Facebook,

Twitter, Tumblr, Instagram, et al) are the conversation. Three, mobile is the location. These three elements create a 'net' with which to catch your customers.

And the fourth element houses the engines that drive traffic (buyers) into your electronic 'net.' I'm talking about search engine optimization (SEO), crowd-vertising (getting others to recommend your products and services), compelling YouTube videos, and other guerrilla marketing stunts. The fifth element is your database. You need to collect or acquire a database that you can break down into micro-demographics and buying habits. When you own a database like that you can go to specific people for advice. You can test market new products with them. You can create a one-to-one partnership that's extremely powerful for customer retention and growth. If you have millions of buyers in your database and you sell broccoli and bananas…and you know a certain group who never buys broccoli, you don't market to them. Digital marketing is an engine of revenue. That's why you need to have millions of names in your database. A large buyer database allows you to drive demand. It is a mistake to think you will be able to sell all you want to sell through a distribution layer like resellers or dealers. The new thinking is to get to intimately know the consumer directly…to drive demand… or to do product testing on their own. "

Rain & Haircuts

One of Klososky's consulting clients is Great Clips. With nearly 3,000 locations, they sell a lot of $12 dollar haircuts. More importantly, at Klososky's urging, they have developed technology mastery. By using big data, the company now knows that you get your haircut every six weeks. So they nudge you via email or cell phone with short alerts, "Need a haircut?" They also built a mobile app that allows you to check the wait times at all locations. By checking the app you can time your day to complete your errands and walk right into your chair.

The next digital level for Great Clips is about influencing business based upon weather conditions. They know that when it rains all day near one of their locations, business can be down by over 30%. So, using real time marketing (Klososky calls it "revenue on demand"), Great Clips can dispatch electronic incentives to drive people into the salon on a rainy day.

Technology Requires Babysitting

You must be 24/7 active in social media. Don't turn it on and leave it alone.

You must find relevant ways to get to your customers before your competition.

You must be facile in managing your databases.

Want a shock? There are hundreds of thousands of small businesses who still do not have websites or mobile apps. The operators who refuse to learn about technology are probably very nice folks, but they will fossilize before they realize they are no longer able to compete.

The ability to market, promote, and sell goods and services, using technology tools, is a must-have.

eCommerce is mission critical to you because people want to use their phones and tablets to buy your stuff.

Phones and Tablets are Cash Registers

As of this writing, there are almost 1.6 billion smart phones in circulation. There are currently 400 million tablets and growing. Phone and tablets are at the epicenter of your communication and buying life.

According to exhaustive Google research, global mobile payment transactions approached $250 billion in 2013 and are projected to be almost $500 billion by 2015.

More than 46 million iPhone apps are downloaded daily. 300,000 TV shows are purchased every day. 50,000 movies are downloaded every 24 hours. And, the most staggering

statistic we could find was that 84% of mobile device owners have researched and made purchases with their mobile
devices. We apparently like our mobile money.

Some smart phone users can click a few keys and influence global financial markets.

Tweeting Wealth!

On August 13, 2013, 77-year old "investor activist" and billion-
aire, Carl Icahn, posted on Twitter, "We currently have a large
position in APPLE. We believe the company to be extremely
undervalued. Spoke to Tim Cook today. More to come." Mere
seconds after the tweet, investors sped to buy Apple stock.
Literally, within minutes, Apple's market value had jumped by
about $13 billion.

For a man of 77 (and worth an estimated $20 billion)
to choose a real time medium like Twitter is a statement of
urgency we (and you) cannot ignore. If the smart phone in his
pocket can accomplish miracles in an instant, why can't yours?

Bots Provide Business Intelligence

What is business intelligence? Let's go back to our tech guru,
Scott Klososky, for an explanation: "BI is the process of mining data across platforms and databases for the purpose of
creating greater insight into the trends, analytics, and abnor-
malities hidden in the data."

Besides financial data crunching, there is also the anec-
dotal equation— knowing what your peeps are posting about

you on social media...and what they are saying about your competitors. Consumers are out there, talking about you, recommending one product, dissing the other, singing your praises or cursing you. If you're a large company, the chatter can be overwhelming. How do you manage the unending stream of blather?

No worries. Hire robots!

Yes, robots can discover BI for you. A "bot" is essentially a computer program that prowls the internet, looking for mentions of your company and products, and then collects and analyzes them, and reports back to you. You have the ability to track your customers' complaints before they even bring them to you! Social media bots will do that for you. Are customers posting negative reviews on Amazon and Twitter? You can find them and fix the problems before their contagion spreads.

One such solution is offered by KANA. KANA's SEM (Service Experience Management) software is incredible with regard to capturing large amounts of customer feedback from email complaints, VM comments, IM results, suggestions, etc., and then cross-referencing social media feedback using an algorithm to chart behavioral trends and emerging topic analytics. They can take a Fortune 2000 company, do experience analytics, and give almost real-time feedback in 60 minutes. That's right, in about an hour you can get a complete picture of your online reputation, and begin responding to it immediately. Other programs like ICC SMART (Social Media Assessment and Response Tool) and Oracle's RightNow CX perform similar functions.

Whichever bot you choose, the goal is the same—having the ability to respond to your customers, even when they haven't bothered to contact you.

Do You Know About Humalogy?

We have talked a lot about bots and automated rules and artificial intelligence as ways of using technology to make your business smarter. But, what about us humans? Do we still have a job? Well, as you saw, the Park Hyatt Aviara was masterful at augmenting the hotel experience with humanity. No robot necessary.

However, at a recent convention, we heard Klososky use the word humalogy—a word that was foreign to us until he explained it like this, "Humalogy is a process every leader should consider for maximizing efficiencies. If you want to produce products or harvest new ideas in the most efficient way, ask yourself, 'how much of this process can be done with technology...and how much must be done by humans?'"

Recently, we had a chance to introduce humalogy to a chain of wonderful hospitals in Florida that were trying to figure out how to make money with Medicare (typically a consistent money loser). After hearing about humalogy, they now have people working to find the perfect marriage of technology and humanity to turn this costly problem into something profitable. One such solution might be to create a "smart watch" worn by patients. The smart watch could wirelessly send the patient's vital signs to the nurse's station so that a nurse wasn't physically required to wake a patient to get blood pressure readings. The hospital would get what they need and the patient could enjoy a night's sleep without frequent interruption.

You see, technology is not denigrating humanity. Technology is augmenting efficiency so we can still afford to employ humans.

Speaking of humans, you will be miles wiser than your competition if you know what changes are taking place regarding humanity in the next chapter.

EIGHT

BE A DOCTOR OF DEMOGRAPHICS

For Team Members/Associates: It is not enough to have product knowledge and superior sales training. These days your customer and client demographics are shifting in age and ethnicity. The people who bought from you in the past may not resemble your future buyers at all. If indispensability is your goal, you will be smart to not just acquaint yourself with these new demographics, but become a studied expert so you can anticipate where your future dollars and co-workers are coming from. This chapter will provide a good start and some valuable resources.

For Leaders: The discussion above applies to you—with one addition. You need to know demographics to be able to manage the future workforce. That said, if you cannot get your Ph.D. in practical demographics, then at least be an eager student of the four known demographic workplace segments. To plan your go-to-market strategies you must know how they see themselves, their work ethics, and your associated sales opportunities. For an overview, we have relied upon the findings of our friend, best-selling author and generational guru, Cam Marston. Marston is recognized as the leading expert in this field and we highly recommend his books, articles, and video commentaries. Go to: www. GenerationalInsights.com

Immerse Yourself in These Four Demographic Segments

Mature Generation
(born between 1928 and 1945)

How many are there? Fifty million were born but only approximately 20 million are alive today. While their numbers don't indicate a high volume of available buyers, many in this generation have substantial disposable income.

What defines them? In a word, scarcity. They grew up in the wake of the Great Depression. Their fathers fought in World War II. Many of their mothers also contributed to the war effort. Our friend Bill Nye (of "Science Guy" fame) visited a museum in London and unexpectedly saw his mother's face in an old photograph. The photograph celebrated the highly classified United States Enigma code breaking team. The Enigma machine was created to decode German communications and was popularized by the Matthew McConaughey movie, U-571. Bill had no clue his mom was involved in this game-changing war effort because she was sworn to silence for 50 years. This demographic is also referred to as "The Silent Generation" because they were often overlooked. These post-war kids had plenty of job opportunities and were able to buy homes and raise large families. Because war was such a recent memory, they also lived under the threat of a global nuclear war. Bomb shelters and school air raid drills were common because they were concerned about safety and security. Modern conveniences like toasters, radio, and cars with power steering, flourished. They are not big agents of change. They prefer familiar, known activities and environments. They work hard, but quietly. What is surprising is that according to research, the "matures" are the "happiest generation," followed by he baby boomers.

Work ethic? They tend to be very dedicated, hard workers. Many worked for only one organization in their lifetime.

How do you sell to them? The Matures are often well off… often from inheritances. It is estimated that they have over 6 trillion dollars remaining to pass to their heirs. Personally, they're after a comforting final chapter in their life. The message to them: "You Deserve This."

Baby Boomers
(born between 1946 and 1964)

How many are there? Of the 76 million born into this segment, only 65 million are alive today. Keep in mind that while this generation is retiring at a rate of 10,000 a day, their spending is only slightly reduced because they already own the luxury items they coveted earlier.

What defines them? Because many of their parents grew up frugal, their parents inadvertently crushed their dreams by promoting the idea that you should, "get one job and keep it for life." Consequently, many in this generation wound up confused and dysfunctional. They experienced social unrest due to the televised assassinations of John F. Kennedy and Martin Luther King, as well as the Viet Nam war. This and various economic struggles (including an oil embargo in 1979) all reinforced a sense of mistrust of both the media and government. The younger boomers adopted an, "I'm out for me" attitude. What followed was extreme narcissism and a focus on self-help.

Work ethic? They were willing to work hard to "stand out." Due to advances in medicine, air and water quality, smoking cessation, and an attitude of being an "active senior" many boomers find themselves able and wanting to work well past 65. Many boomers may actually need to keep working because they didn't plan adequately for retirement.

How do you sell to them? Many boomers will be the recipients of the $6 trillion their parents will pass along. They're frantically prepping for retirement—yet simultaneously spending money on their kids. They will likely continue to do that for some time. Boomers are "buying memories" like exotic trips and reunion concerts. They also like expensive sound systems, upgraded home furnishings, high-end automobiles, wines, pet supplies, expensive pet surgeries, and musical instruments they couldn't afford as teenagers. An idea that resonates for boomers is "nostalgia."

Generation X
(born between 1965 and 1979)

How many are there? Fifty-one million. This number dropped from the baby boomer generation largely due to widespread popularity of birth control.

What defines them? Often referred to as the "lost" generation, this was the first generation of "latchkey" kids, exposed to a cavalcade of daycare and divorce. The Xers are also known as the generation with the lowest voting participation rate of any generation. They are considered the most skeptical and the highest educated; which is why they want full authenticity and sincerity from their chosen merchants and friends. Gen Xers are often characterized by a "what's in it for me" attitude. As a funny side note, Marston claims this generation has a reputation for some of the worst music to ever gain popularity.

Work ethic? This is the generation who pushed for 'casual Friday' because they preferred a laid back environment. While they like a collegial atmosphere they also like things neat and orderly. They want a learning environment that is also functional. Generation Xers don't expect to be given everything. They are happy to make their own way. The movies they watched featured solo outliers saving the day ("Indiana Jones," "Ghostbusters," "Back to the Future," "Batman"). They don't tend to be intimidated by authority. They don't give their respect to others based merely on a title. As youngsters, they grew up watching authority figures fall apart. Their parents got divorced. They saw alcoholism and substance abuse on network television. Similarly, gen X supervisors don't expect to be heralded for their own work title. They expect to earn the respect of their peers and upper management by their own efforts.

How do you sell to them? Surprisingly, the MTV "Slacker" generation is anything but lazy. They are outspending their baby boomer counterparts (in luxury items) by about 18%. They spend money on their children, mortgages, college savings, and quick and cheap vacations. They are buying their next homes now (not vacation homes, but bigger homes for their expanding families) and working to fill them with "stuff." But beware, they don't spend their money foolishly. Their skepticism causes them to research purchases carefully. Marston says, "Mercedes Benz told me the Xer spends an average of 16 hours researching the car online before they test drive it. They will pay more for superior quality, but they won't overpay for it." A sensible group, they're frequently looking for the best possible deal. When you market to this generation, be informed that Xers are not swayed by hype or trends. As natural skeptics, this generation needs constant assurance that your product is real, high quality, and that you stand behind it. They love a solid return policy and/or a money-back guarantee. Marston says, "Beware of the 45-year old Gen X mother. She is the fully engaged super consumer. She talks to everyone in and out of her social network. She is cautious because she is buying for her kids, herself, and her husband. She is also taking it upon herself to buy for her parents, her in-laws, and her peers."

Millennials, aka Generation Y
(born between 1980 and 2000)

How many are there? 82 million strong; making them the largest population segment from which you can enjoy future sales and candidates for your future workforce.

What defines them? They have been called the "ME" generation because they think the world is all about them. Their baby boomer parents have given them advantages *they* didn't have as children. Because many of this generation have difficulty finding a good job (even with a respected diploma under their arms), many boomer parents are letting their adult kids camp at home until age 30. Enabling and entitling, boomer parents have sympathy for their children who are saddled with high student loan debt. Not surprising, millennials have three times more narcissistic personality disorder cases reported than the baby boomer generation.

Work ethic? Pay and compensation are still very important for most millennials seeking a job, but it is not always the primary factor that determines taking the job. They place great value in autonomy, respect, and being treated fairly. They expect employers to provide these conditions at work. They prefer collaborating with other coworkers rather than working in isolation. This stems from the grade school trend to turn classroom tables into "group rounds" rather than the traditional set up where all classroom seats were facing the blackboard. Millennials also want to work for an organization that has a social conscience—a company that contributes to a worthy cause benefitting the less fortunate. They want to feel good about telling friends where they work.

How do you sell to them? As first-time home buyers, they will buy the items that go with new homes like furniture, pets, appliances and dish ware. They are shopping for the life insurance that comes with having kids. The single millennials will likely buy condos and "play toys" like snowmobiles, boats, motorcycles and wave runners. Marketing to this group is more digitally oriented because millennials are known as incredibly sophisticated, technologically savvy, and immune to most traditional marketing and sales pitches. According to Cam Marston's research, you only have 3 seconds to grab their attention. If they like you they will spend another 30 seconds learning about what you sell. If after 33 seconds, they are still interested in your offering, they will "read the fine print" and spend up to another 3 minutes hearing about your offer—but that's it. The best you can expect will be 3:33 seconds to tell your story. Oh, and your pitch better include how you are helping the world with some of your profits. As they want to work for a company with a social conscience, they also want to feel like their purchases are contributing to 'the greater good.' And they want their peers to know they are socially conscious. Millennials feel the pressure to display their purchases on social media. Financial milestones (like buying a home or car) are routinely posted for all to see and envy. The same could be said about 'the selfie' photograph. Millennials love to show their friends what they are doing and where they are doing it. Travel and 'cool hangs' are a sign of achievement without the damage deposit.

How much will millennials eventually have to spend? The answer is more and more. Marston says, "By 2015, 20-30% of all retail sales will be in the hands of millennials." That said, if you can appeal to their personal brand (i.e., who they perceive themselves to be), you will get their attention. Just keep in mind the attention span is short.

Yet, with all of their advantages, 15% of them are still unemployed. Over 25% of them had late payments or are dealing with bill collectors, and well over half are still receiving some form of financial aid from their parents. The 85% who are employed align their desires with their boomer parents. Over three-quarters of millennials want to have the same clothes, cars and technological gadgets as their friends, and around half of them have to use a credit card to pay for basic daily necessities such as food and utilities. (One in nine millennials has a credit card co-signed by a parent).

iGeneration
(born after 2000)

What defines them? While not much is known yet, we do know they are growing up in a highly diverse environment which make the grade schools of the next generation the most diverse ever. Higher levels of technology will make significant inroads in academics. Education will likely revolve around a custom experience based upon even sharper diagnostics of the student's skill sets. Without question, as young adults, the iGens will be schooled in mining and applying big data—an invaluable metric for growing companies.

How do you sell to them? Marston says, "Technology is this generation's pacifier and parents will pay to keep them happy." If you have seen a two year old 'swiping' through games on an iPad you'll see they already know how companies like Apple, Google, Amazon, and Netflix will benefit from their unquenchable thirst for anything 2.0.

The Buyer and the Workforce are Increasingly International

Marston not only studies the intricacies of generational behaviors but he is fascinated by the population base as well. Marston states, "Soon, the 'minorities' in the U.S. will become the majorities. Hispanic and Asian cultures are growing the fastest and the youngest. Look at the population changes between 2013 and 2033. The Hispanic population is going to increase by about 13% and the Asian population will increase between 35-40%. The rest of us will largely be unchanged and the minority. What is also interesting is the evolving size of the household. The rest of us remain unchanged (about 2.5 per household) but Asian and Hispanic cultures typically have more people living per house. Hispanics come in at about 3.5 per household and Asian families a little over 3 people per home. Larger household numbers obviously affect the home buying market. Realtors tell us that Hispanic families are looking for more bedrooms. Asian families are not only looking for more bedrooms but a second kitchen as well; even if they have to install a second one themselves. Food choices are different, too. These burgeoning cultures generally prefer fresh fruits and vegetables...and generally don't buy canned foods."

As cultures collide, you need to adapt. Truly, you will need to become an expert in these important emerging cultures. Insight into the generations is a "must-practice" if you want to be able to serve these new and significant market segments.

The Mobile Workforce
Doesn't Like Your Office

They have nothing against your office per se, they just don't want to work from there. Regardless of the generational or ethnic mix, broadband internet allows your people to take care of business from a coffee shop, a beach or watching a movie inside a cineplex. Entire work forces are checking in at round table collaborative work spaces instead of being isolated in a cubicle. This practice is so popular that the best candidates are asking for this kind of flexibility when interviewing. They want a ROWE. ("Results-only Work Environment") like Best Buy, Gap, IBM and other progressive companies. These companies have developed clear success metrics. If their team members deliver on those metrics, they are encouraged to work in their most productive environment. Believe it or not, the companies above report that productivity soared as a result of this new freedom. Honestly, if you think you have true slackers on your payroll, relax. Laziness will be self-eliminating. They will not survive in a clearly defined success-metric ecosystem.

NINE
ACT WITH EXTREME URGENCY

For Team Members/Associates: By the time an assignment is handed down to you from management, its state-of-urgency has advanced into the 'I need this right now' category. Do not dally. Do not assume you can add the new assignment to the bottom of your already prioritized to-do list. Invaluable people take their bosses' requests with extreme urgency. Completing an assignment ahead of schedule makes you the invaluable go-to person. This chapter will (1) underscore why urgency is so mission-critical to your ascension to "necessary" status and (2) give you ideas for creating an urgent culture that drives profit. When you can create an idea that generates revenue, management is drawn like gravity into your orbit.

For Leaders: A much admired management trait is your ability to operate with calm in a state of extreme urgency. Societal shifts and on-demand customer buying habits dictate it. Fast is the new slow. Now is the new fast. From what we observe in our travels, a culture of extreme urgency is your best insurance policy against becoming irrelevant.

Fast is the New Slow. _Now_ _is the New Fast._

Several times throughout this book we have urged you to embrace doing your job with extreme urgency. Maybe our insistence grates on your nerves when you think to yourself, "I'm already working as fast as I can." We get it. You are terribly busy and your customers and clients will just have to wait…or do they?

In order to convince you of the dire nature of adopting a sense of corporate urgency, let's first make the discussion all about YOU.

You need answers right now, immediately, no waiting, instantly, PDQ, ASAP, quick, and in the blink of an eye. You want your express meal pre-prepared, pre-cooked, ready-mixed, heat-n-serve, and done under a minute. Your smart phone or tablet never allows you to leave work. Work issues follow you home. Customers and coworkers stalk you at your daughter's soccer game. Even from a well-earned vacation, you're still on duty—responding to a staff and/or supplier crisis in a split-second, a jiffy, a flash, in a heartbeat, or at least within a hot second. You find yourself "putting out fires" instead of planning. You are living your life in real time. What is real time? Real time means you must remain productive—and expect results—as you are simultaneously receiving input. Hardly leaves any time to break away for a meal...which is another thing you apparently despise planning. You are starved for time.

Time Starvation is Exhausting, Right?

If that's your life, then you are likely at the teetering edge of your mental, physical, and emotional frontier. You're exhausted. You're stressed. And, tomorrow is relentless. Ah, but there is someone else who wants an even bigger piece of you—your customers.

The people who give you money for your goods, services and time have unceasing demands. They speed-date. They self-checkout. They auto-populate order forms. They IM. They Skype. They text. They post and they tweet. They update their lives in 140 characters or less. They don't hunt for news. An RSS performs at their behest and then pushes the information to them. They seem to dodge, weave, and short cut their way

through life and if we are lucky we get a last minute slice of their time and wallet.

So when you can respond with extreme urgency, you leave your competitors in the proverbial dust.

Amazon's Air Force

Amazon understood extreme urgency before the rest of us.

While Amazon used to be the time-saving bookstore alternative, now they are the alternative to buying everything...from everywhere. Most of you will agree that Amazon has set the expectation high. You hit "1-Click ordering" and within seconds you get an electronic order confirmation. Amazon can make real time feel very close to an instantaneous experience. If you are an Amazon Prime member, they will even pay for the shipping. If you use Amazon, we wager you are continually amazed at how quickly your packages arrive...but Amazon delivery is likely to get much faster.

Amazon is pushing to create the 30-minute (or less) delivery a reality with their Air Drone Project, "Amazon Prime Air." Yes, certain products (under 5 pounds) will ride down a conveyor belt where they will picked up and flown via octocopter to your home. The caveat (at this point) is that you must live within a 10 mile radius of an Amazon warehouse. CEO Jeff Bezos believes this new delivery method will be approved by the FAA by 2016.

Because Amazon has conditioned us to expect such an incredibly timely response, "instantaneous" is now regarded as the expectation. Consider your customer's and client's conditioning. They are thinking, "Dang, if Amazon can do it, why can't you?"

Can You Solve Time Starvation?

So time-starved are your customers that brought-to-your-home services have become a $2 billion dollar business. Look at what your customers (and you) do to save time:

- At-home dog grooming and vet-aided euthanizing of your pet

- At-home car detailing
- On-call concierge doctor visits
- At-home dry cleaning delivery
- Mobile Christmas light hanging
- At-home diet food delivery
- At-home massage & fitness training
- At-home grocery delivery
- At-home closet organizing
- Errand-running personal assistant
- Instant Kindle or iTunes digital delivery of books and movies

RELEVANT REPORT

By Michael Burger

How Fast Can You Plan, Set-up & Mop Up a Child's B-Day Party?

We've been talking about how mobile services save you time. How about planning a birthday party for 15 screaming 9-year olds? I neither have the time, the patience or skill set to pull something like this off. No worries. Call Game Truck! We talked about what a burgeoning business come-to-your-home businesses are. Game Truck offers a turnkey solution for our time-starved lives. Game Truck is a 35-foot tractor-trailer filled with the latest video games and flat screen TV's. The beautiful semi-truck parks in front of your house, and for several hours the kids have the fantasy time of their lives. You do nothing. When the party is over, the kids get out of the truck - and your mess drives away. Parents and children love it. No surprise, right? Aren't you happier when companies bring their services to YOU? You've seen it with mobile dog grooming and the Geek Squad fixing your computers. But it's even happening with high-end services. Concierge doctors that make house calls are trying to make you feel good about doctors again. Companies who rent high end art work and deliver it to your home make you and your home look classy for a few dollars a day. Heck, there's even a company that will adjust your child's braces in your driveway. So…what could YOU do to mobilize YOUR business, and bring your goods and services right to your customers' doorsteps? LINK: http://youtu.be/DqSo3-RMmjc

Will the World Get Even Faster?

As long as we have blazing broadband internet, the answer is "yes."

With such a brisk cultural shift in the way we can buy and communicate, experts are now blaming broadband for shriveling our attention spans. The "attention-span people" (yes, there are such people…like comScore www.comscore.com) say that within the last 18 months Americans have gone from watching seven-minute online videos…to an abbreviated five minutes.

The social media picture app, Instagram, offers 15-second videos (and even some of those seem too long). If 15-seconds is a lifetime to you, try Vine. Vine limits videos to six seconds, and then it disappears. Snapchat is a social app that self-destructs within ten seconds after viewing. Why do we need self-destructing pictures and videos? Because,"photo sexting" has become popular. Vine and Snapchat have supplied their members with the ability to send a private picture without the risk of having it live in infamy in cyberspace.

What about the alleged 3% annual increase in diagnosed ADHD (Attention-Deficit Hyperactivity Disorder)? Does more technology contribute to this lack of focus?

Lesley Alderman of Everyday Health wrote, "The American Academy of Pediatrics is persuaded enough of the detrimental effect that it recommends that children spend no more than one to two hours a day interacting with screen-based media, such as TV and video games. And the recommendation for children under the age of two is no TV at all. The brain is a highly adaptive and sensitive organ, so it makes intuitive sense that something like fast-paced video games could alter the way it reacts to stimuli."

Is Attention Span Nature or Nurture?

It really doesn't matter.

If technology is causing shorter attention spans or more ADHD is the culprit, the genie is out of the bottle. If Amazon can truly deliver within 30 minutes or less, the bar has been raised. Deliverables in real time are the expectation of your customers. Real time is also the expectation of your team members. And, real time is most certainly the expectation of your stakeholders. Whether you are a B2B or B2C operation, ubiquitous broadband internet has empowered your clients and customers to manipulate time and space. They are forever acclimatized to get anything they want – anytime they want it. If you don't respond at near broadband speed, your customer and clients will think you don't care about their business. They might even think you are lazy, or worse—irrelevant.

As businesspeople, let's accept these shifts in human behavior and work with these people—on their terms. Let's sell urgency.

The Dangerous Cost of Being Slow

If you hear a scraping sound, it's likely to be the noise of your feet dragging you into the future. Or maybe you keep hearing the CFO say, "It's too expensive to provide highly urgent, supreme-quality customer service." If either is the case, then rip out this page and take it into your next meeting. Financial folks love numbers. Give them these:

1: Number of bad customer service experiences it takes to cause 70% of the 18-45 demographic to bolt for a competitor.

70%: The percentage of customers who have ended business relationships due to poor service.

85%: The percentage of 18-45 year olds who report bad customer service on Facebook, Twitter, Tumblr, and Instagram.

$243: The average annual value per worldwide customer lost due to poor service

$289: The average annual value per US customer lost due to poor service

$83 billion: The annual cost of poor customer service to the US economy

$100 billion: The annual cost to UK businesses due to *slow* customer service

$340 billion: The annual business loss in major, industrialized economies worldwide due to poor customer service

What is Bad Service?

Service that is considered S-L-O-W is perceived as really bad. Consumer Reports asked 1,000 consumers about their top customer service gripes. On a scale from 1 to 10 (10 being worst), here's how they ranked their gripes:

10: Can't get a person on the phone
8.5: Time-consuming phone menu steps
8:   Long hold times
8:   Wasting my time pitching extras
7:   Stuck on hold with bad music and recorded sales pitches
7:   Waiting to check out
6.5: Waiting for someone to show up

These were seven of the top 12 complaints and they all point to time and urgency! In another survey, consumers were asked how long they were willing to wait on hold for a customer-service representative. One-third said less than 30 seconds. *Seconds!* Two-thirds won't wait more than a minute. Only 10% will wait more than two minutes. Our guess is that these are the 10% who are eager to speak to anyone in the hope of "friendship." (Is that mean?)

Slow Solutions for Fast Problems?

In Chapter 5, we talked about how leaders should make premeditated decisions for routine problems. The goal was to save time and energy when fighting the same dragons over and over again. The same process is essential for the customer experience. Exhaust the potential recurring problems and write a script for how to handle those recurring issues. Sadly, that process rarely happens. Why not? A lack of accountability by management and lack of basic empathy for the socially vocal customer won't be tolerated.

If you are like us, you think, "I don't understand why a cell phone carrier can't be superb at customer care." A cell carrier's world of "issues" are finite. There are only so many things that can go wrong, right? Well, from a customer's point of view, they bought a cell phone primarily to make phone calls. The cell carrier promised to provide the most comprehensive cell phone coverage. The carrier went on TV and boldly told us, "Look at our coverage map!" Yet, there are times when you try to load an app or make a call, and your app won't boot or your call gets dropped.

So, you call your carrier's support line.

Every carrier's support line must routinely field thousands of the exact same kinds of requests and complaints every few minutes. How could they not have a solution for every possible scenario? But you've been there. Your inbound call for help is greeted with one or more of these familiar phrases:

"Thank you for your patience. Your call is very important to us. Please stay on the line and an operator will be with you shortly."

"We are experiencing unusually high-call volume. We appreciate your patience."

"Most questions can be answered on our web site at www._____. Please go there now."

"If you cannot wait and prefer to have us call you back, please leave your number at the beep."

"Calls are answered in the order they were received. Your wait time is approximately one year."

"Please say or punch in your account number using your touch tone keypad."

"I will transfer your call but first I need you to answer a few questions."

We ask you, was there any hint of extreme urgency in any of those automated responses? Automated people do NOT buy your product or service. Live people do. So, why should an automated voice be the preferred choice in solving a problem?

Fix It Now

Customers want their problems addressed quickly...and that's *after* they have already bought your product. Customers fume at wasting time finding out why your product or service doesn't live up to your publicized brand promise. Every second they spend trying to resolve the problem (FYI: the one you created for them) potentially doubles the personal cost of your product *for them*.

Think about that for a moment. If a customer buys your product for $50, and then has to call you because the product doesn't work, the customer does the mental math to add their lost time in talking to you about it.

According to "The Customer Shouts Back, 2006," if you ask most people how much their time is worth they will say, "I am worth between $25 and $100 an hour."

So if your customer has to spend 30 minutes on the phone, writing a letter, visiting an FAQ page, or any other time-consuming activity to solve *your* product's problem, the customer's realized cost of a $50 item can balloon up to $100. And, that's if they decided to keep your product. But if they get so frustrated they decide to return your product, your losses increase exponentially:

- You've probably made them angry enough to eliminate you from a future purchase.

- You have risked being widely exposed on a social network.

- You have a returned item which you now have to refurbish, repackage, or recycle.

- (4) You have lost the marketing cost it took to land that customer in the first place.

The urgency we are describing doesn't just apply to consumer goods and services. You need to remember your B2B community (aka Business to Business). When a person has been conditioned to get anything they want at nearly light speed, they expect your organization to respond on-demand as well. If you don't, your customer, client, supply chain partner or manufacturer will assume you don't understand *their own* sense of urgency. Don't assume bankruptcy could never happen to your organization. The courts are littered with Chapter 11 and Chapter 7 filings from companies that never understood the profit principles of extreme urgency.

Measure Urgency in Dollars

Did you notice what else the complainers had in common? They all declared their intention to bolt for a competitor, or worse, "to never do business with this company again." This is proof positive that s-l-o-w service translates into lost revenue.

How much money?

Last year, banks lost over $44 billion in revenue, cable providers lost $36 billion, and telecom saw more than $69 billion walk out the door to a competitor due to slow, poor service. And that's from just three industries.

Measure Urgency in Seconds

The difference between customer satisfaction and dissatisfaction is truly measured in seconds. Consider the public humiliation endured by Bank of America and Verizon, who tried to impose minor but annoying fees on their customers for everyday transactions. The ensuing social media outcry was measured in the hundreds of thousands of tweets and status updates. Soon the social media firestorm was covered in the old fashioned media.

The appearance of an angry virtual flash mob with digital torches and pitchforks was instantaneous. Bank of America rescinded its policy within days. Verizon apologized within hours. The moral of both stories: These days your dissatisfied customers have the ability to marshal an instant army, demanding you do what *they* want.

It's expensive to deliver slow, bad service. Conversely, smart organizations can make bundles of cash by being fast and great. In the next chapter, we will meet some organizations that "get urgency."

TEN
ASPIRE TO VIRAL SERVICE

For Team Members/Associates: Viral service (we coined this phrase, thank you) is when your service is so amazing, your fans can't wait to tell others. Viral service becomes infectious when your company adopts the attitude: "We want to be famous for our service." It's good to be famous, especially when being famous for good customer service directly translates into high profitability.

People in high-demand deliver viral service over and over again. These people seem to create relationships effortlessly. Service, the act of serving others, appears to come naturally to the people we like the most. Their exploits become legendary. Their good character is talked about behind their backs. Their increased paychecks and elevated titles inspire others to see the correlation between service and achievement. For external customers and clients, promise yourself to be responsive and pleasant. "Out-friendly" your competition. Be easy to deal with...easy to buy from. Realize that you are an extension of your company brand. Represent that brand in a way that casts sunlight on your organization. Management will notice.

For Leaders: The best and brightest "new economy" entrepreneurs have made their fortunes by showing us we no longer have to wait. We honor their obsessive dedication to "impatience."

Lessons From Google, Apple, & Amazon

Ever wonder why the home page of Google consists of only a logo, a box, and two buttons? It was designed that way so your search can load *milliseconds* faster than competitor search engines. Google's founders, Larry Page and Sergy Brin, are similar to Steve Jobs of Apple and Jeff Bezos of Amazon. They are all followers of Donald Norman, author of the product design masterpiece "The Psychology of Everyday Things." Norman's mantra was, "The user is always right." If the user expects a product to work a certain way, that's how it should be designed to work. And, they understood that users wanted things to work *fast* and *easy*. Fast and easy were the founding principles of what have become the world's three most recognizable brands.

Apple taught us to expect the world at the click or tap of a fingertip, even in our pockets. Ease of use is Apple's main innovation and it appeals to us because "easy" makes every-thing _seem_ faster. Apple sold us fast and easy products even before we knew we needed them.

Google taught us to access the knowledge of the world by typing a word or two into a box. Amazon gave us 1-Click ordering and access to just about any product we want deliv-ered in less than 24 hours.

RELEVANT REPORT

By Michael Burger

Apple's Secret Weapon is Understanding Humanity

We've all heard our share of Apple stories, but I urge you to read this one.

I'll say this upfront. I'm not an Apple groupie, nor do I own any of its stock. I'm not that smart. I did however buy an iPhone. On that very same day, while on a bike ride, I hit a bump in the road that tossed me from the bike, dislodged my iPhone headset/ear buds that in turn got caught in my spinning spokes and, wait for it...jerked the phone from its safe handle-bar holder, crashing it to the ground! It then rode shotgun, glass face down, over the asphalt for a good 100 feet! The phone itself was not in a case, it was on backorder from Apple. Timing! I called Apple Customer Care and shared my bike ride/iPhone mishap and explained that I was an idiot and it was my fault and what are my options? My customer care representative asked if the glass was cracked on the phone. I said yes it was; she said, "Well don't touch it, I don't want you to cut your finger."

Who was she, my mother? How sweet and kind was that? She suggested I bring the iPhone into my nearest Apple retail store and she'd make note of our conversation. What did my trip and honesty get me? Twenty minutes later, I left the store with a brand-new iPhone. Free of charge. Look, I'm not telling you to give your product away; nobody stays in business like that. What I am saying is if you're at that tipping point with your customer, perhaps a gray area where it could go either way, why not combine customer care with customer happiness? Apple did, and I'm happy. Here's the direct link to my Apple Relevant Report, see for yourself.

LINK: http://youtu.be/JKGdsQlj5dM

The Value of Service

How much do we like great customer service? We'll pay extra for it, that's how much. According to a key survey, consumers will pay about 9% more for great customer service. Online customers will pay almost 11% more. Great customer service generates an additional $268 billion dollars (yes, with a "B") for U.S. businesses alone.

Exceptional = Fast

In the same survey mentioned above, customers were asked what makes for exceptional service. Here's their top-10 list:

1. **Speed** of delivery
2. **Ease** of access to information
3. Helpfulness and knowledge of CSRs (customer sales representatives)
4. **Time** to resolve an issue
5. **Ease** of reaching a CSR
6. Issue resolved **immediately**
7. **Ease** of returns

8. Proactive service

9. Access to Customer Service online

10. Personalized service

As you can see, at least 70% of exceptional customer service is making it fast and easy.

Cheaper to Keep 'Em

Let's throw one more factor into the mix. Let's say you've got a nice cadre of customers. If your service is too slow and they go elsewhere, you may think your marketing efforts can simply replace them, right? Well, maybe, but it's going to cost you. Karl Stark of the strategic advisory firm Avondale writes that most companies that depend upon continuing relationships with clients can generate growth simply by keeping existing customers longer. He cites a typical company would grow an additional 3% by keeping all their customers for one additional month. If they can keep their customers for four additional months, the cumulative annual growth would be in the double digits. The plain truth is that ramping up your customer care program—to keep current customers happy—is more cost-effective than marketing efforts to attract new ones.

Customer Service IS a Business

So here's what we know so far:

• Bad customer service costs billions.

• Exceptional customer service earns billions.

- The world's biggest brands are built on great customer service.

- Customer service is more cost-effective than marketing.

- Consumers judge customer service mostly based on how fast it is — how *urgent* it is.

A clear picture, right? If you have customers, then customer service is <u>not</u> *part* of your business—it *is* your business. Customer service is a business based on urgency.

A few companies have embraced these truths and built hugely successful businesses based on providing the best and fastest service.

Netflix

Netflix is a business built on customer service. The company was founded by Reed Hastings in 1997. He launched Netflix in response to Blockbuster's bad customer service. He set out to provide consumers with fast and friendly video rentals with no nickel-and-dime fees that penalized customers. Netflix's first motto, "No Late Fees," endeared them to customers. The service was also designed for ease of use. Select a video from their website and it arrives in the mail. Put it back in the mailbox and your next video is on its way. How easy was that?

What really made Netflix flourish was *speed*. Fifty-eight regional distribution hubs enabled overnight service for 97% of customers. Then they added "Watch Instantly," introducing streaming video to Main Street America in 2007. Netflix now has 48 million subscribers. In 2014, Netflix's revenues topped $3.2 billion! "The vast majority of folks are really happy with the service because we are that fast," says Netflix's director of communications. Not just fast, "Instant."

Not to say that fast growing companies don't make mistakes along the way. In 2011, Netflix made headlines when it lost sight of the prime directive, "the user is always right," and attempted to charge approximately 60% more for both the mail subscription service and their streaming video option. Customers revolted. So, Netflix backtracked by trying to spin off its DVD service. Millions of customers dropped the service. Customers responded with an "instant" uproar. The company was forced to create two separate entities – one for digital delivery of content and the to mail out DVDs.

You see, Netflix was a victim of hubris—thinking they could do anything they wanted and the customer would blindly follow. They violated a basic human behavior tenant: "If you rigidly dictate how and when we will buy, we will stop buying." Netflix was trying to manipulate buying behavior and the pushback had violent ramifications. The strategy sadly cut their market cap by two-thirds. (On July 15, 2011, their stock price was $286, but by November 17, 2011, the stock dropped to $76.) Despite the setback, Netflix's earnings rose 63% in that very same fall quarter. At one point in 2014, Netflix stock rebounded to over $450 a share. Why? Because their service is still instant — and instant sells. Instant "empathy" causes your service to go viral.

• ———— RELEVANT REPORT ———— •
By Michael Burger

Empathy is the New Expectation of Service

Ever buy something from a store and try to take it back and they won't let you? A while back, I bought new living room furniture from a store called Room & Board. www.roomandboard.com/

It got delivered right on time, yet I couldn't have been more disappointed. All my fault—the couch I bought looked great in the showroom, not so much in my house—wrong color, wrong size. I called customer care and asked if they could come pick it up. I offered to pay any restock fee. The customer care rep said, "Yes, but it's December 18th." I asked if that was a problem and she replied with, "Maybe. Do you have family coming over for the holidays? Why don't you keep furniture until after the holidays so you and your guests have something to sit on?" Her first response was not how to get her couch back, but how to resolve MY issue! I told her, "You're very kind, but no thank you. You don't know my family. I've got relatives that underestimate the usefulness of flat-ware. By the end of the night that sofa is gonna look like the kids' booth at an International House of Pancakes." Here's the point— she had a sense of urgency about my situation, and resolved it on the spot. Even with Christmas days away. Would it not be great if we all had that kind of urgency for each other?

Also, to all you business owners looking for ways to save money on advertising, this happened to me in 2007. I've shared my positive customer experience with anyone who would listen. Friends, family, the cashier at Trader Joe's .... oh and to my key-note audiences in the corporate world. Consider this, I've never met the CEO of Room and Board, I don't work for the company, and yet since 2007 I'm guessing 40 thousand people have heard me share this great experience. I've become an unpaid spokesperson for Room and Board all because of one customer service representative on one phone call took one moment to hear my story and solve my issue with urgency and kindness. Look, I just shared it again with you reading this chapter. You can watch the report here:

LINK: http://youtu.be/o0FTAYczcLA

"Good" Listens

While Apple, Amazon, Google and Netflix are well-known examples of responsive "dot-com" giants, their urgent customer service approach is transferable to non-tech companies and small businesses. Think about the last time you went to a busy restaurant and the host person gave you an electronic pager/buzzer so that you wouldn't be tethered to the waiting area. You can actually leave the restaurant to shop elsewhere until your table is ready.

Consider a few examples of companies that *get it* and are making service faster and more customer-considerate:

- USAA allows customers to snap a picture of a check – for immediate deposit – and even transfer funds with a quick text message.

- Amica's customer service system routes calls to insurance agents in other offices when the home office staff (that you dialed) is already on the phone.

- Charles Schwab has trained their brokers to take customers service calls when call centers are overwhelmed.

- BB&T sets a 20-minute time limit on customer calls before they are bumped up to a team of experts who can resolve them.

- Southwest Airlines emails vouchers within 24 hours to customers who experience significant delays.

- Ally Bank has "real person" Customer Service Reps are available 24 hours a day, 7 days a week.

Even the pioneers of urgent customer service are finding ways to improve upon their already fast service:

- As we mentioned earlier, Amazon now offers same-day shipping in seven cities. Soon, they expect to offer Amazon Prime Air...a drone that will deliver packages within 30 minutes (if you are within a 10 mile radius of an Amazon warehouse).

- Apple stores now have roving checkout clerks so you don't have to wait in line to checkout.

- Starbucks deploys a headset-wearing barista to take orders on our side of the counter when the counter line exceeds four people.

Be Easy to Buy From

"Make your product easier to buy than your competition. If you don't you will find your customers buying from them, not you."
    — Mark Cuban, Founder of Broadcast.com and owner of the Dallas Mavericks NBA team

Ease of use makes everything feel faster.

Steve Jobs understood ease of use early on. Apple always tried to see things from the consumer perspective. For years, when you opened an Apple product, there was an envelope or box right inside the crate that said "OPEN ME FIRST!" Once you opened that box, the instructions guided you step-by-step as to what to remove next and what to do with it. The easiest user experience shows you respect the customer's time. You respect their need for urgency.

Ask Yourself These Questions

Ease of use is the part of urgency that doesn't have anything to do with your response time or attentiveness to customer needs. Ease of use is about the hoops your customer has to jump through just to try to do business with you. Quiz yourself.

- Do customers have to read a badly organized owner's manual?

- Do customers have to stare at a self-checkout kiosk for five minutes before finding the "Start" button?

- Do you make your customers click through 10 pages of your website to find basic contact info?

- Does your website load too slowly because it's loaded down with flash animation on a low-rent server?

- When customers call you, do you make them navigate a phone tree or do you have live people available to answer their questions?

Make it Easy for People to Leave You

Nobody likes customer to leave but if they want to go, make it easy on them. Don't hide your exit requirements. You've seen this (or done this) on your "unsubscribe" button buried at the bottom of your email advertising page. Don't try to trick people into staying with you. You've all gone to a polling booth and had to "Check YES if you don't want this referendum to pass. Vote NO if you like this proposal."

Don't rope your customers into arrangements that prevent them from leaving when they want to buy elsewhere. Unhappy customers talk to their friends. They will splash their bad experiences all over social media. And, don't penalize people for leaving you. Expensive termination fees are a slap in their face—a slap that will continue to whittle away at your reputation. Instead, graciously wish them well and thank them for their business.

Attempting to keep customers against their will doesn't work. It will only consume hours of your time (and maybe your lawyer's). Regardless, insisting the customer stay with you will erode any goodwill they may have had left.

ELEVEN
INSIST ON BEING WORLD CLASS

For Team Members, Associates, & Leaders: In this book, we have outlined what we consider not just best practices, but rather the *must*-practices we believe are vital for staying relevant in this accelerated society—not to mention this unforgiving economy.

Sometimes World Class
Dares Not to Conform

We have worked hard to give you tactics to compete at the highest levels. We've talked about having the best digital marketing and big data, watching your competition carefully, course correcting, spotting trends, operating with extreme urgency, and market watching to make sure you sell the most innovative products and services. Yet, sometimes being world class breaks those rules. Sometimes being world class is enough.

When you are personally regarded as best-in-class, *you* go viral. Customers and clients race to hand you their money even when you don't have all of the other elements nailed. That's why we like to say, "Being world class at what you do is an unfair advantage."

Leah Shafer, Ross's wife, is a perfect example. Leah has been singing professionally for over 20 years. She has recorded six albums. She has headlined major venues in North America. And, she appeared as a regular performer on NBC's hit show, "The Singing Bee," as well as multiple appearances on the Trinity Broadcast Network's international TV show, "Praise the Lord." Yet, you probably won't know Leah's songs until you visit her website. www.LeahShaferMusic.com.

Still, when the American Football Conference (AFC) and CBS Television were looking for a singer to sing the National Anthem for the 2013 championship game (Denver Broncos vs New England Patriots), they ended their search when they saw and heard Leah Shafer. That afternoon, Leah sang for a packed stadium of 78,000 fans and an estimated television audience of 50 million viewers. It was not luck. Leah was ready. Leah does what every other world class performer does—she practices every day. She takes her art very seriously. Even though she may not yet be a "household name" like Beyonce or Pink, Leah's talent is respected by her peers and those who make big network TV decisions. Since her exposure at the AFC Championship game, (proving she can deliver under enormous pressure) she has been in demand for many other world class events.

Our Closing Hero

Finally, you're about to meet a man who doesn't sing. He doesn't dance. He's never been on network television. He doesn't advertise. He is not on YouTube. You won't find him on Facebook. He doesn't have a fancy e-commerce website. He doesn't collect big data. He doesn't print two-sided business cards. And he doesn't chase down sales leads. Yet he is the perfect example of a non-networking success story. In his case, it isn't "who you know" but rather "who knows you." His work is so spectacular (within his niche) that he is renowned for his attention to detail, his unwavering discipline and a singular expertise that has kept him busier then he wants to be for almost four decades. That's why we like to say, "Being world class at what you do is an unfair advantage."

This is a story about a 1966 Ford Mustang fastback, a guy named Dean and a tremendously successful company that has never spent a dime on advertising. Dean is so busy he routinely turns away work.

Michael Burger's Car Guru

Here's the backstory. I love 60's muscle cars. Six months ago, I bought a sight-unseen 1966 Ford Mustang fastback from a gentleman in Crosby, Minnesota. The greatest thing going for this car, for those of you who know your Fords, was that this car was rust-free, authentic "A" code, 289 / 225 horsepower, factory 4-speed car. After seeing the car in my own driveway I faced the full reality of what the car needed. Enter a guy named Dean. 99.9% of you won't know who this man is, but his story and his approach to business and customer service is aspirational. Quite simply, Dean is the best at what he does. His meticulousness to detail has earned him world class status without advertising or outbound marketing. He doesn't have a PR person. He doesn't use any social media. He doesn't even have a website. Yet, he has more work than he can get to.

If you truly are an expert, and the best at what you do, you'll have an unfair advantage over your competition.

Dean's story is a reminder that we should all find what we love to do—and build a business around that passion. In high school Dean would fix everybody's cars. Business got so good he rented some space in an industrial complex. He's still there, 30 years later. His reputation grew on its own because Dean does what he does—so specifically, so detailed and so precisely.

Let me give you an example. Do you know what a Phillips screw looks like? Here's a mental picture, it's cross shaped. When Dean installs a screw in a piece of trim molding or a dashboard, he takes the time to line up every screw's "cross" so they match. Top to bottom, left to right. This doesn't take much more time, but it demonstrates his attention to detail and complete obsession with perfection. "There's only one way to do something, and that is the correct way," Dean would say.

By the way, you know the auto-rebuild TV shows where they completely disassemble and reassemble a car in three days? Yeah, that doesn't happen outside the TV world.

In fact, it doesn't happen in the TV world either. I'm just saying. I'd be remiss if I didn't share another story about Dean. He's not a flashy guy. He is very literal and focused in his routines. I spent a few days working alongside him. I explained my love for cars and my desire to learn and work on them. He was generous enough to let me help out. Whatever I could do, he let me participate. He was my Sensei and I was the student. Let me give you an example of his daily routine. He always ordered two tacos for lunch, nothing more. No fries. No nuggets. Just two tacos. On our first day of working together, I hooked him up with 'the combo' at Del Taco. Dean was gracious and thankful, but the next day when we broke for lunch he said, "Thank you very much for the combo yesterday, but I just wanted two tacos and nothing more." There is strict sense of order and economy about the way he works. He doesn't like to waste time and he isn't a micromanager. He let me turn a few wrenches. . .when it clearly took cash out of his pocket. And as I must reiterate, he's got more business than he can ever get to. He is clearly using his world class expertise to his advantage.

When Will *You* Become Absolutely Necessary to Your Organization?

As we stated at the beginning of this book, our goal was to give you specific tactics to keep yourself, and your company, in high demand. Hopefully, you've been inspired and motivated to act upon your own 'mission of indispensability.' The key word in that last sentence was "act" because it's not enough to be motivated. You must actually get off the couch and do it.

Successful people and companies get off the couch and make things happen. They act on a commitment to execute on their well-strategized tactics. Success simply doesn't happen by wishing.

We'll close with one of the most significant quotes we've ever heard regarding the path to success. It's a shortcut, really. With that, we wish you all the success and growth you can muster on your own.

> *"The world's greatest achievements*
> *were accomplished by tired, discouraged people...*
> *who just kept on working."*
> —Albert Einstein

How's that for a career shortcut?

SOURCES

Chapter 1

1. Huttig Building Materials quick decisions lead back to profits http://huttig.com/press_releases.aspx & http://finance.yahoo.com/news/huttig-building-products-inc-announces-100000074.html

2. For more on Sears' troubles visit http://www.cnbc.com/id/101299103

3. Sam's Club & Macy's http://www.csmonitor.com/Business/Latest-News-Wires/2014/0125/Sam-s-Club-layoffs-hit-2-300-workers.-Why

Chapter 3

1. 7-11 beefs up menu with great food http://corp.7eleven.com/Newsroom/2013NewsReleases/7ElevenBeefsUpFreshFoodsMenu/tabid/558/Default.aspx

Chapter 4

1. How did Motorola lose the cell phone business?
   http://www.reuters.com/article/2011/08/15/
   us-motorola-idUSTRE77E5TJ20110815

2. How did Nokia become the market share leader?
   http://www.telegraph.co.uk/technology/picture-
   galleries/9818080/The-20- bestselling-mobile-phones-of-
   all-time.html?frame=2458999

3. Stephen Elop's infamous memo to the Nokia troops
   http://www.torbenrick.eu/blog/change-management/
   change-management-need-a-sense-of-urgency/

4. Henry Cloud "Necessary Endings" http://www.amazon.
   com/Necessary-Endings-Businesses-Relationships/
   dp/0061777129

Chapter 5

1. The Day Lehman Brothers blew up
   http://www.thestreet.com/story/12438988/1/the-story-
   of-the-federal-reserve-the-day-after-lehman-brothers-
   collapsed.html

2. Malcolm Gladwell's "Blink" is a must read. http://
   www.amazon.com/Blink-Power-Thinking-Without/
   dp/0316010669/ref=sr_1_1?s=books&ie=UTF8&qid=140
   7089756&sr=1-1&keywords=blink

Chapter 7

1. 2. Tech Guru Scott Klososky should be your expert, too.
   http://www.fpov.com

2. Carl Ichan tweets himself even richer.
   http://finance.yahoo.com/blogs/the-exchange/

---

carl-icahn-multibillion-dollar-tweet-boosts-apple-stock-205938760.html

Chapter 8

1. Generational guru Cam Marston knows how you think, work, and play. http://www.generationalinsights.com/shop

2. Who is the Millennial, really? http://thesocietypages.org/graphicsociology/2011/10/04/who-is-the-millennial-generation-pew-research/

3. The Silent Generation is still very important http://education-portal.com/academy/lesson/the-silent-generation-definition-characteristics-facts.html#lesson and http://www.socialmarketing.org/newsletter/features/generation3.htm

4. The New Luxury Buyers you must know. http://www.mediapost.com/publications/article/175754/gen-x-the-new-luxury-buyers-and-how-to-reach-them.html

5. Millennial money habits might surprise you. http://www.investopedia.com/articles/personal-finance/021914/money-habits-millennials.asp

6. How people want to work in the future R.O.W.E. http://www.gorowe.com

Chapter 9

1. Amazon's Air Force is coming. http://www.amazon.com/b?node=8037720011

2. Snapchat and Vine create and then destroy photos. https://www.arkovi.com/2013/02/snapchat-and-vine-sharing-your-message-in-ten-seconds-or-less/

3. The Cost of Being Too Slow (sources: 2009 Genesys/Greenfield Survey http://www.mynewsdesk.com/se/

pressreleases/survey-underscores-economic-impact-
of-the-customer-experience-across-all-channels-of-
communication-310717, 2009 STELLA/Greenfield survey,
2010 Vodaphone survey, 2010 Avaya and Teleperformance
surveys) http://blog.teleperformance.com/tag/survey/

4. What is Bad Service? Consumer Reports, July 2011

5. Top Complaints (2010 STELLA/Greenfield survey)

6. Yes, customers will pay more for better service. http://www.
    fastcasual.com/news/study-customers-will-pay-more-for-
    better-service/

7. The Customer Shouts Back http://www.ama-
    zon.com/s/?ie=UTF8&keywords=the+custom-
    er+shouts+back&tag=googhydr-20&index=stripbooks&h-
    vadid=21119708785&hvpos=1t1&hvexid=&hvnetw=g&h-
    vrand=5154530763881169300&hvpone=&hvptwo=&h-
    vqmt=b&hvdev=c&ref=pd_sl_3xd659hxv7_b

8. Game Truck drives a party to your house. http://www.
    gametruckparty.com

Chapter 10

1. Fast Service is the new service. (source: 2010 Stella/
    Greenfield survey)

2. Listen to Karl Stark on building customer relationships.
    http://www.inc.com/karl-and-bill/keep-your-friends-close-
    and-your-customers-closer.html
    http://www.crmbuyer.com/story/78631.html

3. Netflix started this way.
    http://en.wikipedia.org/wiki/Reed_Hastings

4. Netflix fumbles a pretty big ball
    http://research.gigaom.com/report/connected-consumer-
    q3-netflix-fumbles-kindle-fire-shines/

ABOUT THE AUTHORS

Ross Shafer should probably use this space to tell you about his best-selling books, his Emmy awards, his network television shows, his wonderful family, and his business windfalls. But for this book, he wants the reader to know he has probably endured more devastating failures than you have. His path to becoming "absolutely necessary" has been derailed by five cancelled TV shows, seven failed businesses, and too many relationships-that-went-sideways to mention…and *that* is what he feels qualifies him to talk about the concept of indispensability. Ross will tell anyone who will listen, "If you're not failing, you have no chance of sustaining success."

Other Books by Ross Shafer

Are You Relevant?
Twelve Reasons Smart Organizations Thrive in Any Economy

Nobody Moved Your Cheese
How to Ignore the Experts and Trust Your Gut

Grab More Market Share
How to Wrangle Business Away From Lazy Competitors

The Customer Shouts Back
10 Big Changes You Need to Make if You Want
Their Lifetime Loyalty

Customer Empathy
Inspirational Stories of Internal and External Service
from the Heart

To learn about Ross Shafer and his speaking schedule go to
www.RossShafer.com

Michael Burger has been a successful real estate entrepreneur for three decades and recently cofounded The Relevant Report is an internationally acclaimed innovative video blog designed to inspire individuals and companies. Like Ross, he also has a network TV-hosting and producing background, as well as a stand-up comedy career. He started his career on cruise ships. As Michael says, "When I got to the point I could keep 1500 passengers from going to the buffet, I knew I was ready." So ready that 10 television shows followed, including the ABC talk show "Mike and Maty." In Michael's spare time he enjoys tennis, golf, cycling, room service—basically everything in the hotel brochure.

To learn more about Michael Burger and his speaking schedule go to www.MichaelBurgerTV.com